Rhetorical Power

Also by Steven Mailloux:

Interpretive Conventions: The Reader in the Study of American Fiction

RHETORICAL POWER

Steven Mailloux

Cornell University Press
Ithaca and London

First published 1989 by Cornell University Press.

International Standard Book Number (cloth) 0-8014-2245-0
International Standard Book Number (paper) 0-8014-9602-0
Library of Congress Catalog Card Number 89-42878
Printed in the United States of America
Librarians: Library of Congress cataloging information
appears on the last page of the book.

The paper in this book is acid-free and meets the
guidelines for permanence and durability of the
Committee on Production Guidelines for Book Longevity
of the Council on Library Resources.

For Molly

Contents

Preface

Rhetorical Power can be read in (at least) two ways, according to two competing critical genres relating theory and practice. One of these genres presents an approach or method that is then applied to a series of texts. Here theory simply introduces the practical criticism or literary history that is its reason to be: theory serves practice. Read in light of this genre, my book proposes a critical perspective on the rhetorical politics of various texts. This perspective is then applied to the institutional rhetoric of academic criticism in Chapters 1 and 2, to the ideological production of literature in Chapter 3, and to the cultural reception of literature in Chapter 4. The next two chapters clarify the notion of rhetoric applied throughout, and then the Conclusion provides a final example of rhetorical analysis in an examination of the text of a congressional hearing.

Another genre, however, reverses the relation of theory and practice. Rather than theory justifying interpretive methods, critical and historical readings simply illustrate the theoretical argument: practice serves theory. Read within this genre, Rhetorical Power never leaves off theorizing. Chapter 1 begins by proposing a rhetorical hermeneutics, a neo-pragmatist argument that claims interpretive accounts must move as quickly as possible from therapeutic critiques of hermeneutics to rhetorical histories of specific acts of interpretation. Chapter 2 uses New Critical formalism and reader-response criticism to demonstrate how this theoretical claim works for acts of literary interpretation within academic discourse. Chapter 3 refines the thesis by clarifying its theoretical metaphors, especially "cultural conversation" and "rhetorical exchange," through a reading of *Huckleberry Finn*, and ends by contextualizing this reading within the critical history of the novel's interpretations.

Chapter 4 then provides the book's most detailed illustration of its theoretical claims, revealing the unlimited complications in accounting exhaustively for even a single act of interpretation. This chapter incompletely locates the Concord Library's 1885 banning of *Huckleberry Finn* in the rhetorical context of social practices surrounding juvenile delinquency in nineteenth-century America. Such extensive cultural histories are a necessity for any rhetorical hermeneutics. What can be lost in the historical detail of the chapter is the fact that doing a rhetorical history of an interpretive act is a form of theorizing about interpretation. In other words, in rhetorical hermeneutics the traditional distinction between doing theory and doing history breaks down. Chapter 5 restates these claims in an argument against foundationalist theory, an argument carried out through readings of three texts, one literary, one historical, and one philosophical. Chapter 6 clarifies the theoretical project further by giving a rhetorical history of the theory itself and placing rhetorical hermeneutics in the context of other recent antifoundationalist accounts. The Conclusion summarizes the book's argument by examining the role of rhetoric and theory in the 1985 congressional hearings on the Reagan administration's reinterpretation of the ABM Treaty.

Rhetorical Power, then, can be read either as a practical proposal about how to approach various texts rhetorically or as a theoretical argument about the historical specificity of every interpretive act and thus the impossibility of foundationalist accounts of interpretation. But a book called *Rhetorical Power* should be even more explicit about its own rhetorical strategies, especially the particular arguments within arguments that characterize the overall organization of the text.

First, within the larger theoretical claims for a rhetorical hermeneutics, there is an evolving argument about doing rhetorical histories of academic discourses. This argument within an argument makes up Chapters 2 and 3, which present a series of rhetorical histories, each building on the incompleteness of the previous one. Chapter 2 begins with a schematic rhetorical narrative and analysis of the institutional emergence of New Criticism. Though this analysis is a useful starting point for understanding the rhetorical politics of an institutional discourse, it is not fine-grained enough to suggest how such a discourse functions as a set of rhetorical strategies with relative autonomy from more widespread cultural exchanges outside the institution. Chapter 2's detailed description of one reaction to New Critical formalism, a version of reader-response criticism, attempts to fill out this picture of interpretive rhetoric within the institutionalized discipline of literary studies in the 1970s. This localized history of rhetorical assumptions and tactics is itself incomplete and needs further elaboration, in terms of both a still more focused rhetorical analysis of academic interpretations of a specific text, here *Huckleberry Finn,* and a more expansive history of the interpenetration of cultural politics and professional arguments making up the societal conversation that incorporates and transcends academic disputes. The rhetorical narrative of how my interpretation fits into the interpretive history of Twain's novel thus builds on rather than supplants the schematic institutional history of New Criticism and the detailed rhetorical analysis of reader-response criticism.

In a similar way, another argument within my larger argument develops step by step a specific reader-response approach to literary discourse. Here the developing sequence extends over Chapters 2, 3, and 4. In Chapter 2 I present a schematic reader-response interpretation of *Moby-Dick* as an example of the traditional, more or less ahistorical, apolitical approach to the reader, and then the rest of the chapter rhetorically analyzes the assumptions and moves involved in this approach. Chapter 3 then adopts many of the rhetorical strategies demonstrated and analyzed in Chapter 2 but uses them in an interpretation of *Huckleberry Finn* which historicizes the reading experience by placing it within a specific context of political debate over racism after the end of Reconstruction. But once a reader-response criticism has begun to ask questions about history, politics, and ideology, it cannot stop with the interpretation of a hypothetical 1880s reading experience described from the perspective of the 1980s. It must also ask questions about how the novel was actually received in the 1880s, and such a reception study leads from questions of racism to questions about literary censorship and juvenile delinquency, what I describe in Chapter 4 as the cultural reception of *Huckleberry Finn* within the context of the "Bad-Boy Boom." This sequence of reader-oriented analyses, each developing or inspiring the other, leads to a proposed approach to fiction that goes some way toward revising the ahistorical, apolitical formalism that continues to dominate American reader-response criticism.

Throughout its various theoretical and historical accounts, *Rhetorical Power* sets to work a specific definition of its key term: *rhetoric* as the political effectivity of trope and argument in culture. Such a working definition includes the two traditional meanings of rhetoric—figurative language and persuasive action—and permits me to emphasize either or both senses, differently in different discourses at different historical moments, in order to specify more exactly how texts affect their audiences in terms of particular power relations. Thus sometimes I emphasize how interpretive arguments and metaphors establish texts as meaningful and significant in institutional contexts (as in Chapter 2 on reader-response criticism and Chapter 3, section II, on the critical history of *Huckleberry Finn*). At other times I locate critical or literary arguments and figures within the surrounding cultural conversation (as in Chapter 3, section I, on *Huckleberry Finn* and post-Reconstruction debates about white supremacy and in Chapter 4 on juvenile delinquency and the reception of the novel). Less frequently, I show how tropes function as arguments (for example, the river metaphor figuring white supremacist arguments in late-nineteenth-century debates about racial amalgamation); and, conversely, I note how arguments work as tropes (for example, arguments about juvenile delinquency functioning as tropes for a disciplinary society's fears and frustrations). In these complementary ways, the following chapters describe the workings of rhetorical power: how various discourses—literary, critical, and theoretical—function in producing the specific historical effects they do.

The debts incurred in the course of writing a book are always more than can be completely acknowledged. The following is only a partial reckoning. I thank

—for advice and encouragement, Charles Altieri, Arthur Brown, William Cain, John Bender, Louis J. Budd, John Crowley, Stanley Fish, Gerald Graff, Jean Howard, W. J. T. Mitchell, Felicity Nussbaum, Richard Ohmann, Hershel Parker, Louise Rosenblatt, John Paul Russo, Edward Said, William Spengemann, Mihoko Suzuki, Brook Thomas, and Mas'ud Zavarzadeh.

—for a year of challenging questions and helpful suggestions, my associates at the Stanford Humanities Center, especially W. B. Carnochan, Hamilton Cravens, Jay Fliegelman, George Fredrickson, Estelle Freedman, Harriet Ritvo, Kevin Sharpe, and Mort Sosna.

—for invitations to do projects that became a part of this book, Louis J. Budd, Ihab Hassan, Victor Kramer, Frank Lentricchia, and Thomas McLaughlin.

—for hospitality and a generous sharing of knowledge and resources, Robert Hirst and Victor Fischer of the Mark Twain Project, Bancroft Library, University of California, Berkeley.

—for continuing interest in a field not their own, Tom Clark and Terry Lyle.

—for research assistance, Martha Dawson and the interlibrary loan departments at the University of Miami, Stanford University, and Syracuse University.

—for copies of Franklin B. Sanborn's correspondence, Wilbur E. Meneray of the Howard-Tilton Memorial Library, Tulane University.

—for typing, Dee Marquez, and for proofreading, Michael Murphy and Mary Ann Young.

—for careful copy editing, Patricia Cantor.

—for their playfulness, enthusiasm, and much more, Mary Nell, Roman, and Tess Mailloux.

I am especially grateful to Paul Armstrong, Peter Carafiol, Peter Rabinowitz, Ellen Rooney, Adena Rosmarin, and Warwick Wadlington for their detailed criticisms of the entire manuscript at various stages. I also express my deep appreciation to Bernhard Kendler of Cornell University Press for his confidence in this project and for his continuing support of my work.

I gratefully acknowledge the financial assistance received from the University of Miami, the School of Criticism and Theory (Northwestern University, summer 1982), the National Endowment for the Humanities (summer 1983), the Stanford Humanities Center (1985–1986), and Syracuse University. Permission has been granted to use material that originally appeared in the following publications: *Studies in the Literary Imagination*, 12 (Spring 1979), published a very early version of Chapter 2, sections II–IV, and a shorter version of Chapter 3 appeared in *New Essays on Adventures of Huckleberry Finn*, edited by Louis J. Budd, copyright © Cambridge University Press, 1985. The University of Chicago Press has granted permission to use material from *Critical Inquiry*, 11 (June 1985), in Chapter 1 and in Chapter 2, section I; from *Critical Inquiry*, 9 (June 1983), in Chapter 6, section I; and from *Critical Terms for Literary Study*, edited by Frank Lentricchia and Thomas McLaughlin (1989), in the Conclusion.

S. M.

Syracuse, New York

PART ONE

Rhetoric and Interpretation

1

Rhetorical Hermeneutics

The Space Act of 1958 begins, "The Congress hereby declares that it is the policy of the United States that activities in space should be devoted to peaceful purposes for the benefit of all mankind." In March 1982, a Defense Department official commented on a phrase used in this statute: "We interpret the right to use space for peaceful purposes to include military uses of space to promote peace in the world."[1] The absurdity of this willful misinterpretation amazed me on first reading, and months later it readily came to mind when I was looking for an effective way to illustrate the politics of interpretation. With just the right touch of moral indignation, I offered my literary criticism class this example of militaristic ideology blatantly misreading an antimilitaristic text.

"But . . . the Defense Department is right!" objected the first student to speak. Somewhat amused, I spent the next ten minutes trying, with decreasing amusement, to show this student that the Reagan administration's reading was clearly, obviously, painfully wrong. I pointed to the words of the statute. I cited the traditional interpretation. I noted the class consensus, which supported me. All to no avail. It was at this point that I felt the "theoretical urge": the overwhelming desire for a hermeneutic

[1]"National Aeronautics and Space Act of 1958," *United States Statutes at Large* (Washington, D.C., 1959), vol. 72, pt. 1, p. 426; Robert Cooper, director of the Defense Advanced Research Projects Agency, quoted in Frank Greve, "Pentagon Research Retains Vision of 'Winning' N-war," *Miami Herald*, 27 March 1983, sec. D, p. 4.

account to which I could appeal to prove my student wrong. What I wanted was a general theory of interpretation that could supply rules outlawing my student's misreading. This little hermeneutic fable introduces the three topics of Part One. One topic is the *theoretical moment* that concludes the narrative; another is the simple plot, a brief *rhetorical exchange;* and finally there's the *institutional setting* (a university classroom) in which the exchange takes place. These three topics preoccupy the sections that follow. Section I analyzes the problems resulting from the theoretical urge, an impasse in contemporary critical theory. Section II proposes my solution to this impasse, a solution I call rhetorical hermeneutics, which leads in Chapter 2 to a rhetorical version of institutional history.

I. The Moments of Theory

The theoretical urge is a recurrent phenomenon within the present organization of American literary studies. Within that discipline, explicating individual texts remains the privileged activity, and, historically, this primary task has always brought in its wake a secondary one: critical practice inevitably leads to its self-conscious justification in critical theory. Every time a new challenger to the critical orthodoxy comes along, the discipline's theoretical discourse renews itself in an attempt to provide a rationale for interpretation. In simplified form, the institutional catechism during the last forty years has gone something like this: What is the purpose of literary studies as an institutionalized discipline? To produce knowledge about literature. How can such knowledge best be achieved? By the explication of texts. What is the goal of explication? To discover the correct interpretation, *the* meaning of the text.[2] Once the theoretical dialogue gets this far, agreement among theorists begins

---

[2]This answer is only implicit in the most popular forms of American deconstruction—what Richard Rorty calls "weak textualism"—whose practitioners "think that they have now found the true method for analyzing literary works because they have now found the fundamental problematic with which these works deal": *Consequences of Pragmatism (Essays: 1972–1980)* (Minneapolis, 1982), p. 153; and see Rorty, "Deconstruction and Circumvention," *Critical Inquiry,* 11 (September 1984), 2, 19–20. Cf. J. Hillis Miller: "The readings of deconstructive criticism are not the willful imposition by a subjectivity of theory on the texts but are coerced by the texts themselves": "Theory and Practice: Response to Vincent Leitch," *Critical Inquiry,* 6 (Summer 1980), 611; and see Miller, *The Ethics of Reading* (New York, 1987).

to break down. How can we guarantee that critics produce correct interpretations? Formalists respond, "By focusing on the text"; intentionalists, "By discovering the author's meaning"; reader-response critics, "By describing the ideal reader's experience"; and so on.

As dissimilar as these theoretical answers appear, they all share a common assumption: validity in interpretation is guaranteed by the establishment of norms or principles for explicating texts, and such rules are best derived from an account of how interpretation works in general. In other words, most traditional theorists assume that an accurate theoretical description of the interpretive process will give us binding prescriptions for our critical practices, prescriptions that can ensure (or at least encourage) correct readings. The classic statement of this assumption is E. D. Hirsch's in "Objective Interpretation": "When the critic clearly conceives what a correct interpretation is in principle, he possesses a guiding idea against which he can measure his construction. Without such a guiding idea, self-critical or objective interpretation is hardly possible."[3]

In this way, contemporary literary theory comes to focus on a question it takes as basic: How does interpretation—the accomplishment of meaning—take place? Two hermeneutic positions have developed in response to this central question: textual realism and readerly idealism. Hermeneutic realism argues that meaning-full texts exist independent of interpretation. From this perspective, meanings are discovered, not created. The facts of the text exist objectively, before any hermeneutic work by readers or critics, and therefore correct interpretations are those that correspond to the autonomous facts of the text. Realism often views the interpreter's mind as passive, simply acted upon by the words on the page. Though the text must be read, in correct interpretation it speaks itself. If the reader needs to do anything, it is only the mechanical activity of combining word meanings into larger thematic units and formal relationships. This is a "build-up" model of interpretation. For hermeneutic realism, texts are the primary source and test of readings; they constrain and ultimately determine interpretations.

Hermeneutic idealism, in contrast, argues that interpretation always creates the signifying text, that meaning is made, not found. In this view, textual facts are never prior to or indepen-

[3]E. D. Hirsch, Jr., "Objective Interpretation" [1960], in *Validity in Interpretation* (New Haven, Conn., 1967), p. 212.

dent of the hermeneutic activity of readers and critics. Idealism claims not only that the interpreter's mind is active but that it is completely dominant over the text. There are no semantic or formal givens; all such textual givens are products of interpretive categories. This is a "build-down" model of interpretation. From this perspective, what counts as a correct reading depends entirely on shared assumptions and strategies, not on autonomous texts. In hermeneutic idealism, a text doesn't constrain its interpretation; rather, communal interpretation creates the text.

As theories of interpretation, textual realism and readerly idealism share a common institutional concern: to establish a foundation for validating knowledge. I call this an *institutional* concern because traditional theorists claim that, without principles of correct interpretation, an institutionalized discipline has no way of grounding its production of new knowledge. Once again Hirsch is the paradigmatic theorist. He claims that, without a proper theory of correct interpretation, we cannot avoid "subjectivism and relativism" and cannot think of "literary study as a corporate enterprise and a progressive discipline."[4] It follows from this view that theory serves the corporate enterprise by making explicit the norms and principles of valid readings. Any such theory attempts to derive these norms and principles from its general account of how interpretation works. Whether the account is realist, idealist, or some combination of the two, it must provide an *intersubjective* ground for correct interpretation, and it is traditionally thought that only by the establishment of such a ground can the dangers of relativism and subjectivism be avoided.

With such a high value placed on intersubjective foundations for interpreting, it should come as no surprise that the concept of conventions plays an important—even central—role in hermeneutic accounts, whether realist or idealist.[5] Thus, with some justification, the following discussion takes the conventionalist version of the realist/idealist debate as a synecdoche for all "foundationalist" arguments in recent critical theory.

Theorists of the realist persuasion have long turned to textual conventions to explain literary interpretation. Formalists, intentionalists, structuralists, and even some reader-response crit-

---

[4]Ibid., p. 209.

[5]In this book "conventions" refers to *instances of shared practices*. See the discussion in my *Interpretive Conventions: The Reader in the Study of American Fiction* (Ithaca, N.Y., 1982), pp. 126–39.

ics locate conventions in a text in order to guarantee intersubjective foundations in their hermeneutic accounts. An especially interesting case of realist conventionalism can be found in the work of Monroe Beardsley, who with W. K. Wimsatt codified the prescriptions of New Critical formalism. In essays on the affective and intentional fallacies, Wimsatt and Beardsley proposed an "objective criticism" that would avoid the dangers of "impressionism," "skepticism," and "relativism."[6] In his *Aesthetics* Beardsley later developed this formalism into a foundationalist theory, asking, "What are we doing when we interpret literature, and how do we know that we are doing it correctly?" and answering, "There are *principles of explication* for poetry in terms of which disagreements about the correctness of proposed explications can be settled."[7] These principles can be summed up in the realist's slogan "Back to the text."[8]

Beardsley explains his realist hermeneutics further in *The Possibility of Criticism*, where he argues that the "literary text, in the final analysis, is the determiner of its meaning."[9] At this point conventions enter into Beardsley's account. In his chapter "The Testability of an Interpretation," he attempts to defend his formalist theory by arguing that "there really is something in the poem that we are trying to dig out, though it is elusive" (*PC*, p. 47). This "something"—the meaning in the text—is the object of interpretation, and Beardsley proposes to define it more rigorously by appropriating the conventionalism of speech-act theory. In another place, Beardsley succinctly describes J. L. Austin's account of language use: "To know what illocutionary action [requesting, promising, asserting, and so on] was performed is to know what action the production of such a text generated by the appropriate conventions."[10]

[6]Monroe C. Beardsley and W. K. Wimsatt, Jr., "The Affective Fallacy" [1949], in Wimsatt, *The Verbal Icon: Studies in the Meaning of Poetry* (Lexington, Ky., 1954), p. 21.

[7]Beardsley, *Aesthetics: Problems in the Philosophy of Criticism* (New York, 1958), pp. 403, 49.

[8]Beardsley, "Textual Meaning and Authorial Meaning," *Genre*, 1 (July 1968), 181.

[9]Beardsley, *The Possibility of Criticism* (Detroit, 1970), p. 37 (hereafter cited in text as *PC*).

[10]Beardsley, "Intentions and Interpretations: A Fallacy Revived," in *The Aesthetic Point of View: Selected Essays*, ed. Michael J. Wreen and Donald M. Callen (Ithaca, N.Y., 1982), p. 195. The central texts on conventions and speech acts are J. L. Austin, *How to Do Things with Words* (Oxford, 1962), and John R.

Austin's conventionalism can be pushed in two very different directions: toward readerly idealism, with conventions placed in hearers, or toward textual realism, with conventions posited in texts. Predictably, Beardsley's adaptation of speech-act theory takes the realist route. Rather than have authors or readers "take responsibility" for performing certain illocutionary acts and for committing themselves to certain conventional conditions (for example, in promising a speaker commits to do a certain act in the future), Beardsley prefers to say that literary texts imitate illocutionary acts and "represent" that certain conditions are in fact the case (*PC*, p. 115n). This is a shrewd maneuver: instead of readers taking responsibility for conventions of language use, texts represent those conventions; conventions move from outside to inside the text. This realist placement of conventions gives Beardsley just what his formalist theory requires—an autonomous text against which all interpretations can be tested. "I am arguing that there are some features of the poem's meaning that are antecedent to, and independent of, the entertaining of an interpretive hypothesis; and this makes it possible to check such hypotheses against reality" (*PC*, pp. 57–58). And these semantic features that test interpretations include conventions embedded in the text.

Realist theories such as Beardsley's emphasize that conventions display shared practices for writing literature and that readers and critics must recognize these textual conventions in order to achieve valid interpretations. But such theories inevitably suffer from incomplete coverage and lack of specificity as exhaustive accounts of interpreting. No matter how comprehensive it tries to be, the realist conventionalism of genre critics, formalists, and semioticians remains unsatisfying as a complete description of even a single text's literary meaning. The common notion of an artwork's irreducible uniqueness refuses to go away, even when a significant portion of the text's sense is attributable to an author's following, modifying, or rejecting traditional conventions. But perhaps the literary text's uniqueness is simply an illusion fostered by the humanistic tradition, on the one hand, and supported by the needs of a critical profession, on the other. Even if this were the case and a text's meaning in fact could be explained as completely conventional, realist accounts would continue to be embarrassed by their contradictory descriptions of the uninterpreted givens in the text and by their many unconvincing explanations of how such textual givens cause interpretations. Realist conventionalism only re-states these essentialist and causal problems: How exactly are conventions manifested in the text? How do such textually embedded conventions determine interpretation? The latter question usually leads realists toward some kind of correspondence model: interpreters recognize conventions in a text because they have literary competence, an internalized set of interpretive conventions.[11] Realists who take this route move toward idealist solutions and in so doing also move toward idealist incoherencies.

In contrast to realism, idealist theories emphasize conventions as shared practices for interpreting literature, conventions present in readers and critics, not in texts. Important idealist theories include those of Stanley Fish in "Interpreting the *Variorum*" and Jonathan Culler in *Structuralist Poetics*. Fish argues that communal interpretive strategies are the only constraints on the production of meaning. Texts are products of interpretive communities, which "are made up of those who share interpretive strategies not for reading . . . but for writing texts, for constituting their properties."[12] In *Structuralist Poetics*, Culler more fully elaborates an idealist-oriented account of using conventions in interpretation. Though at times he refers to "potential" properties "latent" in the text itself, he more often emphasizes interpreters' reading conventions, which determine the sense they make of the literary work. He talks of the poem as offering a structure for the reader to fill up, but he stresses the interpretive conventions competent readers use to invent something to fill up that structure. He suggests that it is not the text but the reading conventions that "make possible invention and impose limits on it."[13]

Whereas realist accounts posit textual conventions that are

[11]See, e.g., the comments on "literary competence" in Beardsley, *Aesthetics: Problems in the Philosophy of Criticism*, 2d ed. (Indianapolis, 1981), p. li; and Beardsley, "The Philosophy of Literature," in *Aesthetics: A Critical Anthology*, ed. George Dickie and R. J. Sclafani (New York, 1977), pp. 329–33.

[12]Stanley Fish, "Interpreting the *Variorum*" [1976], in *Is There a Text in This Class?: The Authority of Interpretive Communities* (Cambridge, Mass., 1980), p. 171.

[13]Jonathan Culler, *Structuralist Poetics: Structuralism, Linguistics, and the Study of Literature* (Ithaca, N.Y., 1975), pp. 113, 126. For a more extreme example of idealist conventionalism, see my *Interpretive Conventions*, pp. 192–207.

recognized by readers, idealist accounts place interpretive conventions in readers, who then apply them to create meaningful texts. Idealists fare no better than realists, however, in using conventions to avoid epistemological embarrassment. True, they do avoid the realist problems connected with essentialism and causation by arguing that the content of the text is produced by the interpretive conventions employed and that texts do not cause interpretations at all. But entirely new problems arise out of these supposed solutions. The two most important involve the infinite regress of conventions and the unformalizable nature of context. In a particular case of interpretation, what determines the interpretive conventions to be used? Idealists cannot answer by proposing metaconventions, because to do so would lead to an infinite regress within their theories. Each set of conventions at a lower level requires metaconventions at a higher level to determine the appropriate lower-level conventions. Then these metaconventions themselves need metaconventions, and so on. One way to avoid this pitfall is to argue that context always determines the interpretive conventions to employ. But such a claim leads only to a more difficult question for the idealist: What constrains the use of interpretive conventions in a specific context?

Both Fish and Culler, among others, have suggested the impossibility of adequately answering this question. As they fully realize, such a suggestion entails a critique of their past conventionalist accounts of interpretation. I will limit my discussion here to Culler's observation that the interpretive conventions on which he focused in *Structuralist Poetics* should be seen as part of a "boundless context."[14] He states his new position in this way: "Meaning is context-bound, but context is boundless" (*OD*, p. 123). Culler seems to be claiming two rather different things, only the first of which helps explain why the contextual nature of interpretation makes idealist conventionalism inadequate.

Culler first seems to be arguing that any full account of meaning must include a notion of boundless context. By characterizing context as boundless, Culler means that any hermeneutic

---

[14]Culler, "Convention and Meaning: Derrida and Austin," *New Literary History*, 13 (Autumn 1981), 30n (hereafter cited in text as CM). This essay was revised and incorporated into Culler, *On Deconstruction: Theory and Criticism after Structuralism* (Ithaca, N.Y., 1982) (hereafter cited in text as OD).

theory trying to specify a particular context exhaustively is doomed to failure: "Any given context is always open to further description. There is no limit in principle to what might be included in a given context, to what might be shown relevant to the interpretation of a particular speech act" (CM, p. 24). Every specification is open to questions asking for further specifications.[15] In such an account, conventions are, at best, only first approximations of boundless context. Conventions begin the specification of relevant contextual features, designating the relation of the words, persons, and circumstances required for a speech act to have the specific meaning it has in a given context (compare OD, p. 121).

But conventions alone are inadequate as explanatory concepts. Either the description of the conventions must reductively and arbitrarily leave out relevant contextual features or the specification of the relevant conventions would have to be so open-ended that conventions would become indistinguishable from context and lose their identity. A hermeneutic theory using conventions in conjunction with other contextual features will fare no better as an exhaustive account of meaning, because there is no limit in principle to the features relevant to the interpretation of specific speech acts. Another way of putting this is to say that context is impossible to formulate completely. Thus any account that attempts to use "context" to constrain interpretation precisely and completely has only two options: either it must simply name "context," "situation," or "circumstances" as a constraint and not elaborate any further or it must carry out an infinite listing of all aspects of context and their interrelations, that is, bring everything in.[16] In other words, "definitive" theories of interpretive context must either never begin the process of specification or never end it.

Culler's first claim about boundless context agrees with what I have been saying so far: boundless context determines meaning, and context is boundless because it is ultimately not formaliz-

[15] See Harold Garfinkel, Studies in Ethnomethodology (Englewood Cliffs, N.J., 1967), pp. 24–31, and Hubert L. Dreyfus, What Computers Can't Do: The Limits of Artificial Intelligence, rev. ed. (New York, 1979), pp. 256–71.

[16] On the first option, see Walter Benn Michaels, "Philosophy in Kinkanja: Eliot's Pragmatism," Glyph, 8 (1981), 184–85; on the second, see Dreyfus, What Computers Can't Do, p. 289. For further discussion of context as an explanatory concept, see my "Convention and Context," New Literary History, 14 (Winter 1983), 399–407.

able. Unfortunately, Culler confuses things with a second, entirely different argument about meaning and context, in which he asserts the "impossibility of ever saturating or limiting context so as to control or rigorously determine the 'true' meaning" (CM, p. 28). In this deconstructionist claim, context is boundless not in the first sense—that it is impossible to formalize—but in a second sense: new contexts can always be imagined for a particular speech act, and thus meaning is in principle radically indeterminate (see OD, pp. 124, 128). Culler ends up using context here as an interpretive device for making meaning undecidable rather than as an explanatory concept in accounting for meaning's determinate shape.

Culler's two uses of context are not necessarily irreconcilable. But to make them strictly consistent, he needs to give up his assertion about the absolute indeterminacy of meaning. As it happens, it would not be difficult for him to do so, given his initial explanatory use of "context." Indeed, though he claims to be doing otherwise in his deconstructive maneuvers, Culler actually demonstrates not that meaning is always indeterminate but that meaning has one determinate shape in one situation and another in a different situation. Though a speech act's meaning can change from context to context, this meaning is always determinate *within a given context*. In the cases Culler suggests—situations in which the proposal of an imagined context shows how a meaning could change—one of two things happens: the meaning remains the same, because in the present situation the proposed context is perceived as imaginary; or the meaning changes, because in the present situation the proposed context is incorporated into the present circumstances. In the second possibility, meaning changes because the context changes. In neither situation is meaning indeterminate; it is determinate (even if ambiguous) because of the context it is in.[17]

But whichever way Culler uses "context"—as explanatory concept or interpretive device—he goes far beyond simply

[17]See Fish, *Is There a Text?*, pp. 277–84, and Fish, "With the Compliments of the Author: Reflections on Austin and Derrida," *Critical Inquiry*, 8 (Summer 1982), 693–721. In this analysis I have followed Dreyfus, Fish, and others in using "context" and "situation" interchangeably. For a suggestive discussion of evaluation related to my analysis of interpretation, see Barbara Herrnstein Smith, "Contingencies of Value," *Critical Inquiry*, 10 (September 1983), 1–35.

showing that "if language always evades its conventions, it also depends on them" (CM, p. 29). What he demonstrates instead is something he admits in a footnote: that the distinction between convention and context breaks down (see CM, p. 30n). Indeed, all idealist theories of interpretive conventions tend to self-destruct when they adopt the notion of context to solve their conventionalist problems. Do either realist or idealist uses of conventions, then, provide a full account of literary interpretation? The answer must be no, for both theoretical positions fail to avoid radical embarrassments in their accounts.

Nor do theories combining realism and idealism avoid the hermeneutic problems. Typically, such theories argue that realism and idealism are each only partially right, that neither the text alone nor the reader alone determines meaning, that meaning is contributed by both text and reader. This comfortable compromise is understandably popular in contemporary theory, but it solves none of the realist/idealist problems.[18] What it does do is cagily cover up those problems by continually postponing their discovery. In conventionalist theories, for instance, we noted how some realists move from conventions in a text to conventions matched in a competent critic's mind. Such theories, by moving toward idealism, avoid the realist problem of explaining textual causation. But when those same theories run up against the idealist problem of determining appropriate interpretive conventions in a given situation, they turn back to the text for a solution. Thus we end up with a cunningly circular argument: stay a realist until you have problems, then move toward idealism until you get embarrassed, then return to realism, and so forth ad infinitum. No amount of tinkering or conflating can save realist and idealist conventionalism from similar dead ends and vicious circles.

It would be a mistake, however, to think that any other account—objective or subjective, conventionalist or nonconventionalist, or some admixture of these forms—could provide a general theory of interpretation, something we can call Theory with a capital T, something that could solve the hermeneutic problems I have discussed in this section. As Steven Knapp and Walter Benn Michaels have argued, Theory is impossible if it is defined as "the attempt to govern interpretations of particular

[18]See the discussion of Wolfgang Iser's phenomenological theory of reading in my *Interpretive Conventions*, pp. 49–56.

texts by appealing to an account of interpretation in general."[19] My critique of realist and idealist conventionalism is another version of the attack on Theory so defined. The solution to the realist/idealist debate in hermeneutics is not, then, the proposal of still another Theory. The way to answer the realist/idealist question "Is meaning created by the text or by the reader or by both?" is simply not to ask it, to stop doing Theory.

II. From Hermeneutics to Rhetoric

The anti-Theory argument opens up two possibilities: Theorists can remain unpersuaded by the argument and continue business as usual, or they can be convinced by it and stop doing Theory. Let's take up the more likely scenario first. If Theory simply continues, what will happen? According to Knapp and Michaels, Theory depends on logical mistakes such as Hirsch's separation of meaning from intention in *Validity in Interpretation*.[20] Since to see a text as meaningful *is* to posit an author's intention and vice versa, a Theory built on the separation of meaning and intention includes prescriptions—"Discover meaning by first searching for intention"—that are impossible to follow. Thus, according to Knapp and Michaels, Theory in its general descriptions is illogical and in its specific prescriptions is inconsequential.

But Knapp and Michaels' thesis needs to be qualified in an important way. Certainly they are right in claiming that Theory cannot have the consequences it wants to have, that it cannot be a general account that guarantees correct interpretations. It can, however, have other kinds of consequences. In advocating a search for the historical author's meaning, for example, intentionalists promote the critic's use of history and biography, what formalists call external evidence. If critics are convinced by intentionalist Theory, their interpretive methods would employ historical and biographical as well as textual facts and thus

---

[19]Steven Knapp and Walter Benn Michaels, "Against Theory," *Critical Inquiry*, 8 (Summer 1982), reprinted in *Against Theory: Literary Studies and the New Pragmatism*, ed. W. J. T. Mitchell (Chicago, 1985), p. 11.

[20]See Knapp and Michaels, "Against Theory," pp. 13–18. See also, in *Critical Inquiry*, 9 (June 1983), Hirsch's rebuttal in his "Against Theory?" and Knapp and Michaels' response in "A Reply to Our Critics," both reprinted in Mitchell, *Against Theory*, pp. 48–52 and 100–104, respectively.

could establish a meaning for a text that was different from one in which external evidence was scrupulously ignored. Misguided or not, Theory can have consequences.[21]

This, then, is my answer to the first question, "If Theorists continue doing Theory, what are they doing?" If a Theory persuades critics, it continues to have consequences, but such consequences are not those of its claims. The Theory has not provided an idealist or realist account of interpretation that can be successfully invoked to adjudicate readings. It may, however, affect critical practice by encouraging one type of interpretive method rather than another: formalist, intentionalist, deconstructive, historicist, or some other. But now I turn to the second question, "What will happen to theory if the anti-Theory argument *is* accepted?" Of course, Theory would end, but what can take its place? What happens when theorists stop searching for that general account that guarantees correct readings? Where do they go once they quit asking realist or idealist questions about interpretation?

One route to follow takes a turn toward rhetoric. I take this path by proposing a *rhetorical hermeneutics*, an anti-Theory theory. Such a hermeneutics views shared interpretive strategies not as the creative origin of texts but rather as historical sets of topics, arguments, tropes, ideologies, and so forth which determine how texts are established as meaningful through rhetorical exchanges. In this view, communities of interpreters neither discover nor create meaningful texts. Such communities are actually synonymous with the conditions in which acts of persuasion about texts take place. Concepts such as "interpretive strategies" and "argument fields" are, we might say, simply descriptive tools for referring to the unformalizable context of interpretive work, work that always involves rhetorical action, attempts to convince others of the truth of explications and explanations.[22]

A rhetorical hermeneutics must, of necessity, be more thera-

[21]I take up the "Against Theory" argument in more detail in chap. 6.

[22]See Fish, *Is There a Text?*, pp. 356–70, and "Change," *South Atlantic Quarterly*, 86 (Fall 1987), 423–44. Also, cf. Thomas S. Kuhn, *The Structure of Scientific Revolutions*, 2d ed. (Chicago, 1970), pp. 152–59 and 198–206. On "argument fields" and related concepts, see Charles Arthur Willard, *Argumentation and the Social Grounds of Knowledge* (University, Ala., 1983), esp. pp. 5–11 and 89–91.

peutic than constructive.[23] To be otherwise, to construct a new account of interpretation in general, would simply reproduce the same old problems of realism and idealism. Rather than propose still another interpretive system on all fours with realist and idealist theories, rhetorical hermeneutics tries to cure theoretical discourse of its Theoretical tendencies. It might, then, restate the critique made in section I: various hermeneutic accounts make the Theoretical mistake of trying to establish the foundations of meaning outside the setting of rhetorical exchanges. All Theories believe that some pure vantage point can be established beyond and ruling over the messy realm of interpretive practices and persuasive acts. Only in this way, it is thought, can correct interpretation, privileged meaning, be accounted for. Hermeneutic realism, for example, assumes a stability of meaning before any rhetorical acts take place. Meaning is determinate, objective, and eternally fixed because of constraints in the text itself which are independent of historically situated critical debates. In a strangely similar way, hermeneutic idealism also assumes stability of meaning outside situated practices. Meaning is determinate, intersubjective, and temporarily fixed because of constraints provided by the communal conventions in readers' and critics' minds. When hermeneutic idealists attempt to describe the system of interpretive conventions that determine meaning, either they describe this system as independent of rhetorical situations or they do not realize that the conventions themselves are the topic of critical debate at specific historical moments. In either case, idealists make a mistake similar to that of realists by presupposing the possibility of meaning outside specific historical contexts of rhetorical practices.

But pointing out the problems with hermeneutic realism and idealism is only an initial, therapeutic step. Rhetorical hermeneutics must also explain why realism and idealism are such attractive theories of interpretation in the first place. We can best do so by redefining realist and idealist claims in terms of their rhetorical implications. What exactly do these past theories teach us about rhetorical exchanges in interpretation? The realist's claim about constraints in the text testifies to the com-

[23]This distinction is nicely elaborated in Richard Rorty, *Philosophy and the Mirror of Nature* (Princeton, N.J., 1979), pp. 5–6.

mon assumption in critical debates that interpretive statements are about texts. References to the text are therefore privileged moves in attempts to justify interpretations. The idealist's claim about the constitutive power of critical presuppositions exemplifies the common pluralist belief that if you change the questions being asked about texts, you change the answers you get, and if you can persuade someone else to ask *your* questions, you are that much closer to persuading him or her to accept your interpretation of a specific text. A rhetorical hermeneutics does not reject any of these assumptions. In fact, it uses their widespread acceptability to explain the rhetorical dynamics of academic interpretation in late-twentieth-century America. But to acknowledge the power of these assumptions in rhetorical exchanges today is *not* to make any claims about whether they are epistemologically true. Such epistemological questions are simply beside the point for a rhetorical hermeneutics. They always lead back to the dead ends of realism and idealism.

Rhetorical hermeneutics, then, gives up the goals of Theory and continues to theorize about interpretation only therapeutically, exposing the problems with foundationalism and explaining the attractions of realist and idealist positions. But a rhetorical hermeneutics has more to do: it should also provide histories of how particular theoretical and critical discourses have evolved. Why? Because acts of persuasion always take place against an ever-changing background of shared and disputed assumptions, questions, assertions, and so forth. Any thick rhetorical analysis of interpretation must therefore describe this tradition of discursive practices in which acts of interpretive persuasion are embedded.[24] Rhetorical hermeneu-

---

[24]Relevant here is the intersection of Hans-Georg Gadamer's hermeneutics with Chaim Perelman's rhetoric. Cf. Gadamer's analysis of tradition and interpretation throughout his *Truth and Method*, trans. and ed. Garrett Barden and John Cumming (New York, 1975), e.g., pp. 250–51, and the analysis of tradition and argumentation in Perelman and Lucie Olbrechts-Tyteca, *The New Rhetoric: A Treatise on Argumentation*, trans. John Wilkinson and Purcell Weaver (Notre Dame, Ind., 1969), e.g., pp. 464–65. More generally, see the "Rhetoric and Hermeneutics" section of Gadamer, "On the Scope and Function of Hermeneutical Reflection (1967)," trans. G. B. Hess and R. E. Palmer, in Gadamer, *Philosophical Hermeneutics*, ed. David E. Linge (Berkeley, 1976), pp. 21–26. Also see recent work in speech communication influenced by Gadamer and Heidegger, e.g., Robert L. Scott, "On Viewing Rhetoric as Epistemic: Ten Years Later," *Central States Speech Journal*, 27 (1976), 258–66; Michael J. Hyde and Craig R.

tics always leads to rhetorical histories, and it is to versions of these histories that I turn in the next three chapters.

By presenting these narratives, I mean to illustrate how a rhetorical hermeneutics is composed of therapeutic theory *and* rhetorical histories. More exactly, such narratives are not simply added onto theory; rather, interpretive theory must become rhetorical history. Thus rhetorical hermeneutics joins other recent attempts to incorporate rhetoric at the level of interpretive theory and its analysis of literary and critical practice.[25] Such attempts share a suspicion of Theory and a preoccupation with history, a skepticism toward foundational accounts of interpretation in general and an attraction to narratives surrounding specific rhetorical acts and their particular sociopolitical contexts. Such attempts place theory, criticism, and literature itself within a cultural conversation, the dramatic, unending conversation of history which is the "primal scene of rhetoric."[26]

Smith, "Hermeneutics and Rhetoric: A Seen but Unobserved Relationship," *Quarterly Journal of Speech*, 65 (December 1979), 347–63; and, for a counterview plus additional bibliography, Richard A. Cherwitz and James W. Hikins, *Communication and Knowledge: An Investigation in Rhetorical Epistemology* (Columbia, S.C., 1986).

[25]See esp. Terry Eagleton, *Walter Benjamin, or, Towards Revolutionary Criticism* (London, 1981), pp. 101–13; Eagleton, "Wittgenstein's Friends," *New Left Review*, no. 135 (September–October 1982), reprinted in his *Against the Grain: Selected Essays* (London, 1986), pp. 99–130; Eagleton, *Literary Theory: An Introduction* (Minneapolis, 1983), pp. 204–14; Edward W. Said, "Opponents, Audiences, Constituencies, and Community," *Critical Inquiry*, 9 (September 1982), 1–26; Robert Wess, "Notes toward a Marxist Rhetoric," *Bucknell Review*, 28, no. 2 (1983), 126–48; and James A. Berlin, *Rhetoric and Reality: Writing Instruction in American Colleges, 1900–1985* (Carbondale, Ill., 1987), pp. 3–18. Also see the works cited below in chap. 3, n. 8.

[26]Frank Lentricchia (discussing Kenneth Burke's fable of history), *Criticism and Social Change* (Chicago, 1983), p. 160.

2

The Institutional Rhetoric of Literary Criticism

> Where, indeed, but to rhetoric should the theoretical examination of interpretation turn?
> —Hans-Georg Gadamer, "On the Scope and Function of Hermeneutical Reflection"

If a rhetorical hermeneutics merges theory with history, what *kinds* of rhetorical histories shall we have? The examples throughout *Rhetorical Power* will answer this question: histories that are interpretive, institutional, and cultural. Each of my historical narratives and rhetorical analyses builds on what has gone before. In this chapter I begin with a schematic history of the academic rhetoric of a once-dominant critical mode, New Criticism. Next I analyze in more fine-grained detail the rhetorical strategies of one institutional challenger to this formalist discourse, reader-response criticism. Then Chapter 3 develops the rhetorical analysis further by extending it outward beyond the academic institution toward the rhetoric of literature and criticism within a cultural conversation.

I. A Synoptic Rhetorical History

Increasing attention has recently been paid to the institutional politics of interpretation, and this attention has proven salutary for histories of literary criticism.[1] Traditional histories

[1] The work of Michel Foucault stands behind many recent inquiries into criticism's institutional politics. See especially Paul Bové, *Intellectuals in Power: A Genealogy of Critical Humanism* (New York, 1986); Jim Merod, *The Political Responsibility of the Critic* (Ithaca, N.Y., 1987); and Jonathan Arac, *Critical Genealogies: Historical Situations for Postmodern Literary Studies*

tended to minimize the importance of social, political, and economic factors in the development of American literary study and to focus almost exclusively on abstract intellectual history. In the introduction to one paradigmatic text, *Literary Criticism: A Short History*, W. K. Wimsatt and Cleanth Brooks claimed to "have written a history of ideas about verbal art and about its elucidation and criticism," stressing "that in a history of this sort the critical *idea* has priority over all other kinds of material."[2] Such histories of critical ideas not only downplayed the political and economic context in which those ideas developed; they also ignored the effects of literary study's institutionalization within the American university of the late nineteenth century. This historical event transformed the critical tradition by adding specific institutional requirements to the more general cultural and political determinations that affected the rhetorical shape of American literary study.

More comprehensive than descriptions of critical ideas is a newer kind of critical history: explanations of literary study in terms of social, political, and economic forces. In *English in America*, for example, Richard Ohmann shows how "industrial society organizes the labor of people who work with their minds"; in *The Critical Twilight*, John Fekete situates modern critical theory within the American network of social ideologies

---

(New York, 1987), pp. 125–38. Foucault's archaeology reveals the "relations between discursive formations and non-discursive domains" such as institutions, while his genealogies trace the history of "the effective formation of discourse" within institutions, "the field of the non-discursive social" (*The Archaeology of Knowledge and the Discourse on Language*, trans. A. M. Sheridan Smith [New York, 1972], p. 162; "The Order of Discourse," trans. Ian McLeod, in *Untying the Text: A Post-Structuralist Reader*, ed. Robert Young [Boston, 1981], p. 71; and "The Eye of Power," trans. Colin Gordon, in *Power/ Knowledge: Selected Interviews and Other Writings, 1972–1977*, ed. Gordon [New York, 1980], p. 198). More specifically, we might say that an institution "includes both the material forms and mechanisms of production, distribution and consumption *and* the ideological rules, norms, conventions and practices which condition the reception, comprehension and application of discourse" (Vincent Leitch, "Institutional History and Cultural Hermeneutics," *Critical Texts*, 2 [July 1984], 7; Leitch acknowledges his debt to Foucault on p. 10n). On the relation of rhetorical, especially discursive, practices to a cultural background of nondiscursive practices, see Hubert L. Dreyfus and Paul Rabinow, *Michel Foucault: Beyond Structuralism and Hermeneutics*, 2d ed. (Chicago, 1983).

[2] W. K. Wimsatt and Cleanth Brooks, *Literary Criticism: A Short History* (New York, 1957), pp. ix, vii–viii.

manipulated by corporate capitalism.[3] Such studies take account of literary criticism as part of a discipline that is situated within an institution, the modern university. Indeed, Ohmann, Fekete, and others have done valuable work in revealing the institutional mechanisms that constrain the development of academic literary study. But though these historical analyses do acknowledge the importance of institutional constraints, such determinations are secondary to their primary interest in economic and political formations in society at large. The result is that (at least in Fekete's case) such accounts sometimes overlook or distort the institutional role of literary studies in the development of critical ideology. Whereas Fekete argues that, in the modern critical tradition, "cultural methodology reveals its politics directly,"[4] I would say that social and political formations reveal themselves only indirectly, through the mediation of criticism's place within institutions for producing knowledge—universities generally and literature departments specifically. That is, the establishment, maintenance, and development of literary study in universities can be only partially explained through analysis of factors originating outside these institutions. No easy inside/outside distinction is implied here. More widespread social, political, and economic formations traverse the institutional space established for academic literary study. Once that space has been established, however, the *specific* interpretive work and rhetorical practices within the space develop with some relative autonomy even when they are affected by practices centered outside the academy.

Let me use the institutional history of New Critical formalism to illustrate what I mean. Traditional accounts of critical ideas and more recent sociopolitical analyses of critical practices give a prominent place to the hegemony of New Criticism in American literary study during the 1940s and 1950s. Traditional histo-

---

[3]Richard Ohmann, *English in America: A Radical View of the Profession* (New York, 1976), p. 4; and see John Fekete, *The Critical Twilight: Explorations in the Ideology of Anglo-American Literary Theory from Eliot to McLuhan* (London, 1977). See also Terry Eagleton, *Literary Theory: An Introduction* (Minneapolis, 1983), pp. 47–53. For related histories of literary studies in other countries, see Chris Baldick, *The Social Mission of English Criticism, 1848–1932* (Oxford, 1983); Brian Doyle, "The Hidden History of English Studies," in *Re-Reading English*, ed. Peter Widdowson (London, 1982), pp. 17–31; and Peter Uwe Hohendahl, *The Institution of Criticism* (Ithaca, N.Y., 1982).

[4]Fekete, *Critical Twilight*, p. 49.

ries of criticism usually recount the evolution of New Critical ideas but fail to explain adequately why those ideas came to dominate literary study. Sociopolitical analyses such as those of Ohmann and Fekete have much more explanatory power. For instance, Fekete skillfully shows how Agrarian social ideology, which attacked modern industrial civilization, was easily accommodated to corporate capitalism through the institutionalization of New Criticism within English departments. But Fekete's otherwise insightful analysis does not grant the institutional setting of literary study its full share in determining the shape and hegemony of New Criticism; in fact, Fekete distorts the nature of the institutionalized discipline when he suggests that New Criticism filled a vacuum created in the 1930s by the failure of socialist criticism within the discipline.[5] Actually, there was no vacuum: literary study within the academy was dominated by historical scholarship, which provided the discipline with a professional training program, shared research goals, and interpretive conventions for viewing literature. The rhetoric of New Criticism was influenced significantly by its institutional attempt to displace this scholarship as the dominant approach to literary texts. To understand exactly what was required of New Criticism, we need to trace the institutional history of literary study. In what follows I will briefly present a rhetorical version of this history, emphasizing only those institutional forces and events that help explain why New Criticism achieved its persuasive authority in the American study of literature. Such a rhetorical history follows directly from the rhetorical hermeneutics I have proposed, because in order to understand the discursive practices of interpretive rhetoric, we must also understand their past and present relations to the nondiscursive practices of institutions.

In the 1870s and 1880s the American university expanded its collegiate curriculum to include scientific and humanistic disciplines previously ignored, and it relied on the model of German scientific research for its conception of knowledge produc-

---

[5]See ibid. Fekete does go on to say that "the New Criticism introduced a technicism and an accommodation with science, and it mercilessly attacked and destroyed left-wing aesthetic forms, including the totally reformist forms of historiographic or sociological criticism."

tion.[6] The influence of this scientific ideology can be seen in the particular way literary study was institutionalized. Various critical approaches were available to those in the university who wanted literature to be made part of the curriculum—for example, moral or didactic criticism, impressionism, and liberal social criticism. But the approach that made possible the institutionalization of literary study was German philology, the scientific study of modern languages and a linguistic and historical approach to literature.[7] Philology provided the scientific rhetoric needed to justify the study of literature and linguistics to the rest of the academic community. Though it did not go unchallenged, this scholarship did allow the discipline to take advantage of all the mechanisms for the production and dissemination of knowledge that other institutionalized disciplines were developing.[8] Philological study provided a methodology that could be used for the classroom practices derived from the German scientific model: the seminar, the specialized lecture, and the research paper. It also made use of the agencies that the emphasis on research had created for the diffusion of knowledge: scholarly journals, university presses, and the annual conventions of learned societies.

But philology did not simply plug into an institutional compartment set aside for literary studies; it also effectively designed the interior of that compartment. In the early twentieth century, philology allowed the discipline to develop historical scholarship in all its forms (source and influence studies, examinations of historical backgrounds, and so forth). Indeed, philological research provided much of the agenda for the future of the discipline. The narrower view of philology gave literary

[6]For a recent general history, see The Organization of Knowledge in Modern America, 1860–1920, ed. Alexandra Oleson and John Voss (Baltimore, 1979).

[7]See William Riley Parker, "The MLA, 1883–1953," PMLA, 68, no. 4, pt. 2 (September 1953), 3–29, and his "Where Do English Departments Come From?," College English, 28 (February 1967), 339–51; Arthur N. Applebee, Tradition and Reform in the Teaching of English: A History (Urbana, Ill., 1974), pp. 25–28; and Phyllis Franklin, "English Studies: The World of Scholarship in 1883," PMLA, 99 (May 1984), 356–70.

[8]See the valuable rhetorical histories in Michael Warner, "Professionalization and the Rewards of Literature: 1875–1900," Criticism, 27 (Winter 1985), 1–28; and Gerald Graff, Professing Literature: An Institutional History (Chicago, 1986), chaps. 4–6. Also see Michael Warner and Gerald Graff, eds., The Origins of Literary Studies in America: A Documentary Anthology (New York, 1989).

study such basic projects as textual editing, variorum commentaries, bibliographical descriptions, and linguistic analyses. The broader view of philology gave historical scholarship its most ambitious rationale: philology as the cultural history of nations.[9] As philology modulated into a less linguistically oriented historicism in America, it maintained this ideal of studying a country's "spirit" through its literary productions.

In the first quarter of the twentieth century, then, philological research and historical scholarship dominated the institutional space provided for literary studies. These communal practices shaped and were shaped by the institutional nature of the discipline, and the functions they served became an important part of the institutional demands that the rhetoric of any new approach needed to address. We can now survey some of the ways in which New Criticism effectively served and, in its turn, revised institutional functions when it came to dominate the discipline by displacing historical scholarship.[10]

First of all, New Criticism provided an ingenious rhetorical accommodation to scientific ideology. As I've noted, scientific research provided the model of knowledge production through which literary study and several other disciplines were institutionalized. The prestige of science continued to grow within the academy during the early twentieth century, but at the same time some members of the humanistic disciplines grew increasingly discontented with scientific ideology and its positivistic assumptions. In literary study, these two conflicting trends came together in the way the New Critics theorized about literature and criticism in the second quarter of the century.

On the one hand, New Critics defended literature against the onslaught of positivist values by claiming that literary discourse presented a kind of knowledge unavailable in scientific discourse. On the other hand, New Criticism itself was sometimes promoted as a "scientific" method of getting at nonscientific, literary knowledge. This strategic manipulation of scientific ideology can be seen in the rhetoric of John Crowe Ransom. In

[9]Applebee, *Tradition and Reform*, pp. 25–26.

[10]For details of the conflict between criticism and scholarship in American literary study, see Phyllis Franklin, "English Studies in America: Reflections on the Development of a Discipline," *American Quarterly*, 30 (Spring 1978), 21–38; William E. Cain, *The Crisis in Criticism: Theory, Literature, and Reform in English Studies* (Baltimore, 1984), pp. 95–101; and Graff, *Professing Literature*, chaps. 7–8.

the early 1940s, Ransom distinguished science from poetry, arguing that poetry recovers "the denser and more refractory original world which we know loosely through our perceptions and memories." Poetry treats "an order of existence . . . which cannot be treated in scientific discourse."[11] Though he distanced literature from science, Ransom advocated a closer relationship between literary criticism and science: "Criticism must become more scientific, or precise and systematic, and this means that it must be developed by the collective and sustained effort of learned persons—which means that its proper seat is in the universities."[12] Here Ransom recognized the importance of proposing a "scientific" method of criticism to replace the "scientific" method of philological scholarship dominating the discipline. In this way, New Criticism accommodated itself to the institutionally entrenched model of knowledge production and simultaneously provided a defense of its subject matter as autonomous and uniquely worthy of study. Actually, New Criticism laid claim to only a few characteristics of scientific method (technical precision, objectivity, neutrality), but these few were enough for it to adapt rhetorically to the scientific ideology in such a way that it provided continuity as well as revitalization for the discipline.

This revitalization included a humanistic critique of carefully chosen aspects of scientific ideology. Some New Critics extended a humanistic attack on scientific relativism to the scientism of historical scholarship. In "Criticism, History, and Critical Relativism," Brooks took exception to Frederick Pottle's historical study, The Idiom of Poetry, and was particularly upset with the book's historicist premises. Critical evaluation is always relative, Pottle argued, because "poetry always expresses the basis of feeling (or sensibility) of the age in which it was written," and therefore earlier poetry can never be judged by

[11]John Crowe Ransom, The New Criticism (Norfolk, Conn., 1941), p. 281. In chap. 1 Ransom works out his distinction between science and poetry in a critique of I. A. Richards' parallel distinction between two uses of language proposed in his Principles of Literary Criticism (New York, 1925).

[12]Ransom, "Criticism, Inc.," in The World's Body (New York, 1938), p. 329. Also see Ransom's call for a "critical attitude" that is "tough, scientific, and aloof from the literary 'illusion' which it examines": "Strategy for English Studies," Southern Review, 6 (Autumn 1940), 235; cited in Kermit Vanderbilt, American Literature and the Academy: The Roots, Growth, and Maturity of a Profession (Philadelphia, 1986), p. 486.

twentieth-century standards. "*The poetry of an age* [in a collective sense] *never goes wrong.*"[13] Brooks opposed these historicist assumptions with his own formalist claims about poetic structures that are transhistorical: "functional imagery, irony, and complexity of attitude" can be used to evaluate poems in all ages (CHCR, p. 209). Brooks argued further that a debilitating relativism would certainly result if historical study continued to ignore the universal criteria of formalist evaluation. "I am convinced," he wrote, "that, once we are committed to critical relativism, there can be no stopping short of a *complete* relativism in which critical judgments will disappear altogether" (CHCR, p. 212). Attributing this growing danger to the fact that "teachers of the Humanities have tended to comply with the [scientific] spirit of the age rather than to resist it," Brooks argued that in literary studies we have tried "to be more objective, more 'scientific'—and in practice we usually content ourselves with relating the work in question to the cultural matrix out of which it came," thus irresponsibly avoiding normative judgments (CHCR, pp. 213, 198). The New Critical accommodation to scientific ideology, then, simultaneously approved one form of objectivity and criticized another: Ransom advocated a "good" kind of formalist objectivity in the interpretation of literary works, while Brooks condemned a "bad" kind of historicist objectivity for failure to evaluate those works. In this strategic way, New Criticism incorporated into its rhetorical appeal the strengths of both scientific and humanistic programs within the institutionalized discipline.

New Criticism satisfied a second institutional requirement when it became an effective means for increased specialization. The New Critical assumption that literature was an ordered object independent of social and historical context entailed a formalist methodology that could reveal the unified complexity of that literary object. Since literary meaning was also assumed to be independent of authorial intention and reader response, New Critics stressed the details of the text-in-and-of-itself. They therefore developed their methodology by focusing on the literary text in a vacuum, or, as they preferred to say, on literature as

[13]Frederick A. Pottle, *The Idiom of Poetry* (Ithaca, N.Y., 1941), quoted in Brooks, "Criticism, History, and Critical Relativism," in *The Well Wrought Urn: Studies in the Structure of Poetry* (New York, 1947), p. 207 (hereafter Brooks's work will be cited in text as CHCR).

literature. New Critics thus tried to elaborate a technical criticism that derived its interpretive categories exclusively from literature and not from psychology, sociology, or history. This rejection of "extrinsic" approaches conveniently included a rejection of the historical assumptions of philological scholarship. The rhetoric of the new "intrinsic" criticism served the institutional function of reinforcing the independence of literary study within the academy, an accomplishment that was part of a general institutional tendency in American universities between 1910 and 1960. As Stephen Toulmin points out:

> During those years ... the academic and artistic professions moved into a new phase of specialization. Each "discipline" or "profession" was characterized by, and organized as the custodian of, its own corpus of formal techniques, into which newcomers had to be initiated and accredited, as apprentices. So, there was a general tendency for each of the professions to pull away from its boundaries with others, and to concentrate on its own central, essential concerns.[14]

In literary study, New Criticism helped fulfill the institutional need for increasing differentiation and specialization.

A third function of New Criticism was its usefulness as a means of further professionalization. Since institutional specialization also requires professionalism, the discipline of literary studies needed an approach that fulfilled what Ohmann calls "the professional mission of developing the central body of knowledge and the professional service performed for clients."[15] New Criticism easily satisfied both of these professional requirements. It redefined the nature of the knowledge produced by the discipline; where once literary studies produced the historical and linguistic knowledge of philology, they now produced formalist knowledge about the literary text in-and-of-itself. New Criticism also changed the priority of

[14]Stephen Toulmin, "From Form to Function: Philosophy and History of Science in the 1950s and Now," *Daedalus*, 106 (Summer 1977), 159.

[15]Ohmann, *English in America*, pp. 239–40. See also Magali Sarfatti Larson, *The Rise of Professionalism: A Sociological Analysis* (Berkeley and Los Angeles, 1977), esp. chaps. 4 and 12; and Dietrich Rueschemeyer, "Professional Autonomy and the Social Control of Expertise," in *The Sociology of the Professions: Lawyers, Doctors, and Others*, ed. Robert Dingwall and Philip Lewis (New York, 1983), pp. 38–58.

the discipline's practices as literary studies moved away from scholarship to criticism, giving ultimate value to explication of individual texts. The formalist assumptions and textual explications presented the discipline with a new pedagogy, one that Brooks and Robert Penn Warren's *Understanding Poetry* (1938) rapidly taught to members of the profession. More slowly, these same New Critical assumptions and practices also displaced philological scholarship as a methodology for training and accrediting the growing number of new recruits to the profession.

The close readings of New Critical formalism represent the fulfillment of the final institutional function I will point out. New Criticism constituted a discursive practice for the discipline, one that could be easily reproduced and disseminated within a growing profession. It gave the members new things to do with old texts; now they had an interpretive machine they could operate without the traditional and lengthy training of philology. Literary critics exploited this machine to fill the increasing number of monographs and journals the expanding institution demanded.

In the 1940s and 1950s, New Critical formalism showed that it could fulfill all of the institutional demands I have outlined. It did so more persuasively than any other available critical approach, even as it simultaneously modified these demands. Again, as with philology, the dominant critical practice and the institutional space were mutually defining. Today debates in critical theory take place in terms set by New Critical formalism: Is authorial intention relevant to correct interpretation? Is textual meaning separate from reader response? Is the literary work independent of historical context? But even more important than setting the current agenda for theoretical debate is the authoritative legacy contributed by New Critical close readings, the detailed explications of individual texts. It is no accident that among the most popular forms of poststructuralist criticism are those that closely resemble the interpretive rhetoric of New Criticism, a rhetoric emphasizing the complexity of the unique literary work. Thus, despite being constantly attacked and supposedly outmoded, formalist rhetoric still remains a significant presence in literary thought and critical practice within the discipline of American literary studies.[16]

[16]For useful discussions of this New Critical legacy, see Frank Lentricchia, *After the New Criticism* (Chicago, 1980); Jane P. Tompkins, "The Reader in

II. Reader-Response Criticism Revisited

One problem with the schematic history of the previous section is that it remains much too general in its analysis of the institutional rhetoric of academic interpretation. To provide more detail, we need to focus on a specific interpretive convention and its rhetorical tactics. First and foremost, interpretive conventions are shared procedures for establishing meaning, which consist of hermeneutic assumptions manifested in specific rhetorical moves. A critic adopts (and is adopted by) these conventions in his or her attempt to describe, explicate, and explain any discourse, whether it be one line of poetry, a complete novel, or an entire literary tradition. The history of recent literary criticism is a chronicle of rhetorical changes in these shared interpretive strategies. While the conventions of New Criticism dominated in the United States during the 1940s and 1950s, the kind of text rhetorically constituted by that criticism became known for its levels of unity, patterns of imagery, ironic tensions, and objective meanings. In the sixties and seventies, reader-response criticism joined many imported and domestic challengers to the New Critical hegemony, and like them it defined texts in terms of formal properties and literary effects different from those identified by the old New Criticism. In the rest of this chapter, I analyze the most widely reviewed version of reader-response criticism, that practiced by Stephen Booth, Stanley Fish, and Wolfgang Iser.[17]

History: The Changing Shape of Literary Response," *Reader-Response Criticism: From Formalism to Post-Structuralism* (Baltimore, 1980), pp. 201–32; Jonathan Culler, "Beyond Interpretation," in *The Pursuit of Signs: Semiotics, Literature, Deconstruction* (Ithaca, N.Y., 1981), pp. 3–17; Cain, "The Institutionalization of the New Criticism," in *Crisis in Criticism*, pp. 104–21; and Edward W. Said, *The World, the Text, and the Critic* (Cambridge, Mass., 1983), pp. 140–77.

[17]Subsequent references to works by these critics will be cited in the text as follows: Wolfgang Iser, *The Implied Reader: Patterns of Communication in Prose Fiction from Bunyan to Beckett* (Baltimore, 1974) (IR); Stephen Booth, "On the Value of *Hamlet*," in *Reinterpretations of Elizabethan Drama: Selected Papers from the English Institute*, ed. Norman Rabkin (New York, 1969), pp. 137–76 (VH); Stephen Booth, *An Essay on Shakespeare's Sonnets* (New Haven, Conn., 1969) (ESS); Stanley E. Fish, *Surprised by Sin: The Reader in "Paradise Lost,"* 2d ed. (Berkeley, 1971) (SS); Stanley E. Fish, *Self-Consuming Artifacts: The Experience of Seventeenth-Century Literature* (Berkeley, 1972) (SA). Here I am interested only in these early texts of practical criticism (with

In the early seventies, the critiques of formalism gained added force from political discourses, such as feminism and neo-Marxism, that transcended the debates within academic literary criticism. Similarly, in the reader-response attack on New Criticism and the affective fallacy, there appears to be a connection between the early talk of "reader liberation" and the liberationist rhetoric of the New Left. Efforts to free the reader-student from the authority of the author, text, or teacher at first seemed to be allied with the more broadly based attacks on political oppression and authoritarianism, attacks taking place on and off college campuses in the late sixties and early seventies. This connection was made explicit by some reviewers of early reader-response criticism. Objecting to Walter Slatoff's *With Respect to Readers* (1970), Harry Woelfel wrote: "In times such as these when subjectivity has been raised to Godhead and students everywhere are goaded to 'express themselves,' . . . Slatoff . . . plays guru to the new cult of subjectivism." More sympathetically, Jan Pinkerton began a 1972 review of several books with the observation that "there are some sorts of criticism that should be spiritually (if not materially) implicated in the recent disruptions of the American university," but implied that Slatoff's notion of "relevance" was a positive remedy to a naive critical objectivity and an undesirable "authoritarianism."[18] In "The Revolt of the Reader," Terry Eagleton wittily sums up this view of the counterculture origins of reader-response criticism: "The growth of the Readers' Liberation Movement (RLM) over the past few decades has struck a decisive blow for oppressed readers everywhere, brutally proletarianized as they have been by the authorial class."[19]

But the shift in the seventies from talk about authors and texts

---

their similarities in interpretive rhetoric) and not in the theoretical disagreements that arose later between, for example, Fish and Iser. For these later disputes, see Iser, "Interview," *Diacritics*, 10 (June 1980), 72–73; Fish, "Why No One's Afraid of Wolfgang Iser," *Diacritics*, 11 (March 1981), 2–13; and Iser, "Talking Like Whales: A Reply to Stanley Fish," *Diacritics*, 11 (September 1981), 82–87.

[18]Harry W. Woelfel III, Review of Slatoff's *With Respect to Readers*, *Southern Humanities Review*, 9 (Summer 1975), 339; Jan Pinkerton, "Reflections on the Classroom and Recent Literary Criticism," *College English*, 33 (February 1972), 600, 605.

[19]Terry Eagleton, "The Revolt of the Reader," in his *Against the Grain: Selected Essays* (London, 1986), p. 181.

to talk about readers and reading actually had only a very mediated connection to any radical politics. In fact, the critical shift owed much more to its rhetorical situation within the discipline of literary studies than it did to any New Left rhetoric active within the larger cultural conversation. In the first place, the extremely divergent approaches to readers reading would probably never have been grouped together under the rubric reader-response or reader-oriented criticism if it were not for the institutional hegemony of New Critical formalism with its proscription against the affective fallacy. Reader-critics themselves encouraged this antiformalist framing by explicitly rejecting and writing against the affective fallacy. However, this apparent similarity and the shared critical vocabulary covered over very different ways of talking about the reader and his (and, only later, her) reading experience.[20] Throughout the seventies, for example, reader-response critics began with differing conceptions of the relation between reader and text: Gerald Prince and Peter Rabinowitz often focused on the reader *in the text*; David Bleich and Norman Holland on the actual reader's complete dominance *over the text*; and Stephen Booth, Stanley Fish, and Wolfgang Iser on the ideal reader's interaction *with the text*. Or again: for Prince and Rabinowitz the inscribed readers (the narratees and other implied audiences) were part of the meaning in the narrative; for Bleich and Holland meaning was a creation by and in the individual reader; for Booth, Fish, and Iser meaning was a product of the interaction of readers and texts.[21]

[20]For detailed comparisons of various reader-response approaches, see my *Interpretive Conventions: The Reader in the Study of American Fiction* (Ithaca, N.Y., 1982), pp. 19–65, and Susan R. Suleiman, "Introduction: Varieties of Audience-Oriented Criticism," in *The Reader in the Text: Essays on Audience and Interpretation*, ed. Suleiman and Inge Crosman (Princeton, 1980), pp. 3–45. Also see Tompkins, "An Introduction to Reader-Response Criticism," in *Reader-Response Criticism*, pp. ix–xxvi; Elizabeth Freund, *The Return of the Reader: Reader-Response Criticism* (London, 1987); and Leitch, *American Literary Criticism from the Thirties to the Eighties* (New York, 1988), pp. 211–37, 252–59. On the issue of gender and the identity of "the reader," see *Gender and Reading: Essays on Readers, Texts, and Contexts*, ed. Elizabeth A. Flynn and Patrocinio P. Schweickart (Baltimore, 1986). Throughout this section I have attempted to use the inclusive "readers" and the corresponding plural pronouns, except when the reader-response critic I am quoting uses singular, masculine forms.

[21]The distinctions made here are provisional and approximate, useful only as a way of initially mapping the reader-oriented perspective. For example,

Thus, only the slippage of critical terminology and the convenience of metacritical grouping made possible the collection of such different theoretical assumptions under one critical label. But such slippage and grouping were almost inevitable given the institutional hegemony of New Criticism. That is, every new American approach to criticism in the sixties and seventies defined itself and was itself defined against the dominant critical discourse. This is one way, then, in which the rhetorical situation of early reader criticism was relatively independent of a larger cultural conversation extending beyond the academy. Reader-oriented criticism's obstacles and opportunities were demarcated quite specifically by its time and place within the professional discourse of academic literary criticism in the early seventies.[22]

This relative autonomy is even more pronounced for the reader-response criticism of Booth, Fish, and Iser. It is probably true that certain forms of subjectivist, psychologically oriented reader criticism did achieve some influence pedagogically because of an apparent consistency with liberationist rhetoric on college campuses.[23] And perhaps all forms of reader criticism benefited from (or became guilty by association with) this same

Prince's and Rabinowitz's theories go well beyond talk about inscribed readers; see Prince, Narratology: The Form and Functioning of Narrative (Berlin, 1982) and Rabinowitz, Before Reading: Narrative Conventions and the Politics of Interpretation (Ithaca, N.Y., 1987). Bleich and Holland also have much more complex approaches to reading than are suggested by my easy distinctions here; see especially their more recent work: Bleich, "Intersubjective Reading," and Holland, "The Miller's Wife and the Professors: Questions about the Transactive Theory of Reading," both in New Literary History, 17 (Spring 1986), 401–21 and 423–47; Holland, Laughing (Ithaca, N.Y., 1982) and The I (New Haven, Conn., 1985); and Bleich, The Double Perspective: Language, Literacy, and Social Relations (Oxford, 1988). Cf. Robert C. Holub's comment about the ex post facto labeling of "reader-response" critics, in Reception Theory: A Critical Introduction (London, 1984), pp. xii–xiii.

[22]I should, of course, talk of the re-emergence of reader-oriented criticism in the late sixties, not only because of the long rhetorical tradition of audience-centered criticism and theory in the West, but also because of the twentieth-century work of such theorists as I. A. Richards, Kenneth Burke, Wayne Booth, and especially Louise Rosenblatt. A revised edition of Rosenblatt's classic Literature as Exploration (New York, 1938) appeared in 1968 and a third edition in 1974. See also Rosenblatt, The Reader, the Text, the Poem: The Transactional Theory of the Literary Work (Carbondale, Ill., 1978).

[23]See, e.g., R. W. Lid and Philip Handler, "Radical Chic and the Liberation of the Reader," Theory into Practice, 14 (June 1975), 149–55.

liberationist rhetoric simply by using a reader vocabulary in the context of the terminological slippage described above. Far more important, however, were the institutional continuities offered by the reader-response criticism of Booth, Fish, and Iser. It is the institutional combination of formalist continuities with reader-oriented variations, rather than any extra-institutional affiliations with New Left rhetoric, that accounts most decisively for whatever persuasiveness this type of reader-response criticism attained.

In many specific and general ways, New Critical formalism still influences the way American criticism rhetorically functions in theory and practice. Ever since New Criticism established the explication of individual texts as the privileged activity of literary study, every new approach has had to prove its worth by effectively applying its proposed methods in close readings and then defending its procedures and results in an accompanying theoretical justification of its assumptions. Thus, the rhetorical project for an emerging critical perspective necessarily involves a threefold strategy: providing persuasive, detailed interpretations of valued literary texts; presenting a strong case for the theoretical assumptions underlying the interpretive method; and displaying a tight fit between the critical theory and the interpretive procedure. As we will see with reader-response criticism, these three rhetorical concerns involve every aspiring critical approach in several different institutional debates at once, debates embedded in both the most recent discussions of critical theory and the evolving interpretive history of specific literary texts. By describing the assumptions and tactics of one form of reader criticism, I intend my analysis to illustrate how, though they differ in detail, all critical approaches function rhetorically as institutional sets of interpretive conventions.

Before enacting and describing the interpretive rhetoric of reader-response criticism, we should look more closely at the interpretive assumptions underlying the project. The crucial, indeed the founding, theoretical claim of all reader-response critics is their explicit rejection of New Critical formalism and its purported assumption of an inactive reader, a reader simply acted upon by the text. Since the late sixties, reader-response critics have championed the reader as an active participant rather than a passive observer during the reading process. In his practical criticism, Wolfgang Iser focuses on "gaps" in the text that stimulate the "reader's creative participation" (IR, p. 275), and Stephen Booth's analyses of Shakespeare's sonnets emphasize the "reading experiences that result from the multiplicity of organizations [formal, logical, ideological, etc.] in which, over the course of fourteen lines, the reader's mind participates" (ESS, p. ix). Therefore, a typical (and, for my purposes here, central) act of readerly participation is the contribution readers make to the lessons they learn from a text. For example, Iser describes many reading experiences in which readers work things out instead of being told (e.g., IR, pp. 41–45, 154), and Stanley Fish often examines a text that "does not preach the truth, but asks that its readers discover the truth for themselves" (SA, p. 1).

In such practical criticism, the stage for action moves from the literary work to the reader's mind. What Fish says of *Paradise Lost* is true for most texts discussed by reader-response criticism: the mind of the reader becomes the "poem's scene" (SS, p. 1). In its strongest form, such criticism sees meaning itself as "an *event*, something that happens, not on the page, where we are accustomed to look for it, but in the interaction between the flow of print (or sound) and the actively mediating consciousness of a reader-hearer" (SS, p. x). Reader-response critics offer descriptions of this interaction, descriptions that often take the form of talk, not about "what a work *says* or *shows*" but about "what it *does*" (Booth, VH, p. 138).

A crucial issue for these critics is the identity of the reader whose experiences they portray: *whose* reading responses are being described? Iser refers to the "implied reader" of his book's title as a term incorporating "both the prestructuring of the potential meaning by the text, and the reader's actualization of this potential through the reading process" (IR, p. xii). Iser also refers to the "educated reader" (p. 58), a close relative of the "ideal" or "informed reader," whom Fish describes as a person "sufficiently experienced as a reader to have internalized the properties of literary discourses, including everything from the most local of devices (figures of speech, etc.) to whole genres" (SA, p. 406). In actual critical practice, all of these theoretical constructs become indistinguishable from the "intended reader," the person "whose education, opinions, concerns, linguistic competences, and so on make him capable of having the experience the author wished to provide."[24] In this version of reader-response criticism, the author becomes a *manipulator* of readers, with his or her techniques guiding the reader to the intended response.

To describe these reactions, reader-response critics adopt a temporal model of the reading process. Fish has made the following helpful distinction between formalist and reader-response enterprises:

> The lines of plot and argument, the beginnings, middles, and ends, the clusters of imagery, all the formal features that are observable when we step back from the reading experience, are, during that experience, components of a response; and the structure in which they are implicated is a structure of response. In other words, there is no necessary relationship between the visible form of a work and the form of the reader's experience—one is a complex of spatial, the other of temporal, patterns—and since it is in the context of the latter that meaning occurs, a criticism which restricts itself to the poem as 'object' will be inadequate to its pretentions. [*SS*, pp. ix–x]

Iser and Booth share Fish's preference for a temporal over a spatial model of the reading experience. Booth describes a "succession of actions upon the understanding of an audience" (*VH*, p. 139), while Iser focuses on the "potential time-sequence which the reader must inevitably realize" (*IR*, p. 280).

The interpretive assumptions of every critical approach form the enabling beliefs upon which its enterprise is founded. So it is with reader-response criticism. Interpretive assumptions about the reader and the temporal reading process provide a basis for the rhetorical strategies of its practical criticism. In the following section, I will provisionally adopt the interpretive conventions of reader-response criticism in order to provide a specific critical performance for further analysis. This brief ex-

---

[24]Fish, *Is There a Text in This Class?* (Cambridge, Mass., 1980), pp. 160–61. Cf. Jonathan Culler, *Structuralist Poetics* (Ithaca, N.Y., 1975), esp. pp. 113–30, on "literary competence," and my *Interpretive Conventions*, pp. 94–113 on "inferred intention."

ample uses in combination some of the rhetorical moves that I will later discuss separately.

III. Learning to Read

The question of the vanishing narrator in *Moby-Dick* has perplexed critics since the earliest reviews of the novel. The reviewer for the London *Spectator* expressed his concern in these words: "It is a canon with some critics that nothing should be introduced into a novel which it is physically impossible for the writer to have known: thus, he must not describe the conversation of miners in a pit if they *all* perish. Mr. Melville hardly steers clear of this rule, and he continually violates another, by beginning in the autobiographical form and changing ad libitum into the narrative."[25] Though the first criticism results from the omission of the "Epilogue" from *The Whale* (the British edition of *Moby-Dick*), the complaint about the change from autobiography to narrative is a precursor to later academic questions about what happens to Ishmael as narrator in the last quarter of the novel. Critics most often arrive at one of two conclusions: one side in the debate claims (with the *Spectator* reviewer) that Melville creates an artistic problem by changing narrators in mid-story; the other side denies that Ishmael actually disappears. Another interpretation is also suggested: Ishmael does vanish as narrator, but his disappearance serves an aesthetic purpose.[26] My own view follows from this last interpretation. I see the vanishing narrator as a consequence of Melville's careful rhetorical plan: teaching the reader to read.

Outside the pages of his fiction, Melville spoke disparagingly of the "tribe of 'general readers' '" who were most responsible for

[25]Review of *The Whale*, London *Spectator*, 25 October 1851, reprinted in *Moby-Dick as Doubloon*, ed. Hershel Parker and Harrison Hayford (New York, 1970), p. 12.

[26]For a sampling of the interpretive debate, see Walter E. Bezanson, "*Moby-Dick*: Work of Art," in *Moby-Dick Centennial Essays*, ed. Tyrus Hillway and Luther S. Mansfield (Dallas, 1953), pp. 30–58; Glauco Cambon, "Ishmael and the Problem of Formal Discontinuities in *Moby-Dick*," MLN, 76 (June 1961), 516–23; Paul Brodtkorb, Jr., *Ishmael's White World* (New Haven, Conn., 1965), pp. 1–10; William B. Dillingham, "The Narrator of *Moby-Dick*," *English Studies*, 49 (1968), 20–29; Edward H. Rosenberry, *Melville* (London, 1979), pp. 80–81; and John Miles Foley, "The Price of Narrative Fiction: Genre, Myth, and Meaning in *Moby-Dick* and *The Odyssey*," *Thought*, 59 (December 1984), 446.

the fact that "it is the least part of genius that attracts admiration." In his novels Melville took forms popular with this audience—whaling adventures, sensational Gothic romances, picaresque travel tales—and used them for his own kind of truth-telling. He wrote with a disguised dual purpose: to entertain and deceive the popular audience with books that sold because they could not be known for what they were by "the superficial skimmer of pages," and in these same books to reveal to the "eagle-eyed reader" the truth "covertly, and by snatches."[27] Thus Melville began *Pierre* with the intention of writing a lady's magazine romance for the popular audience, while he simultaneously composed a profound psychological exploration for his more perceptive readers.[28]

It was on this "eagle-eyed reader" that Melville focused his rhetorical attention in *Moby-Dick*. Early chapters of the novel prepare the way for later ones, not simply by revealing new information but by arming the reader with interpretive habits, specific ways of reading. In the early chapters, Ishmael (a schoolmaster on land) teaches his readers to see the rich significances of the later chapters. Indeed, reading *Moby-Dick* is a process of learning to read it.

From the first, in "Loomings," Ishmael encourages the reader to "dive," to search for the deeper meanings. As Harrison Hayford observes, Ishmael "exhorts us to confront, and, if we can, to explain the meaning of a series of analogical situations, stated in various images."[29] The mysteries of the first chapter are fol-

[27]The first quotation in this paragraph is from Melville's letter to Nathaniel Hawthorne, 1(?) June 1851. All of the other quotations are from Herman Melville, "Hawthorne and His Mosses," *Literary World*, 17 and 24 August 1850. Both of these documents are reprinted in the Norton Critical Edition of *Moby-Dick*, ed. Harrison Hayford and Hershel Parker (New York, 1967), pp. 535–60. All quotations from *Moby-Dick* in this section are from the Norton edition.

[28]Brian Higgins and Hershel Parker, "The Flawed Grandeur of Melville's *Pierre*," in *New Perspectives on Melville*, ed. Faith Pullin (Edinburgh, 1978), p. 162.

[29]Harrison Hayford, " 'Loomings': Yarns and Figures in the Fabric," in *Artful Thunder*, ed. Robert J. DeMott and Sanford E. Marovitz (Kent, O., 1975), p. 123. My interpretation of *Moby-Dick* is derived from the essays and lectures of Harrison Hayford; his readings have been developed further and passed on to me by Hershel Parker. Though neither Melvillean should be held accountable for what I do with his insights, I owe a great debt to both, for they have taught me how to read Melville's masterpiece. I should also note here that in his article "Unnecessary Duplicates: A Key to the Writing of *Moby-Dick*," in Pullin, *New*

lowed by others, as Ishmael makes out of everything a puzzle, a problem: the true identity of the "Black Parliament" (chap. 2); the "boggy, soggy squitchy picture" in the Spouter-Inn;[30] the "mystifying and exasperating stories" told by the landlord; the use of a mysterious "door mat"; "what to make of this head-peddling purple rascal," Queequeg (chap. 3); the meaning of Queequeg's tatoos, which were like "an interminable Cretan labyrinth"; the memory of a childhood "mystery" (chap. 4); Father Mapple's dragging up of his pulpit ladder, an act that "must symbolize something unseen"; the pulpit itself, so "full of meaning" (chap. 8); and the map to the Nantucket Try Pots (chap. 15). At one point Ishmael makes his lesson explicit: "All these things are not without their meanings" (chap. 7). In fact, all of these early puzzles prepare the reader for the more complicated puzzles of Ahab and the Whale. Later, in "Moby-Dick" and "The Whiteness of the Whale," the reader's instruction continues, as Ishmael struggles to explain the "symbol" of the White Whale, first in its unitary significance to Ahab and then in its multiplicity of meanings to himself.

By the last quarter of the novel, the reader's training is complete. If readers have learned their lesson well, they no longer require an explicit guide to encourage them to make a puzzle out of everything. They now see the signifying nature of all things on their own. Thus Ishmael disappears as narrator in the later chapters because he is no longer needed as a teacher. The reader uses him up by learning his lesson—the lesson of how to read the novel.

The structure of the reader's response can be further particularized. The specific habit of mind that Ishamel encourages in the reader is best illustrated (as Harrison Hayford has shown) by the first chapter: the crowds (including the reader) are confronted by the mystery of the sea, and what these inlanders discover is not an easy solution to the mystery, not an obvious signification for the symbol, but rather the "ungraspable phan-

---

Perspectives, pp. 128–61, Hayford provides in passing a very different explanation from the one I suggest for the disappearance of Ishmael as narrator.

[30]In another reader-response analysis of *Moby-Dick*, Carey H. Kirk notes that this picture "provides a useful model as well as a disconcerting initiation for the would-be interpreter of *Moby-Dick*" ("*Moby-Dick*: The Challenge of Response," *Papers on Language and Literature*, 13 [Fall 1977], 384). Cf. Morton L. Ross, "*Moby-Dick* as an Education," *Studies in the Novel*, 6 (Spring 1974), 71–73.

tom of life" (chap. 1). Readers are taught to follow the example of Ishmael (and later Ahab) in turning "every object, situation, and person they confront into a problem, one which cannot be solved, a mystery whose lurking meaning cannot be followed to its ultimate elucidation" (Hayford, " 'Loomings,' " pp. 121–22). The pattern Hayford describes for Ishmael's puzzling is also an accurate depiction of the reader's experience: "confrontation-exploration-nonsolution of a problem." This pattern is repeated in later chapters for both Ishmael and the reader. "Moby-Dick," for example, begins with the problem of what the White Whale means to Ahab. This question is explored and a theory set forth, but the chapter ends with Ishmael's admission that he cannot understand why the crew follows Ahab: "All this to explain, would be to dive deeper than Ishmael can go" (chap. 41). Again and again, Ishmael and the educated reader recognize that, though "some certain significance lurks in all things" (chap. 99), that significance cannot always be captured. The guiding lesson is clear: "Read it if you can" (chap. 79).

The reader's education and the pattern of his or her response indicate the temporal structuring of *Moby-Dick*, the care in Ishmael's "careful disorderliness" (chap. 82). Not only does this interpretation dissolve the problem of the vanishing narrator, it also suggests a perspective on another critical controversy: it is not Ishmael who changes in the telling but *readers* who change in their reading.

IV. Rhetorical Tactics

I will trust in my own readers' interpretive skill to flesh out this bare-bones explication. This brief demonstration of reader-response criticism can now serve as an additional source of examples in the following analysis of that criticism's rhetorical moves. But first some observations. Note how the above interpretation rhetorically situates itself in the critical history of the novel. It does not simply present a reading. Rather, it first identifies an interpretive problem constituted by past critical debates. This is a paradigmatic rhetorical strategy in academic criticism: by claiming that past critics have argued over an interpretive problem, the new interpretation attempts to convince its readers of both the significance of the problem and the value of its proposed solution. The rhetorical importance of this tactic should not be underestimated. Far from being an unnecessary ritual introducing academic interpretations, the rehearsal of past critical debates establishes the reason why the critic's reader should bother to proceed further. Reading a text's critical history in order to produce an interpretive problem cannot be rhetorically separated from the new reading of the text that solves the problem.[31] As we will see in a moment, reader-response criticism often gives a special twist to this rhetorical use of past criticism.

The success or failure of any new critical project depends partly on the persuasiveness of its accompanying theory, the foregrounding of its assumptions, illustrated in section II for reader-response criticism. But even more important in a discipline with a New Critical legacy of close reading, institutional success depends on the persuasiveness of specific interpretations of specific texts. Each new approach to literature therefore develops a set of rhetorical moves that can be repeated and interrelated to produce interpretations that appear as simultaneously original and persuasive—original in that they allow criticism to say something new about old interpretive problems and persuasive in that they connect up with what is already accepted as true. In this section I analyze the rhetorical tactics of reader-response criticism to show how that approach attempts to persuade its readers to accept specific interpretations and the critical project as a whole.[32]

Several of the rhetorical moves below are intricately related to each other, so I will be pulling apart what always appears as a tightly woven unity in any persuasive critical performance. Several of these moves are closely related because they arise from the same interpretive assumptions; for example, the description of successive reading activities and the analysis of response patterns both derive from the adoption of a temporal reading model. Some strategies have an added relationship, being refinements of more basic moves; the variations on the reader-character axis will serve as an example. All critical approaches manifest a similar network of strategies, strategies anchored by an unquestioned core of premises and interrelated either as

---

[31]See Adena Rosmarin, "Hermeneutics versus Erotics: Shakespeare's *Sonnets* and Interpretive History," *PMLA*, 100 (January 1985), 20–37; and Stanley Fish, "Short People Got No Reason to Live," *Daedalus*, 112 (Winter 1983), 175–91.

[32]See Stanley Fish, *The Living Temple: George Herbert and Catechizing* (Berkeley, 1978), pp. 170–73, and *Is There a Text?*, pp. 365–69.

derivations from a common assumption or as variations and refinements of other critical strategies.

The *description of successive reading activities* is the most common move made by the reader-response critics I am discussing. These critics focus on "the mind in the act of making sense, rather than on the sense it finally (and often reductively) makes" (Fish, *SA*, p. xii). Their descriptions of the temporal reading experience often proceed section by section, line by line, even word by word. The following compact example of the strategy is from Fish's analysis of a passage by Augustine: "The first part of the sentence—'He came to a place'—establishes a world of fixed and discrete objects, and then the second half—'where he was already'—takes it away" (*SA*, p. 41). Here readers are first given something and then they lose it. By contrast, Fish would argue, a holistic interpretation of Augustine's sentence ignores this temporal experience and provides only an impoverished meaning extracted after that experience. Booth, Iser, and others use this same strategy on longer passages, just as I do in my analysis of the successive puzzles in *Moby-Dick*. What such a move demonstrates is that form, as Carole Berger points out, "also has a *temporal* dimension, manifest in the reader's sequential experience of a work."[33]

A related strategy is also based on this assumption of a temporal reading model: any patterns found are placed not in the text but in *the structure of the reader's response*. For instance, Booth writes that "the audience's sensation of being unexpectedly and very slightly out of step is repeated regularly in *Hamlet*." This pattern plays a central role in Booth's thesis that the play "is insistently incoherent and just as insistently coherent" (*VH*, pp. 140, 139). Patterns of a similar temporal nature are posited throughout Fish's applied criticism. In one book, he demonstrates how the poems in Herbert's *The Temple* work "by inviting the reader to a premature interpretive conclusion, which is first challenged, and then reinstated, but in such a way as to make it the vehicle of a deeper understanding" (*Living Temple*, p. 35). This pattern is a more complex version of that described in his previous book. In the "self-consuming artifact," the reader "is first encouraged to entertain assumptions he prob-

---

[33]Carole Berger, "The Rake and the Reader in Jane Austen's Novels," *Studies in English Literature, 1500–1900*, 15 (Autumn 1975), 544.

ably already holds and then is later forced to reexamine and discredit those same assumptions" (*SA*, p. 10). Still earlier, Fish found a simpler pattern in *Paradise Lost*: "mistake, correction, instruction" (*SS*, p. 42). Similarly, my analysis of *Moby-Dick* uses the "pattern of confrontation-exploration-nonsolution" that Hayford sees for Ishmael as a description of the reading experience the novel provides.

The attempt to describe these sequential activities and temporal patterns always presents itself as an attempt to close the gap between criticism and reading. As one reader-oriented interpreter puts it, "it may be truer to the reader's experience of the text to speak of a succession of moments that yield varying effects."[34] To be "truer to the reader's experience" is the representational goal of reader-response criticism. Mindful of the New Critics' attack on the "affective fallacy," reader-oriented critics such as Fish in his "affective stylistics" try to beat the objectivists at their own game: Formalist criticism, Fish argues, "is 'objective' in exactly the wrong way, because it determinedly ignores what is objectively true about the *activity* of reading." In contrast, his analysis "in terms of doings and happenings is . . . truly objective because it recognizes the fluidity . . . of the meaning experience and because it directs us to where the action is—the active and activating consciousness of the reader" (*SA*, p. 401). In an institutionalized discipline preoccupied, as we noted in Chapter 1, by fears of interpretive relativism, Fish turns aside the charge of subjective impressionism by advocating a more comprehensive objectivity. He then enhances his objectivist ethos further by arguing that he describes *the* reader's experience, that is, the responsible responses of an "informed reader" with competencies that are potentially formalizable (*SA*, p. 406).[35]

Thus reader-response critics claim to identify the description of reading with the act of criticism and purport to represent accurately the temporal reading process in their analyses. To convince others that this descriptive claim is valid, the reader-response critic often resorts to the device of *citing other readers'*

---

[34]Robert W. Uphaus, *The Impossible Observer: Reason and the Reader in Eighteenth-Century Prose* (Lexington, Ky., 1979), pp. 17–18.

[35]As noted in chap. 1 above, Fish has given up these objectivist pretensions in his most recent theorizing and has himself provided a suggestive analysis of his earlier meta-critical claims (see *Is There a Text?*).

reactions. Booth's "Preface" best illustrates this device of using evidence external to one's own reading experience: "I have attempted to demonstrate that the responses I describe are probable in a reader accustomed to Elizabethan idiom. I have also quoted at length from the responses of the critics and editors who have preceded me in the study of the sonnets; their comments, glosses, and emendations provide the best available evidence that the responses I describe are not idiosyncratic" (*ESS,* p. x). In his discussion of *Hamlet,* Booth also uses other critics' responses in demonstrating the confusion he claims to see in the reader's experience of the play; thus he argues that it is intended incoherencies in the text that cause critics to propose stage directions to "make sense of Hamlet's improbable raging at Ophelia in III.i" (VH, p. 137).

I employ a similar strategy in my analysis of *Moby-Dick,* when I cite the perception by Melville critics that Ishmael disappears as narrator. Their interpretations serve as evidence for the final act I posit in the reader's education—the learning of Ishmael's lesson and his resultant loss as teacher. Fish also uses such evidence but pushes it in different directions. For example, he uses a critical controversy over the meaning of a passage to show that two contradictory meanings are equally available, his usual conclusion being that the recognized ambiguity is to be experienced, not resolved, by the reader. In fact, the reader's recognition of ambiguity *becomes* the meaning (*Is There a Text?* pp. 150–51). Another strategic use of other critics' readings is to show an author's success in trapping the reader; that is, a critic's interpretation is taken not as the "right" response but as evidence that the author encouraged the "wrong" response so that he could later correct the reader (e.g., *SA,* pp. 219–21). In all of these ways, reader-response critics show themselves to be especially adept at making a usable past out of a text's interpretive history.

This first group of rhetorical moves derives from the basic assumption that criticism should analyze the temporal reading experience. Reader-response critics try to describe successive reading activities and patterns of response and validate their descriptions with evidence from other critics' reactions. Another strategy is used to support not individual analyses but the whole enterprise of concentrating on the reader: the accumulation of external evidence to demonstrate authorial concern with readers. This strategy is less a part of the reader-oriented analysis than an argument for its critical respectability. Thus we find Iser referring to letters in which Richardson states that "the story must leave something for the reader to do" and other letters in which Thackeray shows he "did not want to edify his readers, but to leave them miserable" (IR, pp. 31, 116). Roger Easson makes a similar move in his reader-response analysis of *Jerusalem*, which begins: "Repeatedly, in his correspondence, in his marginalia, and in his poetry, William Blake expresses an abiding concern with his audience."[36] My use of a Melville letter and his essay on Hawthorne has the same rhetorical purpose as these other critical moves: to prove that my emphasis on the reader was shared by the author of the text I am analyzing. Whatever is said at the level of the discipline's theory about the "intentional fallacy" or "the death of the author," references to authors continue to purchase rhetorical leverage for one's interpretation, and even a *reader*-oriented criticism exploits this rhetorical tactic again and again.

A still more basic strategy is to cite direct references to the reader in the work being discussed (see Iser, IR, pp. 29, 38). Such a text-based procedure not only justifies the reader-centered focus but also becomes a part of the description of the reading experience. The next series of moves are really only refinements of this basic strategy. All of these moves either place the reader in the text in some way *or* demonstrate correspondences between elements in the text and the reader's experience.

The first rhetorical move in this group is to show that *the reader's response is a topic of the story*. Booth demonstrates, for example, that the "illogical coherence—coherent madness" experienced by the audience of *Hamlet* is "a regular topic of various characters" in the play (VH, p. 172). And in Shakespeare's sonnets, he argues, the author "evokes in his reader something very like the condition he talks about" (ESS, p. 59). This strategy of demonstrating response as topic sometimes expands into a claim that *the subject of the text is the reader*. For Booth, *Hamlet* becomes "the tragedy of an audience that cannot make up its mind" (VH, p. 152). For Fish, *Paradise Lost* has as its center of reference "its reader who is also its subject" (SS, p. 1). The potential self-reflexiveness of this strategy is apparent in

---

[36]Roger R. Easson, "William Blake and His Reader in *Jerusalem*," in *Blake's Sublime Allegory*, ed. Stuart Curran and Joseph A. Wittreich, Jr. (Madison, Wis., 1973), p. 309.

Easson's essay: Blake's *Jerusalem* "is a poem about itself, about the relationship between the author and his reader. . . . *Jerusalem* may be read as a poem about the experience of reading *Jerusalem*" (p. 309).

Instead of putting the reader in the poem, story, or play, a related critical move demonstrates how settings and events already in the text correspond to the reader's experience of that text. "*Jerusalem* mirrors the state of the reader," claims Easson (p. 314). More specifically, Fish shows how in *Paradise Lost* Michael's teaching of Adam in Book XI resembles Milton's teaching of the reader throughout the poem (*SS*, p. 22); and in his discussion of Herbert's poetry, Fish argues that "what is happening in the poem"—the "actions" of the speaker—corresponds to "what is happening in (and to) the reader" (*SA*, p. 165). Booth also exemplifies this recurrent strategy when he writes, "As the king is threatened *in* scene one, so is the audience's understanding threatened *by* scene one" (VH, p. 147).

A refinement of this last move is to point out a specific model in the text for the entire reading experience. Here a section of the reader's response is taken as a type of the whole. In discussing *Vanity Fair*, Iser finds "an allegory of the reader's task at one point in the novel"—a brief scene that "contains a change of standpoints typical of the way in which the reader's observations are conditioned throughout this novel" (*IR*, pp. 110–11). In Hamlet's "little poem on perception and truth," Booth discovers "a model of the experience of the whole play" (VH, p. 173). And in my analysis of Melville's novel I cite the strategy of one reader-response critic who calls Ishmael's attempt to interpret the Spouter-Inn painting "a useful model . . . for the would-be interpreter of *Moby-Dick*" (see n. 30). Ultimately, the set of tactics placing readers and reading experiences in texts presupposes a rhetorical authority given to texts by intrinsic criticism, the dominant perspective that reader-response approaches supposedly challenge. Indeed, the thematizing of one's critical assumptions, the discovery of, say, deconstructive or psychoanalytic premises in the literary work interpreted, remains a powerful argumentative move in even the most avant-garde, "postformalist" critical methods, a fact that testifies not only to the rhetorical legacy of intrinsic approaches but also to the disciplinary assumption that criticism remains at the service of the authoritative literary text.

The next group of rhetorical tactics I will describe focuses on the reader's relationship to the narrator and characters. The simplest of this group is the strategy (traditional in discussions of satire) that points out implicit references to the reader's life outside his or her present reading experience. Robert Uphaus's chapter on *Gulliver's Travels* illustrates this move when it emphasizes that the "transference from manifest fiction to the reader's [life] experience . . . is, perhaps dismayingly, insisted upon" (p. 18). Another move for the reader-response critic is to note how the narrator explicitly comments on the reading activities that the critic has posited. Iser, for instance, points out where Fielding, in *Joseph Andrews*, "makes various observations about the reader's role as producer"; for Iser, this is a reference to the reader's filling of gaps, his imaginative participation (*IR*, p. 39). A refinement of this critical strategy applies a character's comment to reading responses; for example, Booth writes that Horatio's statement "describes the mental condition evoked in an audience by this particular dramatic presentation of events as well as it does that evoked in the character by the events of the fiction" (*VH*, p. 142).

A commonplace of much traditional criticism is the identification of reader with characters, and, not surprisingly, reader-response critics use this device. (See Booth, *VH*, p. 150, and Iser, *IR*, p. 117.) More interesting, however, are the variations performed on this reader-character axis. Distinctions must be made, for example, among critics' (1) having readers identify their life experiences with a character's, (2) having readers become self-consciously aware of resemblances between their *reading* experiences and characters' actions, and (3) simply declaring that a character's act mirrors the reader's activities during the reading process with no reader awareness of that resemblance. Fish uses the second strategy when he argues that "a large part of the poem's meaning is communicated" to readers through their awareness that Adam's experience in the poem "parallels" the reader's experience reading the poem (*SS*, p. 29). Here the resemblance between character actions and reader activities is made a part of the reading experience. The third move mentioned above makes no such claim for reader awareness; the critic simply demonstrates a correspondence between a character's acts and the reader's response, as in Berger's description of *Pride and Prejudice*: "Instead of guiding us to accurate judgements of Darcy and Wickham, Austen creates an experience

analogous to Elizabeth's in its bewildering complexity and sus-
ceptibility to distortion" (p. 539). This is the same tactic Fish
uses in his discussion of Herbert's poetry where the speaker and
reader are associated in similar disorienting and educational
experiences: "'A True Hymne' proceeds in stages, and . . . its
stages represent levels in the reader's understanding as well as
plateaus in the spiritual history of the speaker" (SA, p. 200).

Still another rhetorical strategy involving the reader-character relation detaches the two "actors" from each other: "In the
Phaedrus, there are two plots; Socrates and Phaedrus are busily
building a picture of the ideal orator while the reader is extract-
ing, from the same words and phrases, a radical criticism of the
ideal" (SA, p. 13). In this move Fish does not identify reader
with character but contrasts the two. In a variation on this
strategy, Iser shows that Vanity Fair "denies the reader a basic
focal point of orientation. He is prevented from sympathizing
with the hero" (IR, p. 107). Detachment from characters is a
prerequisite for judging them, even when that judgment is a
result of prior identification or resemblance; for example, Fish
describes a version of the Herbertian "double motion" in which
"the speaker and the reader part company and the latter becomes a critic and corrector of the former's words and thoughts"
(SA, p. 178).

Having the reader judge the characters is often, even in traditional criticism, only a step on the way to having readers judge
themselves. But in reader-response criticism, describing such
self-evaluation becomes a central concern, and this concern
manifests itself in a variety of rhetorical moves. In one the critic
shows how readers are pressured to judge their own actions and
attitudes performed outside the reading of the text. Uphaus, for
instance, argues that in Gulliver's Travels the reader's attention
is called not simply to some of "the arbitrary niceties that are the
domain of royalty" but to some of "the dubious distinctions . . .
that the reader may unconsciously accept or consciously sus-
tain" (p. 17). Here readers judge the characters in the text and
themselves in their everyday lives.

A related strategy describes readers correcting themselves but
not the characters. This move abandons the reader-character
axis, and its depiction here initiates the final series of critical
strategies I will discuss. In this move, readers become judges of
their own reading responses. As Fish puts it for Paradise Lost,

the reader is "simultaneously a participant in the action and a critic of his own performance" (SS, p. xiii). The object of judgment here is not the reader's everyday life but his actions performed during the reading of the text causing those actions. Thus Iser shows how the author of *Joseph Andrews* encourages a feeling of superiority in such a way that the reader eventually becomes embarrassed ("trapped") by the feeling (*IR*, p. 44). Iser does not pinpoint the moment of entrapment; rather he suggests that at some *unspecified* time following the initial feeling of superiority, the reader becomes embarrassed by it. In contrast, Fish and Booth repeatedly describe precise moments when readers turn on themselves because of a specific textual event or statement.

Before describing these more precise specifications of reversal, I need to explain the rhetorical tactic on which they depend: the description of reader expectations and their disappointment. Howard Anderson provides one of many examples that I could cite: "Sterne repeatedly manipulates us by deliberately disappointing expectations of narrative form which we have developed through our prior reading."[37] Shattered expectations result in disappointment, disorientation, confusion; these effects recur again and again throughout applied reader-response criticism. Disappointed expectations especially proliferate in the reading experiences Fish describes in *Surprised by Sin*. His description of the Guilty Reader is typical: Beginning with assumptions about epic tradition and Christian myth, the reader is startled to discover what seems to be an admirable Satan. The speciousness of the devil's argument becomes apparent to the reader only after Milton's epic voice intervenes. Then the reader admonishes himself for "the weakness all men evince in the face of eloquence" (pp. 4–9). This example not only illustrates how Fish uses unfulfilled expectations in his analyses; it also shows how he pinpoints the moment when readers become their own critics.

In reader-response criticism a reader's disappointed expectations are never viewed as ends in themselves; rather, such disorientation always becomes an authorial means for a more significant end, such as the moral trial of the reader. In reader-response analyses we find many statements describing this au-

[37]Howard Anderson, "*Tristram Shandy* and the Reader's Imagination," *PMLA*, 86 (October 1971), 967.

thorial purpose: *Mansfield Park* includes "a test of the reader's moral perceptiveness" (Berger, p. 535); in *Vanity Fair* the reader "is constantly invited to test and weigh the [moral] insights he has arrived at as a result of the profusion of situations offered him" (Iser, *IR*, p. 118); in *Paradise Lost* Milton puts readers on trial by "fitting temptations to our inclinations and then confronting us immediately with the evidence of our fallibility" (Fish, *SS*, p. 41). The last statement in this sampling indicates the specific use to which reader-response critics put the reader's disorientation: the text contradicts readers' expectations as it corrects their actions. Trial thus becomes entrapment. For instance, after being encouraged to judge every word and act of the devils in Hell, the reader of *Paradise Lost* continues this associational and judgmental practice in a totally different and inappropriate situation—unfallen man in Edenic Paradise. The reader is thus "forced to admit again and again that the evil he sees under everyone's bed is his own" (Fish, *SS*, p. 102). Self-criticism is the result, then, of misplaced assumptions, shattered expectations, trial by error, and correction from the text.

According to reader-response critics, even self-evaluation is not the final resting place intended for the reader. The last rhetorical move I want to discuss is the critic's demonstration that self-judgment is simply an authorial means for *educating the reader*. This brings me to a final pair of strategies used in reader-response criticism—the descriptions of two different but related processes: learning by reading and learning to read. Both assume that the reader learns as an active participant rather than as a passive observer. The reader's education is therefore—to use Milton's words—"not so much a teaching, as an intangling."[38] That is, the reader becomes involved "in his own edification" (Fish, *SS*, p. 49). In the experiences Iser portrays, the disappointment of expectations pushes the reader toward discovery, and the entanglement of readers in moral conflicts forces them to formulate solutions of their own (*IR*, pp. 35–45). What Iser describes here are the lessons of the text—learning by reading—rather than a lesson on reading that text.

Describing this latter process—learning to read the text—is the paradigmatic move of reader-response criticism. It is one I make use of in my analysis of *Moby-Dick* in order to resolve an

[38]*Complete Prose Works of John Milton*, vol. 2, ed. Ernest Sirluck (New Haven, Conn., 1959), p. 642, quoted in Fish, *SS*, p. 21.

interpretive crux: Ishmael "disappears" because he has served his purpose of teaching readers to read his book. This critical move is ingeniously duplicated throughout reader-response criticism. Iser describes the essays in *Tom Jones* as "guidelines" for showing the reader "how he is to view the proceedings" (*IR*, p. 47). Discussing *Hamlet*, Booth notes that "after the fact, the play often tells us how we should have reacted" (VH, p. 160). Anderson argues that "Sterne uses the example of false judgments of minor characters to guide the reader's judgment of his major character in the future" (p. 970). And again Iser: "The potential experiences of the first two monologues [in *The Sound and the Fury*] serve to sharpen the reader's critical eye, creating a new background against which he will judge Jason's clear-cut actions" (*IR*, p. 149). In all these examples, critics describe how earlier passages in a text prepare the reader to judge, to interpret, to read later passages.

Descriptions of this cumulative training are made possible by all the groups of rhetorical moves I have discussed: accounts of temporal reading responses, refinements of seeing the reader in the text, variations on reader-character analyses, and versions of having readers judge themselves. Fish uses all of these critical strategies in his analysis of reading *Paradise Lost*. In one place he demonstrates that the result of corrections by the epic voice "is the adoption of a new way of reading." Taken in by Satanic rhetoric, the reader "proceeds determined not to be caught out again; but invariably he is" (SS, p. 14). Here the reader learns to read so that he can be shown how difficult it is to read the text (and the world) correctly. In this case, learning to read ultimately becomes learning by reading.

The critical moves I have discussed are the most common rhetorical strategies used in applied reader-response criticism. It was necessary to go on at such descriptive length with so many specific examples in order to demonstrate the fine detail of the rhetorical activity involved in any critical project. Academic criticism, like other interpretive practices, is rhetorical through and through, from the macro-structures of the institutionalized discipline, discussed in this chapter's first section, to the micro-practices of critical readings, analyzed in the last.

These micro-practices are not merely techniques employed by critics to describe an objective text and a preexistent response. Nor are they manifestations of interpretive conventions that simply create that text and its effects out of nothing. Neither metacritical account of the interpretive strategies adequately explains the rhetorical function of reader-response criticism or any other approach (and when such accounts are repeated as hermeneutic theory they always tend toward realist or idealist foundationalism). It would be more rhetorically accurate to say that reader-response criticism, when successful, convinces its readers to focus on a reading experience in which text and effect come into view simultaneously. Like all critical approaches, reader-response criticism is a set of rhetorical strategies that aims to persuade readers to take on its interpretive point of view for a given literary work.

Moreover, such interpretations (presented as neutral descriptions) not only function as appeals for specific readings; they also serve as an argument for the whole reader-response enterprise. To return to just one illustration from the previous discussion: reader-response critics often interpret the subject of a text to be the reader. This rhetorical strategy works by describing the reader's relation to the text (he or she is the subject of it), and this description simultaneously provides the evidence that legitimizes the reader-centered focus of which it is a part. That is, the description of the reader as subject of the text is at the same time a justification for focusing on the reader. Here an interpretation generates evidence that is taken as validation of the attempt at making that interpretation in the first place. Such a thematization of its assumptions in a literary work serves as a strategic argument for the self-declared priority of reader-response criticism within the institutional competition among different critical approaches, those already established and those newly emergent. Indeed, every act of criticism would persuade us to adopt its conventions as opposed to some others and to "write" the text it "describes." If we are convinced by an interpretation, it is finally the critic who teaches us to read.

Throughout the seventies, reader-response criticism participated in this rhetorical activity within academic literary studies while remaining rather unresponsive to much of the cultural conversation in American society at large. Unlike Marxist and feminist discourses, reader criticism tended to ignore the ideological debates of a wider cultural politics extending beyond the academy, and insofar as most reader-response approaches avoided the issues of race, class, and gender, for example, they supported conservative voices that attempted to cordon off the university in general and literary criticism in particular from directly engaging in any kind of radical politics. In similar ways, all academic literary criticism necessarily involves participation—by omission or commission, as it were—in two interrelated sectors of rhetorical politics: that of the professional discourses within the institutionalized discipline and that of the broader domain of cultural politics reaching beyond the university.

There are still other political domains, interlocking and overlapping with these first two, in which the rhetoric of critical discourse engages quite actively. At perhaps the most general social level, literary criticism participates in the rhetorical construction of everyday common sense.[39] For example, especially in its early theorizing, reader-response criticism often assumed a commonsense distinction between the individual reader and the independent text, a distinction that required a theory regulating their interaction. The belief in the importance of the individual whose activities must nevertheless be carefully constrained is a basic component of American common sense.[40]

[39]See, e.g., Clifford Geertz, "Common Sense as a Cultural System," in *Local Knowledge: Further Essays in Interpretive Anthropology* (New York, 1983), p. 76; Shirley Brice Heath, *Ways with Words: Language, Life, and Work in Communities and Classrooms* (Cambridge, 1983); Chaim Perelman and Lucie Olbrechts-Tyteca, *The New Rhetoric: A Treatise on Argumentation*, trans. John Wilkinson and Purcell Weaver (Notre Dame, Ind., 1969), pp. 510–14; Harold Garfinkel, *Studies in Ethnomethodology* (Englewood Cliffs, N.J., 1967), esp. chaps. 2, 3, 8; and Charles Taylor, "Interpretation and the Sciences of Man," in his *Philosophy and the Human Sciences: Philosophical Papers, 2* (Cambridge, 1985), pp. 15–57. The intersections of these texts should be compared to the more explicitly political projects in Ideology Critique and Critical Legal Studies. See, e.g., Jürgen Habermas, "Technology and Science as 'Ideology,'" in his *Toward a Rational Society: Student Protest, Science, and Politics*, trans. Jeremy J. Shapiro (Boston, 1970), pp. 81–122; Mark Kelman, *A Guide to Critical Legal Studies* (Cambridge, Mass., 1987); and Sandra Harding, *The Science Question in Feminism* (Ithaca, N.Y., 1986), pp. 111–35.

[40]See Roberto Mangabeira Unger, *Knowledge and Politics* (New York, 1975), pp. 63–103; Robert N. Bellah, Richard Madsen, William M. Sullivan, Ann Swidler, and Steven M. Tipton, *Habits of the Heart: Individualism and Commitment in American Life* (New York, 1985); Fredric Jameson, "On *Habits of the Heart*," *South Atlantic Quarterly*, 86 (Fall 1987), 545–65; and Mark Tushnet, *Red, White, and Blue: A Critical Analysis of Constitutional Law* (Cambridge, Mass., 1988).

When forms of reader criticism depended on and reinforced this common sense and its ideological rhetoric of democratic individualism, such criticism was necessarily enmeshed in a rhetorical politics extending outside the academy. Thus the rhetoric of any critical discourse can do work in multiple domains of politics simultaneously, but the degree of its positive involvement is always relative to the historical domain being analyzed.

PART TWO

Cultural History and
Huckleberry Finn

3

Rhetorical Production and Ideological Performance

Report of the Debate had at Huckleberry Hollow, S.C., on the proposition to organize & institute The Society for the Propagation of Esthetic & Intellectual Culture. Let the dispute arise on the *name*—& break up in a row & bloodshed without getting further. Let it begin in a lofty and courtly parliamentary style of dignity, with some chief person . . . who simply wants "Religious" substituted for "Aesthetic," & supports his motion by a dignified but sophomoric speech. Two parties spring up—one for Religious, the other for Aesthetic—& as the debate gradually warms up, they drop into the most magnificent profanity & the most opulent & imaginative obscenity & finally have a fight.

—Samuel L. Clemens, Notebook, 18 July 1879

This chapter develops my argument in several directions. First, it extends the rhetorical analysis to literary as well as critical texts and expands the relevant rhetorical context beyond academic institutions, elaborating thereby the notion of a cultural conversation. Second, the reading of *Huckleberry Finn* in section I extends and historicizes the reader-response criticism of the previous chapter, placing the reading experience within a specific sociopolitical controversy in 1880s America. And third, section II particularizes my earlier general histories of academic rhetoric by focusing on the evolution of critical arguments about one specific text, *Huckleberry Finn*, and then situates my own reader-oriented interpretation within this history. This last move develops further the thesis of a rhetorical hermeneutics: any specific interpretation is best understood in relation to particular historical contexts of institutional and cultural debates.

Mark Twain remains an active presence in the ongoing conversation of American culture. His voice, especially in *Huckleberry Finn*, has been heard for over a century now and shows no signs of falling silent.[1] Today Twain's novels participate in the cultural conversation not only as voices but as topics. Before examining the rhetorical longevity of his masterpiece, we should pause and inquire into this metaphor: What exactly is the "cultural conversation" in which Mark Twain is both agent and object?

We can begin an answer with the help of a literary critic important to many discussions of *Huckleberry Finn*. In *The Liberal Imagination* Lionel Trilling takes to rhetorical task another contributor to Twain's critical history, V. L. Parrington, in his *Main Currents in American Thought*. "Parrington's characteristic weakness as a historian is suggested by his title, for the culture of a nation is not truly figured in the image of the current. A culture is not a flow, nor even a confluence; the form of its existence is struggle, or at least debate."[2] Though, as we will see, the river metaphor functions effectively in the racist rhetoric of the 1880s and more benignly throughout *Huckleberry Finn*'s critical history, Trilling argues correctly that it is not a useful figure for culture, that historical conversation of multiple voices engaged in continuing rhetorical conflict.

In *The Philosophy of Literary Form* Kenneth Burke had earlier drawn a more elaborate picture of this conversation:

> Imagine that you enter a parlor. You come late. When you arrive, others have long preceded you, and they are engaged in a heated discussion, a discussion too heated for them to pause and tell you exactly what it is about. . . . You listen for a while, until you decide that you have caught the tenor of the argument; then you put in your oar. Someone answers; you answer him; another comes to your defense; another aligns himself against you, to either the embarrassment or gratification of your opponent, depending upon the quality of your ally's assistance. However, the discussion is interminable. The hour grows late, you must depart. And you do depart, with the discussion still vigorously in progress.[3]

[1]Among the many echoes of Twain's voice during *Huckleberry Finn*'s centenary, see Roger Rosenblatt, "Huck and Miss Liberty", *Time*, 7 July 1986, p. 25.

[2]Lionel Trilling, *The Liberal Imagination: Essays on Literature and Society* (Garden City, N.Y., 1950), p. 7.

[3]Kenneth Burke, *The Philosophy of Literary Form* (Baton Rouge, 1941), pp. 110–11. I am indebted to the excellent discussion of Burke's fable in Frank

This elaboration of the conversational metaphor seems preferable to more peaceful depictions, where polite dialogues replace impassioned quarrels, where the desire simply to keep the conversation going replaces attempts to win arguments and end debate.[4] Burke's fable involves argumentative battles, rhetorical allies and enemies, and struggles for persuasive power. So that we don't take this scene *too* seriously, Burke even gives a slightly Twainian twist to the ironic deflation of the verbal contests by placing them in a genteel parlor setting.

Burke's fable of rhetorical politics proves useful as a frame for my analysis of *Huckleberry Finn*. This analysis examines the cultural conversation in and around Twain's novel, paying particular attention to the ideological rhetoric of the text and the way its arguments relate both to political quarrels of the 1880s and to academic discussions in the twentieth century. The first section locates *Huckleberry Finn* within the debates over racism after the end of Reconstruction, when the novel was first published; the second deals with the critical arguments of modern literary study when the novel was endlessly interpreted. Rhetoric—as the political effect of trope and argument—will be the focus throughout.

In society and its conversations, power is not simply a negative force, obstructing, suppressing, canceling the energy of action. It also functions in a positive way, creating, enabling, energizing various sociopolitical activities.[5] My focus through-

---

Lentricchia, *Criticism and Social Change* (Chicago, 1983), pp. 160–62. Also see the conversational analogy used in R. W. B. Lewis, *The American Adam: Innocence, Tragedy, and Tradition in the Nineteenth Century* (Chicago, 1955), pp. 1–3. Even more relevant here are some recent uses of the work of Mikhail Bakhtin; e.g., see Don H. Bialostosky, "Dialogics as an Art of Discourse in Literary Criticism," *PMLA*, 101 (October 1986), 788–97.

[4]I'm thinking here of Richard Rorty's utopian vision of an egalitarian conversation. See his *Philosophy and the Mirror of Nature* (Princeton, 1979) and *Consequences of Pragmatism: Essays, 1972–1980* (Minneapolis, 1982), and my discussion in chap. 5, below.

[5]The notion of power assumed here is significantly influenced by Foucault's later work, as he moved his emphasis from an analytics of power to technologies of the self; from, say, *Discipline and Punish: The Birth of the Prison*, trans. Alan Sheridan (New York, 1977), to *The Care of the Self*, trans. Robert Hurley (New York, 1986). Foucault's notion of power/knowledge is discussed in greater detail in chap. 5, below. Especially relevant here are such Foucauldian formulations as: "In human relationships, whatever they are—whether it be a question of communicating verbally, as we are doing now, or a question of a love relationship, an institutional or economic relationship—power is always present: I

out this book is on *rhetorical* power, the specific way discourse achieves its effects on audiences within and without its conventional boundaries.[6] We will see that *Huckleberry Finn* provides ample evidence of this power in its ideological performance, a performance in which the novel continually asks its readers to take on the role of critical audience observing a series of staged debates and speeches. In these dramatized arguments, readers both witness rhetorical power in the narrative and experience its effects in the act of reading.

We can think of *ideologies* as defining positions within the cultural conversation. Ideologies—such as capitalism and socialism, abolitionism and white supremacy—are sets of beliefs and practices serving particular sociopolitical interests in a specific historical context, and these sets appear in the cultural conversation as strategic arguments and rhetorical figures.[7] This rhetorical view of ideology escapes Clifford Geertz's critique of interest theories because it does not ignore "ideologies as systems of interacting symbols, as patterns of interworking meanings." Far from it. By focusing on ideological rhetoric, my analysis demonstrates exactly how ideology makes "politics

---

mean the relationships in which one wishes to direct the behavior of another": "The Ethic of Care for the Self as a Practice of Freedom: An Interview with Michel Foucault," trans. J. D. Gauthier, S.J., in *The Final Foucault,* ed. James Bernauer and David Rasmussen (Cambridge, Mass., 1988), p. 11. Also see Foucault, "The Subject and Power," in Hubert L. Dreyfus and Paul Rabinow, *Michel Foucault,* 2d ed. (Chicago, 1983), pp. 208–26, where he defines the "exercise of power" as a "structure of actions brought to bear upon possible actions; it incites, it induces, it seduces, it makes easier or more difficult; in the extreme it constrains or forbids absolutely; it is nevertheless always a way of acting upon an acting subject or acting subjects by virtue of their acting or being capable of action. A set of actions upon other actions" (p. 220). Cf. Kenneth Burke, *A Rhetoric of Motives* (1950; rpt. Berkeley, 1969), p. 41: "The basic function of rhetoric" is "the use of words by human agents to form attitudes or to induce actions in other human agents."

[6]The tradition linking rhetoric and politics goes back, of course, to the ancient Greeks and extends into the twentieth century. See, e.g., Terry Eagleton, *Walter Benjamin, or, Towards a Revolutionary Criticism* (London, 1981), pp. 101–13; and Chaim Perelman, "Rhetoric and Politics," *Philosophy and Rhetoric,* 17 (1984), 129–34.

[7]See Raymond Williams, *Keywords: A Vocabulary of Culture and Society* (New York, 1976), p. 129; Alvin Gouldner, *The Dialectic of Ideology and Technology: The Origins, Grammar, and Future of Ideology* (New York, 1976), pp. 54–55, 210–28; and Göran Therborn, *The Ideology of Power and the Power of Ideology* (London, 1980), pp. vii–viii, 2–3, 77–78.

possible by providing the authoritative concepts that render it meaningful, the *suasive* images by means of which it can be sensibly grasped." It is precisely the arguments and tropes of cultural debate that provide a community with its ideological "maps of problematic social reality and matrices for the creation of collective conscience."[8] In the case of *Huckleberry Finn*, the ideological performance recharts the social map of the "Negro Problem" and dismantles the racist hierarchies of a society's collective conscience.

The relation of literature to ideology and the cultural conversation varies radically according to material circumstances, discursive genres, authors' public images, and the reading community's assumptions. A literary text can be a topic in cultural discussion or it can be a participant motivated by and affecting the conversation. As a participant, literature can take up the ideological rhetoric of its historical moment—the rhetoric of political speeches, newspaper editorials, book reviews, scholarly treatises, and so forth—and place it on a fictional stage. Readers thus become spectators at a rhetorical performance, and sometimes, as in *Huckleberry Finn*, they also become actors in the drama they are watching.[9]

We will see exactly how the ideological drama of *Huckleberry*

[8]Clifford Geertz, "Ideology as a Cultural System," in his *The Interpretation of Cultures* (New York, 1973), pp. 207, 218 (my emphasis), and 220. In recent American culture studies, critical texts with useful analyses of rhetoric and ideology include Sacvan Bercovitch, *The American Jeremiad* (Madison, Wis., 1978); Houston A. Baker, Jr., *Blues, Ideology, and Afro-American Literature: A Vernacular Theory* (Chicago, 1984); Jane P. Tompkins, *Sensational Designs: The Cultural Work of American Fiction, 1790–1860* (New York, 1985); and Cathy N. Davidson, *Revolution and the Word: The Rise of the Novel in America* (New York, 1986). See also Sacvan Bercovitch and Myra Jehlen, eds., *Ideology and Classic American Literature* (Cambridge, 1986).

[9]For other interpretations of *Huckleberry Finn* in terms of "performances," see James M. Cox, *Mark Twain: The Fate of Humor* (Princeton, 1966), pp. 136–51; and the more extended use of the dramaturgical metaphor in George C. Carrington, Jr., *The Dramatic Unity of Huckleberry Finn* (Columbus, O., 1976). Also relevant here is Eagleton's analogy between ideology in literature and a dramatic production; see his *Criticism and Ideology: A Study in Marxist Literary Theory* (London, 1976), chap. 3. For a discussion of Twain's audience, especially in relation to the subscription trade through which *Huckleberry Finn* was published, see Hamlin Hill, "Mark Twain: Audience and Artistry," *American Quarterly*, 15 (Spring 1963), 25–40. Also see Eileen Nixon Meredith, "Mark Twain and the Audience: A Rhetorical Study" (Ph.D. diss., Duke University, 1976).

Finn relies for its success on the reader's participation in making the novel work. The celebrated humor of the various narratives in the book—its histories, dreams, fictions, and elaborate lies—depends on the reader's perception of both the fictional speaker's purpose and the discrepancy between his tale and the "truth" as the reader understands it. Similarly, the humor and often the ideological point of the novel's many staged arguments—verbal disputes, Socratic dialogues, inner debates, and polemical monologues—rely on readers' ability to recognize patterns of false argumentation, especially their ability to identify the dubious authorities to which the arguments appeal: superstition, clichéd romanticism, institutionalized morality, and, ultimately, racist ideology. The irreverence of Twain's humor, for which he was often criticized, is only the most visible part of his more general attack on social authority, an attack that *Huckleberry Finn* carries out through a relentless questioning of *rhetorical* authorities that serve ideologically dubious ends. Again and again the dramatized arguments make the reader laugh because the rhetorical authorities invoked appear as ridiculous confidence tricks that society plays on its individual members.

The figure of the con man nicely overstates the nature of the rhetorical exchanges that fill *Huckleberry Finn*. This kind of trickster is a self-interested rhetorician and a greedy manipulator. For a con to work, the mark must be convinced by the con man's visual and verbal rhetoric. Actual truth becomes irrelevant; what counts is successful persuasion. But the confidence man is not interested in simply performing tricks for the fun of it. He plays his game for a reason, seeking to turn rhetorical exchanges into economic ones, to transform impassioned rhetoric into cold cash. The confidence man thus attempts not only to convince, to affect belief, but also to modify actions for his own benefit.[10] With the deceptive figure of the con man as our guide, we can turn to the staged arguments that the confidence trick

[10]On the confidence man in Twain's fiction more generally, see Susan Kuhlmann, *Knave, Fool, and Genius: The Confidence Man as He Appears in Nineteenth-Century Fiction* (Chapel Hill, N.C., 1973); Warwick Wadlington, *The Confidence Game in American Literature* (Princeton, 1975); Gary Lindberg, *The Confidence Man in American Literature* (New York, 1982); and William E. Lenz, *Fast Talk and Flush Times: The Confidence Man as a Literary Convention* (Columbia, Mo. 1985).

exploits but does not exhaust. These arguments in the novel are ultimately part of a larger conversation that was taking place in America during the 1880s.

I. Ideological Rhetoric in the 1880s

Adventures of Huckleberry Finn appeared in February 1885 in the midst of a heated political quarrel over the absence of debate on the "Negro Problem." By the formal end of Reconstruction in 1877, a reunited nation had turned its rhetorical attention to matters other than those that had separated the states during the Civil War. This national change of subject included the North's relative silence on the race question, which allowed the southern states to deal with the emancipated slaves on sectional rather than national terms and to roll back Reconstruction attempts to guarantee blacks their political and civil rights.[11] By 1885 the ideological rhetoric of white supremacy, almost uncontested by the North, dominated southern politics and eventually became institutionalized in state laws regulating relations between blacks and whites.[12]

The discussion of the "Negro Problem" appeared muted and sporadic only in comparison with the protracted intensity of debate during the Civil War and Reconstruction. In late 1884, however, one brief, national outburst was precipitated by a presidential candidate's concession speech. Having lost a close election to the Democrat Grover Cleveland, the Republican

[11]On the change in northern political (and thus rhetorical) concerns at the end of Reconstruction and immediately after, see C. Vann Woodward, *Reunion and Reaction: The Compromise of 1877 and the End of Reconstruction* (Boston, 1951), pp. 211–14, 245–46; Rayford W. Logan, *The Betrayal of the Negro from Rutherford B. Hayes to Woodrow Wilson*, 2d ed. (New York, 1965), pp. 23–61, 165–94; and John Hope Franklin, *Reconstruction after the Civil War* (Chicago, 1961), pp. 194–217.

[12]For a detailed examination of white supremacist ideology in southern arguments over politics, education, and labor during and after Reconstruction, see Claude H. Nolen, *The Negro's Image in the South: The Anatomy of White Supremacy* (Lexington, Ky., 1967). Of course, southern rhetoric had no monopoly on racist ideology; for an overview of northern racism, see Forrest G. Wood, *Black Scare: The Racist Response to Emancipation and Reconstruction* (Berkeley, 1970), pp. 1–16. For an interesting analysis of the political failure of the Radical Republicans' antiracist ideology at the end of Reconstruction, see W. R. Brock, *An American Crisis: Congress and Reconstruction, 1865–1867* (London, 1962), pp. 284–304.

James Blaine surprised the North and outraged the South with an acerbic valedictory that included a diatribe against southern election practices in which blacks "are deprived of free suffrage, and their rights as citizens are scornfully trodden under foot." Throughout the southern states, Blaine declared, the "colored population . . . by a system of cruel intimidation and by violence and murder . . . are absolutely deprived of all political power."[13] The response to Blaine's speech was immediate and angry. The *Savannah Morning News* headed its front-page account "Blaine Tries to Bite / The Bitterness of His Defeat Drives Him Mad / He Snaps and Snarls at the South like a Rabid Canine" (19 November 1884, p. 1). Vehement southern editorials answered Blaine's charges in detail as northern Democratic newspapers joined the furious counterattack. "The Beaten Blusterer . . . Vents His Spleen on the South in a Vindictive and Mendacious Harangue," headlined the *Detroit Free Press* (19 November 1884), and the following day it ran an editorial speculating that Blaine's "inflamatory utterances" were part of a scheme to encourage "race conflict" in the South. If such a "war of races" began, the editorial predicted, Blaine and his followers would lay the blame on the election of Cleveland, the first Democratic president since the Civil War.[14]

Soon after the Blaine controversy died down, a new and even more provocative voice was heard, that of George W. Cable, popular southern author of *Old Creole Days* and *The Grandissimes*. From November 1884 to February 1885, Cable joined his friend Samuel Clemens on a widely publicized and highly successful reading tour through several northern and border states. In late December, during the tour, *Century Magazine* published Cable's polemical attempt to reopen the debate on the

[13]"Smarting under Defeat/Mr. Blaine Makes a Very Foolish Speech. / He Waves the Bloody Shirt Vigorously, and Plays upon the Prejudices of the Ignorant," *New York Times,* 19 November 1884, p. 1.

[14]"Mr. Blaine's Malignant Scheme," *Detroit Free Press,* 20 November 1884, p. 4. Even before Blaine's speech, newspapers in both the North and the South reported widespread fears among blacks concerning loss of their rights, even a return to slavery, after Cleveland's election. See, e.g., " 'Re-Enslavement' of the Negroes," *Detroit Free Press,* 11 November 1884, p. 4; "The Colored Situation," *Washington Post,* 16 November 1884, p. 4; and "Unfounded Fears of the Colored People," *Natchez Daily Democrat,* 18 November 1884, p. 2. The anxieties of black citizens were taken seriously enough that within days of Blaine's speech, both President-elect Cleveland and Vice President−elect Hendricks gave public assurances that the rights of all citizens, black and white, would continue to be protected; see *Washington Post,* 21 November 1884, p. 1.

race question. "The Freedman's Case in Equity" would have been controversial enough if its author had been a northerner, but as an essay written in the mid-1880s by a citizen of Louisiana, it was almost unthinkable.

Cable begins by claiming, "The greatest social problem before the American people to-day is, as it has been for a hundred years, the presence among us of the negro."[15] Yet, for all its importance, this problem is no longer seriously discussed. There is an "absence of intellectual and moral debate," partly because the North, "weary of strife at arm's length," has "thrown the whole matter over to the States of the South." Unfortunately, most southerners share an attitude that works "to maintain a purely arbitrary superiority of all whites over all blacks." Cable goes on to analyze this ideology of white supremacy, which perpetuates the power of the ruling race by defining blacks as "an alien, menial, and dangerous class." This ideological definition of the ex-slave allows southerners to justify their abridgment of freedmen's liberties.[16] The result: a social system based on distinctions and separations that are "crude, invidious, humiliating, and tyrannous." Cable continues: "Nothing is easier to show than that these distinctions on the line of color are really made not from any necessity, but simply for their own sake—to preserve the old arbitrary supremacy of the master class over the menial."

Cable's critique of southern ideology and social practice had an immediate effect. Deluged by angry letters attacking the essay, the *Century* editors invited a response from Henry W. Grady, editor of the *Atlanta Constitution* and a spokesman for the New South. Acknowledging that his region had been silent nationally on the "negro question," Grady proposed to break that silence and "speak the mind of the South."[17] His reply, "In

[15]All quotations in this paragraph are taken from George W. Cable, "The Freedman's Case in Equity," *Century Magazine*, 29 (January 1885), 409–18.

[16]In support of this ideological definition, the white supremacists appropriated scientific and religious discourses, especially ethnological discussion and biblical exegesis; see Nolen, *Negro's Image*, pp. 3–10; Wood, *Black Scare*, pp. 5–10; and George M. Fredrickson, *The Black Image in the White Mind: The Debate on Afro-American Character and Destiny, 1817–1914* (New York, 1971), pp. 228–55. And for analysis of a parallel case of interpretive imperialism, see Edward W. Said, *Orientalism* (New York, 1978), discussed in more detail in chap. 5, below.

[17]This and later quotations are taken from Henry W. Grady, "In Plain Black and White: A Reply to Mr. Cable," *Century Magazine*, 29 (April 1885), 909–17.

Plain Black and White," vehemently rejects Cable's "suggestion of the social intermingling of the races." The hierarchy of white over black, which Cable found so invidious and arbitrary, Grady identifies as both healthy and natural. For Cable, the racial distinction is as unjust as it is unnecessary; but for Grady this same distinction is not only justified, it is the foundation of a stable society.

Grady claims that the separation of the races is required by an instinct "that gathers each race about itself." But if there were not such "race instinct," he argues, it would have had to be invented. "Without it, there might be a breaking down of all lines of division and a thorough intermingling of whites and blacks." The racial separation must be preserved because its loss would lead to "the disorganization of society" and "an internecine war." Increasing the decibel level of his rhetoric, Grady embeds his racist ideology in argument and figure: "The whites, at any cost and at any hazard, would maintain the clear integrity and dominance of the Anglo-Saxon blood. . . . Even if the vigor and volume of the Anglo-Saxon blood would enable it to absorb the African current, and after many generations recover its own strength and purity, not all the powers of earth could control the unspeakable horrors that would wait upon the slow process of clarification." As we will see, both the racist argument and its figuring as separated river currents appear in the rhetoric of *Huckleberry Finn*.

Grady's anxiety over amalgamation, or the pollution of Caucasian blood, and his prediction of race warfare recur frequently in the ideological rhetoric of white supremacy.[18] Isolated from this tradition of racist invective, Grady's metaphor of an explosive mixture makes only a vague chemical sense; but when it is juxtaposed to the rhetoric of another respondent to Cable, the tropological argument takes on a much fuller meaning. Grady insists that the black and white races must remain separate, the river currents must not mix, for if they do, "internecine war"

For a discussion of Grady's racial views in the context of the New South's economic program, see Paul M. Gaston, *The New South Creed: A Study in Southern Mythmaking* (New York, 1970), pp. 118–50.

[18]See Nolen, *Negro's Image*, pp. 29–50; Fredrickson, *Black Image*, pp. 228–55; Joel Williamson, *New People: Miscegenation and Mulattoes in the United States* (1980; rpt. New York, 1984), pp. 61–109; and James Kinney, *Amalgamation!: Race, Sex, and Rhetoric in the Nineteenth-Century American Novel* (Westport, Conn., 1985), pp. 105–81.

will result.[19] Why? The more extreme racism of Charles Gayarré provides a gloss on Grady's trope. Gayarré, historian of Louisiana and spokesman for the Old South, most fully articulated his ideology of racial separation and white supremacy not in his direct response to Cable but in his earlier article "The Southern Question."[20] Gayarré argues that laxity in separating the races has led to miscegenation, and that the mulattoes or "hybrids" thus produced have become dangerous sources of racial unrest. "Hybrids" correctly feel superior to pure blacks: "The superiority of the Caucasian blood, even in infinitesimal doses, always tells." Yet the "hybrid" remains inferior to whites: "Surely a bottle of half wine and half water never was equal to a bottle of pure wine." And there resides the problem. Unsatisfied with being grouped with blacks but not equal to whites, "hybrids" make a "tool of the full-blooded African," constantly stirring up trouble by hypocritically exploiting the greater numbers of the race they disdain. Without the "hybrid," Gayarré argues, "the negro element would be perfectly quiet and manageable."

Thus, troublemaking "hybrids" represent one way in which racial mixing leads to violent conflict. But Gayarré goes on to suggest a second, future problem as well. The black race does not really want equality, Gayarré claims. "Nature, which is a kind mother, has put infallible instincts within every created and animated thing for self-preservation, and the negro instinctively feels that equality or the coveted fraternal embrace of the white man would be the rugged and deadly hug of the bear." But

---

[19]In a later speech, Grady reused the river metaphor for race relations but gave a more optimistic turn to its argument. To his white New England audience he said, "When you plant your capital in millions [in the New South], send your sons that they may help know how true are our hearts and may help to swell the Anglo-Saxon current until it can carry without danger this black infusion": "At the Boston Banquet" (December 1889), in Joel Chandler Harris, *Life of Henry W. Grady Including His Writings and Speeches* (New York, 1890), p. 197.

[20]See Charles Gayarré, "Mr. Cable's Freedman's Case in Equity," *New Orleans Times-Democrat*, 11 January 1885, p. 8, and 18 January 1885, p. 8. The quotations in this and the following paragraph are from Gayarré, "The Southern Question," *North American Review*, 125 (November–December 1877), 472–98. On Gayarré's beliefs in the context of residual Old South racism after Reconstruction, see Charles Roberts Anderson, "Charles Gayarré and Paul Hayne: The Last Literary Cavaliers," in *American Studies in Honor of William Kenneth Boyd*, ed. David Kelly Jackson (Durham, N.C., 1940), pp. 221–74. Both Hayne and Gayarré considered Grady to be far too conciliatory in his New South reply to Cable (pp. 235–36).

if, through enforced social equality and contrary "to the teachings of history and science, the negro should rise to an equality of intelligence and energy with the Caucasian," the ensuing "struggle for power" could "inaugurate a war of races." In the end, of course, the whites would triumph and ultimately blacks would face annihilation, but the extended conflict before this climax would be intense and terrible. Since the black race "will never live in peace with the white on a footing of equality," Gayarré argues, southerners must "keep forever distinct the white race from the black, in obedience to the law of God which has established that distinction." Only in this way can blacks be protected "against aspirations and efforts which will end in disappointment and hasten a more active and deadly struggle" ending in race extinction.

After carrying on the same kind of polemic with his own tropological argument, Grady in a calmer register assesses the "separate" but "equal" accommodations for blacks throughout the South and ends with a plea that the South be left alone to solve the race problem: "This implies the clear and unmistakable domination of the white race in the South. The assertion of that is simply the assertion of the right of character, intelligence, and property to rule. It is simply saying that the responsible and steadfast element in the community shall control, rather than the irresponsible and the migratory" ("In Plain Black and White," p. 917). These final sentences confirm Cable's assertion about the ideology of white supremacy: the racist interpretation of the freedman's nature requires that blacks remain "an alien, menial, and dangerous class" properly subjugated to perpetual white authority.[21]

[21]Cable, "Freedman's Case," p. 412. This is not to imply that Cable himself escaped racial prejudice nor that he endorsed miscegenation or even social equality. His responses to Grady and other critics attack only enforced public segregation, not voluntary private disassociation. Blacks have a civil right to occupy the same theaters, train cars, and libraries as whites, he argued, but through social choice blacks and whites will not (and should not) intermarry. See Cable, "The Silent South," *Century Magazine*, 30 (September 1885), 674–91, and the useful discussion of the limits to Cable's "heresy" in Lawrence J. Friedman, *The White Savage: Racial Fantasies in the Postbellum South* (Englewood Cliffs, N.J., 1970), pp. 99–117. On the whole "Freedman's Case" controversy, see Arlin Turner, *George W. Cable: A Biography* (Durham, N.C., 1956), pp. 194–218.

Into this highly charged and polarized argument came *Huckleberry Finn*, and its relation to the renewed debate was more than topical. *Century Magazine* had published an extract in the same issue in which "The Freedman's Case in Equity" appeared, and Twain regularly read to audiences from the novel during his tour with Cable.[22] Indeed, the passages Twain chose to read were often those that most directly involved his humorous critique of white supremacist ideology, a critique carried out through Twain's rhetorical manipulation of his readers. To investigate the novel's rhetoric is to unfold its complicated nature as ideological performance. By staging rhetorical exchanges—in the story and with his readers—Twain maneuvered his audience to cooperate with him in this performance. As we trace the progression of Twain's strategies, we will follow the reader through a series of reading events that encourage him or her to take a stance on the rhetorical authorities invoked and ultimately on a society's ideological politics.

The playful early episodes with Tom Sawyer's gang rehearse the reader for this critical role. In Chapter 2, as the gang debates its plan for "robbery and murder," Tom appeals to his authoritative knowledge of "pirate books and robber books" to convince his followers that they must not only kill and steal but also " 'ransom' " their victims.[23] When Tom admits that he doesn't know what ransoming means, a gang member objects, " 'But how can we do it if we don't know what it is?' " and Tom answers, " 'Why blame it all, we've *got* to do it. Don't I tell you it's in the books? Do you want to go to doing different from what's in the

---

[22]The *Century* extract includes one of the dialogues I will interpret below as an ideological performance of antiracism—"Jim's Investments, and King Sollermun," *Century Magazine*, 29 (January 1885), 456–58. For more on the political context, see Louis J. Budd's helpful discussion in *Mark Twain: Social Philosopher* (Bloomington, Ind., 1962): "Good enough to last a long time, [*Huckleberry Finn*] owes much of its luminosity to a flaming social and literary debate of Twain's own time" (p. 94). For accounts of the Twain-Cable reading tour, see Guy A. Cardwell, *Twins of Genius* (East Lansing, Mich., 1953), and Arlin Turner, *Mark Twain and George W. Cable: The Record of a Literary Friendship* (East Lansing, Mich., 1960).

[23]All of the quotations from the novel will be cited by chapter in my text and are taken from *Adventures of Huckleberry Finn*, ed. Walter Blair and Victor Fischer (Berkeley, 1985). The first American edition of *Huckleberry Finn* was published by Charles L. Webster Co. on 18 February 1885.

books, and get things all muddled up?' " The argument continues as Tom contrives a definition of "ransom"—keeping hostages until they're dead—and then again invokes his authoritative reading of adventure books in response to the question " 'Why can't a body take a club and ransom them as soon as they get here?' " In exasperation, Tom replies, " 'Because it ain't in the books so—that's why. . . . Don't you reckon that the people that made the books knows what's the correct thing to do?' " All this is innocent fun, imaginative play among boys, and it is amusing in its way. But the dialogue is more than just entertainment; it also serves as part of the reader's rhetorical training. For the humor to work, the reader must recognize not only the generic misreading of adventure stories as conduct books, but also the rhetorical appeal to a false authority followed blindly. Mastering this early and simple lesson encourages the reader to question rhetorical authorities invoked later. These subsequent arguments involve more consequential misinterpretations, which the reader must call into question if the humor is to be released and the ideological point made.

Next follows an argument in Chapter 3 which is actually an inner debate about the effectiveness of prayer. This dialogue within Huck begins: "I says to myself, if a body can get anything they pray for, why don't Deacon Winn get back the money he lost on pork? . . . No, says I to myself, there ain't nothing in it." Before the reader has a chance to agree or disagree, the Widow corrects Huck's misreading of Christian doctrine: "I went and told the widow about it, and she said the thing a body could get by praying for it was 'spiritual gifts.' " At most, Twain is satirizing selfish misinterpretations of Christian teaching here. No serious criticism of institutional religion seems intended. In fact, the Widow's explanation of these "spiritual gifts" gives a positive reading to at least one aspect of Christian ideology. Huck accepts the Widow's meaning of "prayer" but rejects its value: "She told me what she meant—I must help other people, and do everything I could for other people, and look out for them all the time, and never think about myself. . . . I went out in the woods and turned it over in my mind a long time, but I couldn't see no advantage about it—except for the other people—so at last I reckoned I wouldn't worry about it any more, but just let it go." The irony, of course, is that what Huck here denies in words he later affirms in action. But at the moment, the reader is simply called on to laugh at Huck's misunderstandings and the boyish egoism of his arguments.

The innocent playfulness continues when Tom returns. He misreads *Don Quixote* and thereby convinces his gang that what they see is not what they'll get. Reading *Don Quixote* non-ironically, he cites Part 1, Chapter 18, as proof that enemy magicians have turned "A-rabs" and elephants into a Sunday school class to frustrate Tom's gang.[24] His concluding insult for the nonbeliever appeals to his own expertise and will be echoed later by Huck with more serious ideological implications. As Huck continues to challenge his claims, Tom says, " 'Shucks, it ain't no use to talk to you, Huck Finn. You don't seem to know anything, somehow—perfect saphead.' " Here, as later, the reader recognizes that the insult comically boomerangs; it is not Huck but Tom who is misguided.

Later, argumentative appeals to superstition work in similar ways. The reader is cast in the role of the critical listener, participating in the fun by recognizing the questionable authority of the interpretations invoked. But up to this point, little political weight has been attached to any of these rhetorical performances. The satire remains directed at the misreaders more than at the ideas misread. Still unexamined is the power of ideologies to misinterpret in a rhetorically self-interested way.

This situation now changes abruptly. Without skipping a comedic beat, Twain slides his readers comfortably into the role of ideological critics, the role they will play for the rest of the novel. In Chapter 6, after the law prevents him from getting hold of his son's money, Pap Finn launches into a wild monologue violently attacking the " 'govment,' " where a " 'man can't get his rights.' " Pap's speech shifts into a racist diatribe when he bitterly complains about news that a visiting " 'free nigger' " from Ohio could actually " 'vote, when he was at home. Well, that let me out. Thinks I, what is the country a-coming to? It was 'lection day, and I was just about to go and vote, myself, if I warn't too drunk to get there; but when they told me there was a State in this country where they'd let that nigger vote, I drawed out. I says I'll never vote agin.' " The satire of the poor white approaches silly burlesque but pulls back in time to allow the righteous indignation of the speech to serve as the reader's first

[24]Olin H. Moore, "Mark Twain and Don Quixote," *PMLA*, 37 (June 1922), 337–38.

extended introduction to the ideology of white supremacy in *Huckleberry Finn*. The entertaining monologue requires little rhetorical work from a reader, especially one familiar with the Blaine controversy over black suffrage in the South. The racism remains on the surface of the discourse, and the striking contrast between the speaker's ethos and his well-educated black target—" 'a p'fessor in a college' "—makes the ideological point, one that prepares the way for the more interesting rhetorical performances to follow.

The rhetoric of the arguments staged later asks readers to perform increasingly more challenging tasks: they must not merely witness but contribute to a debate or judge its winner. In Chapter 14, for example, Huck and Jim argue about the biblical account of Solomon. The debate begins when Jim questions whether anyone with a million wives could possibly be wise. Huck appeals to the authority of Widow Douglas and the traditional interpretation in claiming that Solomon was indeed the wisest of men. Jim contradicts Huck, citing the story " 'bout dat chile dat he 'uz gwyne to chop in two.' " Comparing half a child to half of a dollar bill, Jim asks, " 'What use is a half a chile?' " and argues that the story doesn't show how wise Solomon was, but demonstrates instead his *lack* of wisdom. Huck doesn't explicitly provide an alternative reading for the story; he simply rejects Jim's: " 'But hang it, Jim, you've clean missed the point—blame it, you've missed it a thousand mile.' " Jim counters by elaborating his reading a bit more: " 'Doan talk to me 'bout yo' pints. I reck'n I knows sense when I sees it; en dey ain't no sense in sich doin's as dat. . . . De man dat think he kin settle a 'spute 'bout a whole chile wid a half a chile doan' know enough to come in out'n de rain.' " Again, Huck does not respond by presenting a counterreading; he simply reiterates his objection to Jim's interpretation: " 'But I tell you you don't get the point.' "

But what *is* the point of the biblical story? Readers must supply it themselves: The incident is part of a narrative that tries to demonstrate Solomon's great wisdom. Jim doesn't miss the rhetorical point of the story; he is arguing that the story fails to make the point. As readers supply the traditional reading, they participate in the debate's staging, and this participation is the basis of its humor for them. But the dramatized argument is funny not simply because it displays Jim's ignorance but also because of the discrepancy between the authoritative interpreta-

tion and Jim's surprising rereading. Indeed, Jim shows himself
to be quite adept at interpretive rhetoric when, after first brush-
ing aside the hermeneutic concept of " 'the point' " of a story, he
co-opts the concept and argues that " 'de real point is down
furder—it's down deeper.' " This deeper point is that Solomon
has so many children he doesn't care about any individual one.
" 'A chile er two, mo' er less, warn't no consekens to Sollermun.' " This rhetorical move—going beyond your adversary's
superficial interpretation—neatly returns the conversation to
its beginning, the topic of Solomon's many wives.

Twain again displays Jim's rhetorical skill in the argument
that immediately follows. In this performance, the reader participates by deciding who wins the debate. Jim questions the
obvious statement that it makes sense for a Frenchman to speak
French, and Huck responds by initiating his own version of a
Socratic dialogue:

> "Looky here, Jim, does a cat talk like we do?"
> "No, a cat don't."
> "Well, does a cow?"
> "No, a cow don't, nuther."
> "Does a cat talk like a cow, or a cow talk like a cat?"
> "No, dey don't."
> "It's natural and right for 'em to talk different from each other,
> ain't it?"
> "Course."
> "And ain't it natural and right for a cat and a cow to talk
> different from us?"
> "Why, mos' sholy it is."
> "Well, then, why ain't it natural and right for a Frenchman to
> talk different from us?—you answer me that."

Instead of answering with the generally accepted fact, the logical conclusion to which Jim and the reader have been led by
Huck's argument, Jim retaliates with his own Socratic dialogue
modeled after Huck's:

> "Is a cat a man, Huck?"
> "No."
> "Well, den, dey ain't no sense in a cat talkin' like a man. Is a cow
> a man?—er is a cow a cat?"
> "No, she ain't either of them."

"Well, den, she ain't got no business to talk like either one er the yuther of 'em. Is a Frenchman a man?"

"Yes."

"*Well*, den! Dad blame it, why doan' he *talk* like a man?—you answer me *dat!*"

Who wins the debate? Jim has skillfully replicated the pattern of Huck's argument, and by burying a false premise—"All men should speak English"—he beats Huck at his own game. At first, the rhetorical exchange appears to emphasize Jim's ignorance, but by the time readers get to the end, they realize that the staged argument demonstrates Jim's rhetorical ingenuity. Twain emphasizes the ideological irony of this performance when he has Huck conclude the exchange: "I see it warn't no use wasting words—you can't learn a nigger to argue. So I quit." Of course, readers reject the racist slur as a rationalization. They know Huck gives up because he has lost the argument: it is precisely because Jim *has* learned to argue by imitating Huck that he reduces his teacher to silence. Far from demonstrating Jim's inferior knowledge, the debate dramatizes his argumentative superiority, and in doing so makes a serious ideological point through a rhetoric of humor.

These rhetorical performances, then, function simultaneously as amusing entertainments *and* as ideological critiques of white supremacy. Early readers of *Huckleberry Finn*, we know, appreciated the special humor of these dialogues. Clemens included "King Sollermun" and "How come a Frenchman doan' talk like a man?" in his 1884–1885 reading tour. A warning from Cable had emphasized their direct relevance to the race problem. Asked for suggestions about which passages to include in their program, Cable replied that "King Sollermun" was "enough by itself to immortalize its author," but he raised a question about one of the program titles, "Can't learn a nigger to argue." He cautioned, "In the text, whether on the printed page or in the reader[']s utterances the phrase is absolutely without a hint of grossness; but alone on a published programme, it invites discreditable conjectures of what the context may be."[25] Clemens apparently agreed with Cable because he accepted his partner's new title, "How come a Frenchman doan' talk like a man?"

[25]Cable to Clemens, 25 October 1884, in Cardwell, *Twins of Genius*, p. 105.

Afterward, during the last few weeks of the tour, the "Twins of Genius" could not help remaining sensitive to the race issue when the *Century* published "The Freedman's Case in Equity."

On stage and in print, Jim's two rhetorical performances were potentially just as subversive of racist ideology as Cable's less humorous and more explicit attack. But their impact is perhaps best seen if we contrast the two dialogues with similar rhetorical performances that have an opposite ideological effect. In October 1869 Clemens' *Buffalo Express* published an item that quotes a "darkey's account of a sermon": "Well, sahs, de sermon was upon de miricles of de loaves and fishes. De minister said how de 7000 loaves and de 5000 fishes divided between de twelve apostles; an' de miricle was, dat they didn't bust!"[26] The ignorance revealed in the black's misreading is the only source of humor in the sketch. By contrast, Jim's reading of the King Solomon episode illustrates his ingenuity and skill in interpretive argument. The result is that a reader's racist ideology is, in the former case, reinforced, but in the latter, contradicted.

In November 1869 the *Buffalo Express* published another dialogue between black characters:

"I say, Baz, where do dat comet rise?"

"It rises in the forty-six meridian ob de frigid zodias, as laid down in the comic almanac."

"Well, where does it set, Baz?"

"Set! you black fool! It don't set nowhere. When it gets tired of shining it goes into its hole."[27]

Again, the dialogue appeals to racist stereotypes. As Arthur G. Pettit has argued, these early sketches depend on readers' enjoyment of the "ignorance, superstition, simplicity, gullibility" of the black characters for "what little 'humor' distinguishes them."[28] The contrast to Jim's rhetorical victory in *Huckleberry Finn* is striking. While the ideological presence of white racism

[26]"Gleanings," *Buffalo Express*, 4 October 1869, p. 2.

[27]"Gleanings," *Buffalo Express*, 8 November 1869, p. 2 (paragraphing modified).

[28]Arthur G. Pettit, "Mark Twain and the Negro, 1867–69," *Journal of Negro History*, 56 (April 1971), 95. Unlike Petitt's, my argument here does not depend on the claim that Twain was the author of these 1869 sketches or that he approved their publication.

permeates both early and later rhetorical performances and is in both a necessary ingredient of the humor, in the latter case racist ideology is turned inside out.[29]

In the inner debates staged at the ideological center of *Huckleberry Finn*, Twain again asks the reader to judge the rhetorical authority and help make the ideological point. But the ironic humor of these performances does not depend only on a recognition of the false sociopolitical authority invoked, that of racist ideology. It is almost as important to note that Huck's false arguments take place in the setting that traditionally guarantees the most profitable search for truth, the dialectic of self-deliberation. Plato's idealism and Descartes's rationalism serve as philosophical paradigms for this long-standing assumption. As two twentieth-century rhetoricians have put it, the dialectical logic of self-deliberation has usually been preferred to the argumentative rhetoric of debate because, the traditional view holds, "when a person is thinking, his mind would not be concerned with pleading or with seeking only those arguments that support a particular point of view, but would strive to assemble all arguments that seem to it to have some value, without suppressing any, and then, after weighing the pros and cons, would decide on what, to the best of its knowledge and belief, appears to be the most satisfactory solution."[30] In other words, self-reflection is held to be logical and disinterested, avoiding the distortions of combative debates with others.

But in the staging of Huck's tormented soul-searching, Twain rejects this traditional hierarchy and the dichotomy on which it is based. Self-deliberation takes the form of internalized debate, and Huck's self-arguments are just another version of the staged debates we have seen so far. The reader learns to think in rhetorical rather than dialectical terms and to treat "self-deliberation as a particular kind of argumentation."[31] Still, the humor of the dramatized self-arguments depends at least partly on our reading the rhetorical performance against the background of the

[29]But not completely. As I will argue at the end of this section, Twain's subversion of the blatant racism of typical newspaper "darky" humor takes place within—and leaves untouched—the more incidious racism of Negro stereotypes in blackface minstrelsy.

[30]Chaim Perelman and Lucie Olbrechts-Tyteca, *The New Rhetoric: A Treatise on Argumentation*, trans. John Wilkinson and Purcell Weaver (Notre Dame, Ind., 1969), p. 41.

[31]Ibid.

traditional assumption that self-deliberations are dialectical and not rhetorical, that they are honest and sincere attempts to discover truth and not eristic dialogues.[32] The reader's participation thus involves both a recognition and rejection of the traditional priority, just as it involves a recognition and rejection of the *ideological* authority the debate invokes.

The first internal argument in Chapter 16 sets the stage for later ones. The two disputants are Huck's socialized conscience and his private feelings, primarily his sense of loyalty. Throughout the novel's critical history this inner conflict has usually been conceived as a struggle between a racist ideology imposed from without and Huck's natural goodness within.[33] Viewed rhetorically, the first round of the debate is won by Huck's conscience when it breaks down every one of his justifications for helping Jim escape: "I tried to make out to myself that *I* warn't to blame, because *I* didn't run Jim off from his rightful owner; but it warn't no use, conscience up and says, every time, 'But you knowed he was running for his freedom, and you could a paddled ashore and told somebody.'" Finally, Huck gives up and says to his conscience, "'Let up on me—it ain't too late, yet—I'll paddle ashore at the first light, and tell.'" And so he tries but discovers he "warn't man enough—hadn't the spunk of a rabbit." Huck cannot condone his act of protecting Jim. He must interpret it as weakness because (what Geertz calls) "collective conscience" has initially won the inner debate by appealing to the authority of racist ideology, an ideology so deeply internalized that Huck accuses himself of being a potential ac-

---

[32]See ibid., p. 39, for a discussion of heuristic and eristic dialogues.

[33]Twain himself encouraged this reading in an 1895 notebook entry, in which he referred to *Huckleberry Finn* as a book "where a sound heart & a deformed conscience come into collision & conscience suffers a defeat" (Mark Twain Papers, Notebook 35, typescript p. 35, in *Adventures of Huckleberry Finn*, ed. Walter Blair and Victor Fischer with the assistance of Dahlia Armon and Harriet Elinor Smith [Berkeley, 1988], p. 806). Critics have restaged the inner debate in many ways and for varied purposes. Typical examples: Edgar M. Branch sees a conflict between "self-centered, conventional morality," "conventional conscience," on the one side, and "intuitive morality," "humanitarian idealism" on the other: *The Literary Apprenticeship of Mark Twain* (Urbana, Ill., 1950), p. 200. Henry Nash Smith describes a dramatization of the inner debate between "false belief," the "perverted moral code" of a slave society, and "generous impulse," "the vernacular commitment to freedom and spontaneity," in *Mark Twain: The Development of a Writer* (Cambridge, Mass., 1962; rpt. New York, 1974), p. 122.

cessory to a strange kind of kidnapping: "Here was this nigger which I had as good as helped to run away, coming right out flat-footed and saying he would steal his [enslaved] children— children that belonged to a man I didn't even know; a man that hadn't ever done me no harm." Convinced of his wickedness by a persuasive conscience, Huck can't help condemning himself. But as in the other staged debates, the reader recognizes the false nature of the winning argument—its appeal to false authority— and once again supplies the ideological point and the basis for the episode's ironic humor.

The rhetorical follow-up to Huck's "failure" is one of many instances in which Huck takes on the role of confidence man. Playing this role again and again, Huck repeatedly figures the nature of the rhetorical exchanges throughout the novel. In this particular case, he meets up with two slave hunters while pad-dling to shore to turn Jim in; but unable to betray his friend, he ends up persuading the men to believe a fiction that they them-selves supply. Huck tells them that it's his ill father on the raft. Then from Huck's deliberately hesitant answers to their further questions, the slave hunters infer that Huck's "father" is much sicker than he's letting on: " 'Your pap's got the small-pox,' " they cry, backing away from the raft, " 'and you know it precious well.' " In an ironic inversion of the reader's past performances, the hunters think they are supplying the truth that corrects Huck's lie when actually they are supplying the lie that covers the truth Huck wants to hide. Huck orchestrates the scene per-fectly. Not only is the main purpose of the con achieved—Jim is protected—but, as in many other cases, the rhetorical exchange becomes an economic exchange as well: to assuage their guilt for abandoning the boy, the hunters leave him two twenty-dollar gold pieces. Thus enriched, Huck soon returns to the debate between his public conscience and his private benevolence.

But this traditional characterization of the internal argument oversimplifies the rhetorical situation. Viewing Huck's conflict as a debate between racist ideology and Huck's natural goodness may be a useful way to get at the ideological point of his inner struggle, but it is not very helpful in capturing the rhetorical dynamics of the internal dialogue. Indeed, the critical history's habitual way of characterizing the debate is misleading because it identifies both rhetorical stands as primarily *ethical* posi-

tions, and this is simply not the case.³⁴ Only Huck's public
conscience cites reasons based on the ethical opposition between good and bad. In contrast, Huck's natural "goodness"
bases its argument on pragmatic considerations about feeling
happy and about actions being troublesome, considerations that
tend to break down simple distinctions between good and evil.
Incapable of turning Jim in, Huck describes himself as "feeling
bad and low, because I knowed very well I had done wrong. . . .
Then I thought a minute, and says to myself, hold on,—s'pose
you'd a done right and give Jim up; would you felt better than
what you do now? No, says I, I'd feel bad—I'd feel just the same
way I do now. Well, then, says I, what's the use you learning to
do right, when it's troublesome to do right and ain't no trouble to
do wrong, and the wages is just the same? I was stuck. I couldn't
answer that. So I reckoned I wouldn't bother no more about it,
but after this always do whichever come handiest at the time."
   Huck's personal pragmatism reduces his public conscience to
silence, and the rhetorical triumph is reversed. But this has been
a debate not between ideologies—racism and, say, abolitionism—but between public morality and private feeling. Any
ideological coloring has been supplied by the reader, who—as
the critical history demonstrates—judges Huck's conscience as
racist and his feelings as nonracist and therein naturally "good."
Out of this reader-produced distinction emerge the debate's
more complex ironies. For Huck's natural "goodness" wins the
supposedly ethical debate with an amoral argument, one that
silences his public conscience but ignores its appeal to racist
ideology. Not only must readers supply the relevant ideological
critique, not only must they reject the continued appeal to false
authority, they must also recognize that "goodness" triumphs by
arguing for amorality! This humorous rhetoric works because
the reader has become as active in the ideological performance
as are Huck's conscience and feelings.
   The climactic argument in Chapter 31 simply restages these
earlier inner debates in less complicated and more powerful
form. But before readers arrive at this rhetorical climax, they

³⁴The most interesting ethical staging of the debate is Walter Blair's in *Mark
Twain & Huck Finn* (Berkeley, 1960), pp. 135–44, where he explains that Twain
is carrying on an argument with W. E. H. Lecky's *History of European Morals,
from Augustus to Charlemagne* (1869).

must make their way through a different set of ideological issues. The focus shifts from race to class, from a critique of white
supremacy to an ideological performance of Twain's bourgeois
liberalism, with its simultaneous attack on aristocratic privilege
and mob rule. As Louis J. Budd points out, this ideological
position can be characterized as Manchester Liberalism, which
rejected authoritarianism and protected the rights of the people.
But "the people" were defined as the propertied middle class,
and this liberal ideology was no less suspicious of the unwashed
masses than the gentry elite.[35] Thus, after the dramatized debates that rhetorically critique racism, Chapters 17 through 30
enlarge the ideological stage to enact a liberal attack on aristocracy—southern, British, and French—and on commoners, primarily poor whites. Certainly the middle class does not escape
censure here, but its shortcomings appear minor by comparison.

   In these chapters, the figure of the confidence man returns
with renewed rhetorical vigor as the fake king and fake duke
work their persuasive magic in con after con. By playing up the
"tears and flapdoodle" of the con man's speeches at the camp
meeting and the Wilks funeral, Twain forces the reader to see
the extreme gullibility of the citizens as they are parted from
their money.[36] But if the middle class is satirized for its sentimentality and credulity, the author saves his more serious con-
demnation for the violence of the southern gentry and poor
whites. This is not surprising. Nineteenth-century liberalism
placed ultimate value on individual rights, and thus feuds and
lynchings were ideological anathemas in their violent denial of

[35]See Budd, *Mark Twain*, esp. pp. 60, 68, 105; and Louis Filler, "East and
Middle West: Concepts of Liberalism in America during the Late Nineteenth
Century," in *Late Nineteenth-Century American Liberalism*, ed. Filler (Indi-
anapolis, 1962), pp. xiii–xliv. Budd's description of Twain's ideological com-
mitments is much more convincing than the radical "Left perspective" at-
tributed to Twain by Michael Egan, *Mark Twain's Huckleberry Finn: Race,
Class, and Society* (London, 1977), p. 66. Cf. Philip S. Foner, *Mark Twain:
Social Critic* (New York, 1958).

[36]Revisions in the extant manuscript indicate that Twain worked to increase
the satire on the townspeople's weakness before the con man's rhetoric. As
Walter Blair puts it, "By constantly making the king's language more vulgar and
slangy, Mark makes the cheat's pretense . . . more transparent, his victim's
gullibility more stupid": *Mark Twain & Huck Finn*, p. 352. For the relevant
revisions, see *Adventures of Huckleberry Finn (Tom Sawyer's Comrade) by
Mark Twain: A Facsimile of the Manuscript*, 2 vols. (Detroit, 1983), 1:149–50
(pp. 241–42 in the manuscript pagination).

the right to life. Again, *Huckleberry Finn* rhetorically enacts and leads its readers to enact its ideological critique. Two examples will suffice to show the connection Twain makes between class violence and persuasive power.

In Chapter 18, Huck describes the feud between the Granger-fords and Shepherdsons, two "clan[s] of aristocracy" that were "high-toned, and well born, and rich and grand." Explaining the feud to Huck, Buck Grangerford appeals to tradition in justifying the constant killing. He defines a "feud" with a narrative: "'A man has a quarrel with another man, and kills him; then that other man's brother kills *him*; then the other brothers, on both sides, goes for one another; then the *cousins* chip in—and by and by everybody's killed off, and there ain't no more feud. But it's kind of slow, and takes a long time.'" But when Huck asks about the feud's origin, he finds that no one knows "now, what the row was about in the first place." Buck sees no problem with his appeal to this dubious rhetorical authority—a tradition of self-perpetuating murder originating in an unknown argument. Buck sees no problem, but of course the reader does.

But should the reader also notice that the feud is simply the original lost argument dramatized in physical violence? Certainly a later rhetorical performance shows another close relation between verbal and brute force. In Chapter 22, Sherburn's speech to the lynch mob shifts the critique from gentry to poor whites but stays focused on violence. Sherburn notes how easy it is for a crowd to transform itself into a lynch party. All that's needed is a leader's persuasion and a mob's cowardice. "'The average man don't like trouble and danger. *You* don't like trouble and danger. But if only *half* a man—like Buck Harkness, there—shouts "Lynch him, lynch him!" you're afraid to back down—afraid you'll be found out to be what you are—*cowards.*'" But if the rhetorical point here is that effective rhetoric can lead to violence, it is also the case that Sherburn's speech itself prevents violence from taking place, at least temporarily. Besides criticizing mob rule, then, this speech displays the power of rhetoric, whether for good or ill, whether for deflecting or inciting violence.

Twain had introduced his liberal critique of poor whites much earlier in presenting Pap's racist speech (Chapter 6). The difference between the earlier and later rhetorical performances is that Pap's diatribe illustrates only the inversion of white supremacist ideology. His speech humorously (if too obviously) demonstrates that the black professor is more qualified to vote than the white drunkard. But in the later lynch-mob sequence, the implied violence of Pap's words becomes the issue, and the scene dramatizes not the problems with universal suffrage but the actual dangers of mob rule and the power of rhetoric to manipulate the masses.

Although the performance of bourgeois liberalism dominates the rhetorical stage in these middle chapters,[37] the critique of white racism does not simply wait in the wings. It reappears, for example, in Chapter 26, when Huck tries to convince Mary Jane Wilks that British servants are worse off than American slaves. But the novel's ideological climax takes place in the famous inner debate of Chapter 31, where Huck wrestles with the question of whether to rescue Jim. The argument is simple in its rhetorical lines: on one side, Huck's socially imposed conscience; on the other, his feelings of affection for and loyalty to Jim. At first his conscience appeals not only to racist ideology but also to that ideology's use of Christianity in support of slavery. Huck has no defense. Believing that "people that acts as I'd been acting about that nigger goes to everlasting fire," Huck decides to write Jim's owner that her runaway slave can be found imprisoned at the Phelps farm. "Washed clean of sin for the first time . . . ever," he contemplates how close he had "come to being lost and going to hell." Then, with his conscience's guard down, Huck's feelings make their persuasive counterattack. Thinking over his trip down the river with Jim, Huck finds that he "couldn't seem to strike no places to harden me against him, but only the other kind." Despite himself, Huck begins piling up

[37]Perhaps these central chapters relate to a more specific debate involving partisan politics. Clemens began *Huckleberry Finn* in the summer of 1876 and sent off the completed manuscript in April 1884. This period of over seven years saw the formal end of Reconstruction and the beginning of the Democratically Solid South. Blair argues that the then-Republican Clemens may have been affected by his party's propaganda attacking southern Democrats: "Coupled with his growing misanthropy and his political zeal, campaign documents, fervent oratory, and heated editorials must have caused the author to emphasize rougher aspects of Southern life which lay in his memory" (*Mark Twain & Huck Finn*, p. 224). In any case, Mark Twain did preface a discussion of southern violence with a question about why the "South is 'solid' for one political party" in an 1882 passage written for *Life on the Mississippi* which was deleted from the published book: "The Suppressed Passages," ed. Willis Wager, in *Life on the Mississippi*, ed. Edward Wagenknecht (New York, 1944), pp. 412–16.

Jim's many acts of friendship as good reasons for changing his mind. He looks at the letter to Jim's owner, studies a minute, then says, "All right, then, I'll go to hell," and tears up the paper. Huck's feelings triumph over his conscience; friendship wins out over racism. These rhetorical victories do not change Huck's ideological beliefs in the slightest, however, only his actions. As many critics have observed, Huck's continued acceptance of racist ideology guarantees that he will misread his decision as "wicked." It is the reader who applies the moral label of "good" to the outcome of the inner debate. Once again, Huck's appeal to the false authority of racist ideology ironically enacts a critique that the reader helps perform.

Difference is the essence of debate, and so it is no accident that the debates staged throughout *Huckleberry Finn* are almost always arguments over *differences:* differences between fact and fiction, good and bad, wise men and fools, Americans and Frenchmen, servants and slaves. In one episode, raftsmen get "to talking about differences betwixt hogs, and their different kind of habits; and next about women and their different ways . . . and next about differences betwixt clear-water rivers and muddy-water ones." This last topic becomes a discussion of the specific differences between the Mississippi and Ohio rivers. One man claims that "the muddy Mississippi water was wholesomer to drink than the clear water of the Ohio." The group agrees and then talks "about how Ohio water didn't like to mix with Mississippi water" (Chapter 16). Of the many differences discussed in *Huckleberry Finn*, this last comes closest to figuring the novel's central concern, the ideologically produced differences between the races, and it prefigures (then inverts) the river metaphor used by Grady in his racist response to Cable's *Century* essay.

Throughout *Huckleberry Finn*, dramatized arguments again and again break down all these differences or overturn their hierarchies. Wise men become fools, Frenchmen should talk like Americans, what is socially approved is morally reprehensible, the inferior slave is superior to his master. Although whites don't want to "mix" with blacks, at least one black man proves "wholesomer" than most whites. This turn exposes the black–white difference as an ideological imposition that in the progress of the narrative is slowly but surely undone. In the end,

Huck discovers that Jim is actually "white inside" (Chapter 40). Although this is another of those sincere compliments that presupposes racism, it also works on the level of ideological figure to dismantle the opposition upon which that racism is based: black and white become morally indistinguishable.

However, even as racial oppositions tend to collapse in *Huckleberry Finn*, class hierarchies are maintained. That is, though rhetorical performances demystify the power of white supremacy, they leave untouched the social stratification assumed by bourgeois liberalism. Attacks on racial prejudice in the eighties did not entail a critique of class distinctions, and Twain's novel follows this discursive pattern of selective social criticism.[38] But another reactionary aspect to Twain's ideological performance remains more elusive (at least for most readers).

As some African-American critics have pointed out, Twain's sympathetic portrayal of Jim still participates in a form of racism, a form most vividly expressed through the minstrel tradition in which white performers blacked their faces and "niggered up" songs, dances, and jokes to entertain their middle- and lower-class audiences with caricatures of black people.[39] Minstrelsy was the most popular form of public mass entertainment in nineteenth-century America before vaudeville and musical comedies, and Clemens' reaction to it was typical. In 1906 he wrote: "The minstrel used a very broad negro dialect; he used it competently and with easy facility, and it was funny—delightfully and satisfyingly funny. . . . To my mind [minstrelsy] was a thoroughly delightful thing, and a most competent

[38]Cf. Cable's declaration: "What a godsend it would be if the advocates of the old Southern regime could only see that the color line points straight in the direction of social equality by tending toward the equalization of all whites on one side of the line and of all blacks on the other. We may reach the moon some day, not social equality" ("Freedman's Case in Equity," p. 417). Also see the rhetorical enforcement of hierarchy discussed in Wadlington, *Confidence Game in American Literature*, pp. 257–71.

[39]See Ralph Ellison, "Change the Joke and Slip the Yoke," *Partisan Review*, 25 (Spring 1958), rpt. in his *Shadow and Act* (New York, 1964), pp. 50–51; Fredrick Woodard and Donnarae MacCann, " 'Huckleberry Finn' and the Traditions of Blackface Minstrelsy," *Interracial Books for Children Bulletin*, 15, nos. 1, 2 (1984), 4–13; and Bernard W. Bell, "Twain's 'Nigger' Jim: The Tragic Face behind the Minstrel Mask," *Mark Twain Journal*, 23 (Spring 1985), 10–17. Bell also notes the influence of the racist stereotyping exploited by the southwestern humorists Twain admired. See also Kenneth S. Lynn, *Mark Twain and Southwestern Humor* (Westport, Conn., 1959).

laughter-compeller and I am sorry it is gone."[40] With its music, slapstick, burlesques, and specialty acts of all kinds, the minstrel show depended on far more than racism for its wide appeal. But in its grotesque portrait of blacks, ministrelsy created and reinforced comic stereotypes that permeated the cultural unconscious of a nation. As Bernard Bell has written, "Since minstrelsy was a national symbolic ritual of debasement of blacks for petty profit and for the psychological distancing of whites from their personal responsibility in the tragic perversion of American principles, Twain's taste in humor reveals his socialization as an American, not merely as a Southwesterner, in the ethics of white supremacy."[41]

From this perspective, the rhetoric of *Huckleberry Finn* is much more complicated in its ideological effects than I have suggested. We can see this in Clemens' own acceptance of minstrelsy's caricatures: remembering an endmen exchange from an 1840s minstrel show, he wrote, "Sometimes the quarrel would last five minutes, the two contestants shouting deadly threats in each other's faces with their noses not six inches apart, the house shrieking with laughter all the while at this happy and accurate imitation of the usual and familiar negro quarrel."[42] The ideological effect of the minstrel show is to have its audience accept its distortions as accurate representations, and part of *Huckleberry Finn*'s rhetorical power is that at times it reproduces this ideological effect during the reading experience, as the story recreates the stage character of the ignorant "nigger" and replays the comic arguments so popular in minstrel shows throughout the nineteenth century. In this way, the novel maintains the white supremacist ideology underlying the minstrel tradition even as Twain's rhetorical "lessons"—the outcomes of the staged debates—undermine the more explicit racism of the segregation practices so strongly criticized by his friend Cable and some northern liberals. That is, the very staged debates that I have identified as subverting racism at one ideo-

[40]*Mark Twain in Eruption: Hitherto Unpublished Pages about Men and Events*, ed. Bernard DeVoto (New York, 1940), pp. 111, 115.

[41]Bell, "Twain's 'Nigger' Jim," p. 12; also see Robert C. Toll, *Blacking Up: The Minstrel Show in Nineteenth-Century America* (New York, 1974); Gary D. Engle, *This Grotesque Essence: Plays from the American Minstrel Stage* (Baton Rouge, 1978); and Joseph Boskin, *Sambo: The Rise and Demise of an American Jester* (New York, 1986).

[42] *Mark Twain in Eruption*, p. 113.

logical level (blatant discrimination) work to reinforce it at another (cultural stereotype).

Post–Civil War minstrel shows contained direct social commentary that was more diverse than the sort seen in antebellum performances. What distinguishes *Huckleberry Finn* in its borrowings from this tradition is that the ideological content of its social criticism—its antiracism—works against the grain of its ideological form, the minstrel show dialogue. A typical minstrel show would begin with blackfaced performers sitting in a semicircle and entertaining the audience with music, songs, and jokes. Question-and-answer routines and other kinds of arguments formed a significant part of this opening act. Sometimes a dignified "interlocutor" would converse with the two absurdly comic endmen, Brudder Tambo and Brudder Bones (named for their instruments), or the two endmen would ignorantly argue over some ridiculous topic in heavy "nigger" dialect and with exaggerated facial expressions and bodily gyrations.[43] Twain uses toned-down versions of such dialogues in the staged debates that I have claimed undermine racism. In doing so he does not completely rid those forms of their ideological residue: the reader is still allowed, even encouraged, to condescend to the disputants in the staged debates. True, expectations about Jim's intellectual inferiority are betrayed by his rhetorical victories, but it is still the superior reader who bestows the forensic laurels. The novel's ideological performance thus overturns the more obvious form of racism while leaving another, more subtle form almost completely intact. In this way, racism is both subverted *and* reinforced during the reading of *Huckleberry Finn*.[44]

II. Interpretive Rhetoric in the 1980s

Our reading of *Huckleberry Finn* has stopped short of the concluding "Evasion" episode, where Huck and Tom attempt to

[43]See Toll, *Blacking Up*, pp. 52–55; and cf. the interlocutor–endmen exchanges in Richard Moody, ed., *Dramas from the American Theatre: 1762–1909* (New York, 1969), pp. 485–88.

[44]For a counterargument to my interpretation here, see David L. Smith, "Huck, Jim, and American Racial Discourse," *Mark Twain Journal*, 22 (Fall 1984), 6: "The issue is, does Twain merely reiterate clichés, or does he use these conventional patterns to make an unconventional point? . . . In virtually every instance, Twain uses Jim's superstition [or, one could add, minstrel show ste-

free Jim. Twain wrote this complicated scene to burlesque romantic adventure stories, stories that Tom invokes to authorize his convoluted rescue plans. But many readers have been decidedly unimpressed by the episode, complaining that it is too long and inappropriate, a disappointing ending to Twain's masterpiece. How can my rhetorical interpretation address this, the primary critical problem in readings of *Huckleberry Finn?* The question suggests two others: How did the interpretive problem develop as such? And what effect does that development have on any attempt at a solution? These questions will take us into the critical history in which Twain's life and novel have been publicly debated. Here we move from *Huckleberry Finn* as participant in the cultural conversation to the novel as topic within it; the text talking becomes the text talked about.

But first we must return to Burke's metaphor for cultural debate presented in the introduction to this chapter. In its illustrative simplicity, Burke's fable ignores an important aspect of cultural discourse: its history is composed not of a single conversation but of many. At a particular historical moment, the cultural conversation consists of different threads, several ongoing debates each with a tradition that may or may not intersect with others at various points. A specific contribution to one rhetorical exchange may simultaneously participate in others as well. Thus cultural history proceeds as a complex network of conversations, a network always changing its rhetorical shape over time. In what follows we will listen to the critics of *Huckleberry Finn* as they carry on several discussions at once: one constituting the interpretive history of Mark Twain and his novel, another concerned with critical methods changing within the

---

reotypes and routines] to make points which undermine rather than revalidate the dominant racial discourse." In the terms of this section, Smith would argue, I suppose, that the rhetorical effect of *Huckleberry Finn*'s ideological performance is *consistently* antiracist, that the novel adopts certain stereotypes and forms from minstrelsy and southwestern humor and then *completely* subverts them, leaving no racist residue in its ideological effect. In the end, I am more convinced by Ellison, Bell, and others (cited in n. 39, above) than I am by Smith. Whatever success Jim has in arguing with Huck, and it is substantial, the reader still remains in the superior position accorded him or her by the traditions that Twain appropriates for his antiracist rhetoric. Ultimately, the extreme racism of segregation and white supremacy is debunked by the rhetorical performances but not the more subtle ideological positioning of the reader by the minstrel forms of those performances.

discipline of American literary studies, and still another more generally involved in the cultural politics inside and outside the academy.

In *The Ordeal of Mark Twain* (1920), Van Wyck Brooks introduced the first major problem for Twain scholarship by arguing that a commercial and genteel America had prevented Samuel Clemens from being the great writer he could have been. A few months earlier, Brooks's friend Waldo Frank had made a similar claim about Clemens' failure, but it was the *Ordeal's* more extended argument that later academic critics took up and made the starting point for interpretive and evaluative debates.[45] Brooks's study established the rhetorical terms for these future discussions: Clemens was the victim of social pressure to conform; rather than thoroughly criticize American society, he succumbed to its crass materialism and stifling morality by becoming a mere humorist, abandoning his true artistic genius.

Applying his thesis to *Huckleberry Finn*, Brooks perceived the literary repetition of Clemens' personal struggle. In the author's inner life, the conventional citizen battled the rebelling writer; social conformity suppressed artistic individualism. In the novel, this battle becomes Huck's psychological struggle, "one between conscience and the law, on one side, and sympathy on the other." Brooks argued that "in the famous episode of Nigger Jim, 'sympathy,' the cause of individual freedom, wins." But if the conflict in *Huckleberry Finn* is simply the conflict in Mark Twain, the resolutions turn out to be quite different. Twain solves the conflict "successfully, he fulfills his desire, in the book as an author can. In actual life he did not solve it at all; he surrendered."[46] And this surrender, Brooks claimed, took the form of becoming a humorist. Humor was Twain's compromise with social convention, a compromise forced on him by his need to conform, a compromise that suppressed his artistic spirit. He could have been a committed critic of his society. Instead he became its clown.

Brooks was not just criticizing nineteenth-century America here or simply attacking the apotheosis of Mark Twain as the triumphant "Lincoln of our literature." He was also participating in what he saw as a more pressing controversy in cultural politics, the debate over the artist's situation in twentieth-

[45]Waldo Frank, *Our America* (New York, 1919), pp. 38–44.
[46]Van Wyck Brooks, *The Ordeal of Mark Twain* (New York, 1920), pp. 35–36.

century America. Brooks envisioned *The Ordeal of Mark Twain* as his latest attempt to clear away obstacles inhibiting the writer's self-fulfillment in contemporary society. In his final paragraph he addresses his fellow authors directly: Mark Twain "was the supreme victim of an epoch in American history, an epoch that has closed. Has the American writer of to-day the same excuse for missing his vocation? . . . Read, writers of America, the driven, disenchanted, anxious faces of your sensitive countrymen; remember the splendid parts your confrères have played in the human drama of other times and other peoples, and ask yourselves whether the hour has not come to put away childish things and walk the stage as poets do."[47] Brooks's interpretation of Twain's "wound" thus participated simultaneously in both the fledgling critical history of Twain's texts and the broader cultural discussion among literary intellectuals of the twenties.

The impassioned debates Brooks initiated continued for years. In this phase of the Twainian conversation, the most important contribution was Bernard DeVoto's *Mark Twain's America* (1932), which attacked Brooks's interpretation on several fronts. DeVoto criticized Brooks's use of psychoanalysis, his distortion of facts, his definition of the artist, his political misuse of literature. DeVoto ridiculed Brooks's "helplessness in the presence of humor" and rejected his thesis that Twain was a frustrated artist, unable to rebel against society. Perhaps most important, DeVoto complained about Brooks's ignorance of American history.[48] This last criticism placed the debate firmly in the context of the historical scholarship that dominated the academic study of literature in the twenties and thirties.

DeVoto ended his critique of Brooks with an interesting comment we can apply to academic critical history and its relation to cultural politics: *The Ordeal of Mark Twain* "adds one more wall to an unrealistic edifice which is intended to be a description of America. It exists as a part of a logical structure, on which further masonry may be erected as the city of gold lifts its pinnacles. These sticks and stones, being once in place, make

---

[47]Brooks, *Ordeal*, p. 267. For more details about Brooks's cultural politics, see William Wasserstrom, *The Legacy of Van Wyck Brooks: A Study of Maladies and Motives* (Carbondale, Ill., 1971), pp. 15–50.

[48]Bernard DeVoto, *Mark Twain's America* (Boston, 1932), pp. 225–39; quotation, p. 236.

unnecessary any further consideration of Mark Twain's books when it is desirable to refer to Mark Twain in later ideology about Our America."[49] Though his critique is dismissive in intent, DeVoto did recognize here that Brooks's contribution to Twain's critical history was simultaneously part of an attempt to remake American culture. DeVoto concluded by attacking Brooks's followers, whose treatment of Twain "has no relation to what he wrote but only to what Mr. Brooks wrote about him." DeVoto's sarcasm somewhat misfires in light of his own lengthy rebuttal to Brooks and the arguments of critics who subsequently chose sides in the continuing debate. The later interpretive history testifies that often critics can talk about what Twain wrote only by talking simultaneously about what Brooks wrote about him. The Twainian conversation never takes place in a critical vacuum, and it proves difficult indeed to change the subject.

To understand the next phase of *Huckleberry Finn*'s critical history, we must modify Burke's fable one last time. In his parlor of cultural debate, the disputants participate in a heated discussion, "too heated for them to pause and tell [latecomers] exactly what it is about."[50] In fact, interpretive latecomers to *Huckleberry Finn* criticism find many disputants who will stop and give them the conversational lowdown, supplying ample if not disinterested information about the state of the academic discussion. Indeed, in a sense, a text's critical history is constantly writing (and rewriting) itself in public because of certain institutional practices within literary studies: the introductory summaries of past criticism in interpretive articles, bibliographic essays periodically surveying the state of scholarship, book reviews placing a book's argument in the context of ongoing critical debate, and collections of reprinted commentaries introduced by retellings of a text's critical history. Out of such institutional discourses emerge interpretive problems—frequently identified as such—that later critical rhetoric must often address to stay relevant and persuasive. These publicized

---

[49]Ibid., p. 239. For a useful analysis of the Brooks–DeVoto debate, including later episodes, see Guy A. Cardwell, "Mark Twain: The Metaphoric Hero as Battleground," *ESQ*, 23 (1977), 52–66. Cardwell discusses how DeVoto also viewed himself as participating simultaneously in a cultural debate about America which transcended professional controversies within the academic study of literature. Also see Wallace Stegner, *The Uneasy Chair: A Biography of Bernard DeVoto* (New York, 1974), pp. 96–111.

[50]Burke, *Philosophy of Literary Form*, p. 110.

problems become part of the latecomer's crash course on the Twainian conversation, and soon he or she is able to develop a position and join the problem-solving debates.[51]

In the 1980s this crash course emphasizes two episodes in the critical history: an initial debate over the author's life and a later argument over the form and value of his most important novel. Actually, these two episodes of the Twainian conversation are closely related, the historicist problem of Twain's "wound" becoming the formalist problem of *Huckleberry Finn*'s ending.

When at midcentury Lionel Trilling and T. S. Eliot defended the novel's conclusion, they reiterated Twain's problematic relation to narrative humor and ideological seriousness.[52] But in their analyses, the interpretive problem was translated from the Brooks–DeVoto quarrel about an author's life to a formalist debate about a text's unity. The old question "Did Twain use humor to avoid seriously criticizing his times?" was replaced by another: "Is the story of Jim's escape a farcical betrayal of *Huckleberry Finn*'s earlier ideological critique?" This change of subject resulted partly from a change in the nature of American literary studies. As we noted in Chapter 2, historical scholarship dominated the rhetorical context of academic literary study in the twenties, but by 1950 this form of institutional discourse had been successfully challenged by formalist theory and by intrinsic explications of individual texts. A historicist conversation surrounding Twain's work evolved into a formalist discussion, and the critical history often recorded this transformation. In 1962, for example, Lewis Leary concluded his introduction to *Mark Twain's Wound* with the observation that many critics "have turned to what seems today the legitimate province of literary criticism—concern with what a man wrote rather than with why he wrote it."[53] In 1948, when Trilling published his

---

[51]My thinking about these rhetorical issues has been aided by the theory of interpretive history presented in Adena Rosmarin's "'Misreading' *Emma*: The Powers and Perfidies of Interpretive History," *ELH*, 51 (Summer 1984), 315–42; "Hermeneutics versus Erotics: Shakespeare's *Sonnets* and Interpretive History," *PMLA*, 100 (January 1985), 20–37; and "Forum," *PMLA*, 100 (October 1985), 811–812.

[52]T. S. Eliot, Introduction to *The Adventures of Huckleberry Finn* (New York, 1950), pp. vii–xvi; and Lionel Trilling, Introduction to *The Adventures of Huckleberry Finn* (New York, 1948), pp. v–xviii, reprinted as "Huckleberry Finn" in his *Liberal Imagination*, pp. 100–113.

[53]Lewis Leary, "Standing with Reluctant Feet," in *A Casebook on Mark Twain's Wound*, ed. Lewis Leary (New York, 1962), p. 30.

introduction to *Huckleberry Finn*, he implicitly addressed it to both the interpretive history of Twain's novel and to the more general institutional conversation about how literature should be discussed. His apparent focus on the text rather than on its historical context helped introduce a new problem for Twain criticism, a problem more attuned to the institutional triumph of formalist criticism over historical scholarship.

Trilling began his analysis by asking the question "Wherein does [*Huckleberry Finn's*] greatness lie?" and then started an answer: "Primarily in its power of telling the truth . . . the truth of moral passion; it deals directly with the virtue and depravity of man's heart." One way it does so, Trilling explained, is through the narrative of Huck's "moral testing and development." Huck's character turns "heroic" when, "on the urging of affection, [he] discards the moral code he has always taken for granted and resolves to help Jim in his escape from slavery." Trilling went on to claim that "in form and style *Huckleberry Finn* is an almost perfect work." The only "mistake" ever charged against the novel is that "it concludes with Tom Sawyer's elaborate, too elaborate, game of Jim's escape." After admitting that the episode is in fact "too long" and "a falling off," Trilling came to its defense by claiming it has "a certain formal aptness," for "some device is needed to permit Huck to return to his anonymity, to give up the role of hero, to fall into the background which he prefers." *Huckleberry Finn's* style complements this formal perfection. The prose moves "with the greatest simplicity, directness, lucidity, and grace." It is a colloquial style, in the popular "tradition of humor," which exploited contemporary interest in regional dialects. Trilling's final sentence suggested that *Huckleberry Finn* unites the stylistic detail of its form with the moral truth of its content: Mark Twain "is the master of the style that escapes the fixity of the printed page, that sounds in our ears with the immediacy of the heard voice, the very voice of unpretentious truth."[54]

[54]Trilling, *Liberal Imagination*, pp. 101–2, 107, 110–13. Any theorist writing after Derrida cannot help remarking on this last quote's classic illustration of phonocentricism, the privileging of voice over writing in the representation of truth. Since I endorse Trilling's metaphor of culture as debate at the beginning of this chapter, I should probably pause here to dissociate my own rhetoric from Trilling's logocentricism. By adopting the conversational metaphor in my theoretical critiques and cultural analyses, I am not claiming some transhistorical universality for speech over writing, some transcendental "immediacy of the

With this combination of formalist and phonocentric rhetoric, Trilling's (and later Eliot's) defense of *Huckleberry Finn's* conclusion began to shift the set of problems addressed in Twain's critical history. But if any change of subject is to occur, the conversational participants must recognize the shift and act accordingly. If a new debate is to start, sides must be chosen in the argument and the topic must become generally accepted by those concerned. Leo Marx soon took the first step in his incisive "Mr. Eliot, Mr. Trilling, and *Huckleberry Finn*," where he attacked the claims made for the novel's formal unity.[55]

Marx argued that "to bring *Huckleberry Finn* to a satisfactory close, Clemens had to do more than find a neat device for ending a story. His problem, though it may never have occurred to him, was to invent an action capable of placing in focus the meaning of the journey down the Mississippi." And the meaning of the journey, according to Marx, is the "quest for freedom." Huck's "unpremeditated identification with Jim's flight from slavery is an unforgettable moment in American experience, and it may be said at once that any culmination of the journey which detracts from the urgency and dignity with which it begins will necessarily be unsatisfactory." Marx went on to explain why the burlesque ending is indeed "unsatisfactory" in the extreme. Among other objections, he argued that "the slapstick tone jars with the underlying seriousness of the voyage"; that Huck unaccountably regresses into "Tom's helpless accomplice, submissive and gullible"; and that Jim undergoes "a similar transformation" into a "flat stereotype: the submissive stage-Negro." Worst of all, the ending diminishes Huck's heroic victory over the socially imposed morality justifying slavery.

---

heard voice" in its expression of "unpretentious truth." Quite the contrary, by using the conversational metaphor to focus on rhetorical exchanges, I am historicizing both speech and writing, and speech in writing, to show that the only useful way to talk about "truth" is in local, not universal, terms in hermeneutic theory and cultural history. Indeed, I think that the metaphor of a "conversation"—with its multiple dialogues, overlapping voices, pregnant silences, unanswered accusations, suggestive whispers, overreactions, and misinterpretations—functions quite well to avoid the logocentric myth of presence Derrida has so persuasively demystified. I discuss further this neo-pragmatist use of the conversational metaphor in chap. 5, below.

[55]Leo Marx, "Mr. Eliot, Mr. Trilling, and *Huckleberry Finn*," *American Scholar*, 22 (Autumn 1953), 423–40; all of the quotations in the following two paragraphs are taken from this essay.

Marx completely rejected Trilling's formalist argument for the novel's "symmetry of structure." But what really astounded him was the narrowness of Trilling's apolitical formalism. Marx saw Trilling as essentially a moralist in his criticism and therefore asked how he could "treat so lightly the glaring lapse of moral imagination in *Huckleberry Finn*." Why did Trilling turn away "from a moral issue in order to praise a dubious structural unity?" Marx speculated that criticism of the fifties was "less sensitive to questions of what might be called social or political morality" perhaps "because of the strength of the reaction against the mechanical sociological criticism of the thirties." Certainly Marx was correct in his suggestion that the discipline of literary studies had turned away from such extrinsic approaches and that this formalist shift in institutional rhetoric helps explain Trilling's argument. But the situation was more complex, the conversations more multiple, than this explanation allows.

Trilling reprinted his analysis of *Huckleberry Finn* in *The Liberal Imagination: Essays on Literature and Society* (1950), and in so doing, inserted his interpretation into a larger debate in cultural politics. His book-length contribution to this strand of the cultural conversation set out to criticize the "liberal imagination" from within its own ideology. Trilling defined his task as an attempt "to recall liberalism to its first essential imagination of variousness and possibility, which implies the awareness of complexity and difficulty." This awareness of complexity had been replaced in recent liberal criticism, he argued, by a tendency to simplify. In an attack on *Main Currents in American Thought* (1930), Trilling rejected the narrowness of V. L. Parrington and "his coadjutors and disciples, who make up what might be called the literary academicism of liberalism." That narrowness could most clearly be seen in their severe treatment of Henry James. In liberal criticism "James is traditionally put to the ultimate question: of what use, of what actual political use, are his gifts and their intention?" Inevitably James's work "cannot endure the question." Trilling then argued that this liberal judgment of James "goes back of politics, goes back to the cultural assumptions that make politics. We are still haunted by a kind of political fear of the intellect." Not only academic critics but literary artists as well fell prey to this reductive liberalism. For instance, Sherwood Anderson's "great American heroes were Mark Twain and Lincoln, but when he writes of these two shrewd, enduring men, he robs them of all their savor and masculinity, of all their bitter resisting mind; they become little more than a pair of sensitive, suffering happy-go-luckies."[56]

So goes Trilling's argument against the contemporary "liberal imagination." My reason for reproducing it here is to show that Marx was only partially correct when he cited a shift in academic literary criticism as the explanation for Trilling's formalist reading of *Huckleberry Finn*. Equally important was the rhetorical context of Trilling's cultural politics, his more general attack on recent liberal claims about literature in society. Moreover, this broader critique feeds back into Twain's critical history, for Trilling condemned liberal interpretations closely akin to those of Van Wyck Brooks. In *The Pilgrimage of Henry James* (1925), for example, Brooks speculated about the literary costs of expatriation and criticized the later James for "an art in which all the cleverness of the manipulation cannot conceal the poverty of the material."[57] In this judgment of James, as well as in his reading of Twain, Brooks's interpretations resemble those of Parrington, and this affiliation suggests that Trilling's strictures on liberal critics applied equally to both literary historians.[58] Indeed, how better to caricature Brooks's evaluation of Twain than by what Trilling condemned as Anderson's view: Twain as a sensitive, suffering happy-go-lucky? Whether Trilling was directly addressing Brooks or not, his rereading of *Huckleberry Finn* in the context of *The Liberal Imagination* functions as a response within the novel's critical history and thus serves as a connecting point of transition from historicist to formalist debates.

What is especially ironic about Trilling's contribution to the Twainian conversation, as Marx pointed out, was the particular shape of his interpretive rhetoric. The liberal critic of past cultural liberalism chose a formalist argument that cuts literature off from society in order to prove Twain's cultural significance.

[56]Trilling, *Liberal Imagination*, pp. xii, 8–10, 28–29.

[57]Brooks, *The Pilgrimage of Henry James* (New York, 1925), p. 135. Cf. Vernon Louis Parrington, *The Beginnings of Critical Realism in America, 1860–1920*, vol. 3 of *Main Currents in American Thought* (New York, 1930), pp. 239–41.

[58]Parrington approvingly cited Brooks's argument that Mark Twain's "creative genius" was thwarted "by a disastrous surrender to the ideals of the Gilded Age" (*Beginnings of Critical Realism*, p. 89).

For Trilling, *Huckleberry Finn* is "one of the world's great books and one of the central documents of American culture" at least partly because of its unified form and content, its style and truth, which Trilling described in a formalistic rhetoric that downplayed the novel's relevance to either its own specific political context or Trilling's own cultural moment. Granted, Trilling did remark on the universality that makes the book "subversive," forcing readers to question their unexamined moral beliefs. But this is a subversiveness that has lost its historical specificity. Furthermore, when Trilling did briefly discuss the specific historical context of Twain's novel, he focused not on political debates after Reconstruction but on post–Civil War nostalgia for the antebellum innocence and simplicity symbolized by the river.[59] Trilling neglected the most vital historical relationship between *Huckleberry Finn* and American society, and it was precisely this sort of political objection that Leo Marx raised in the essay that did the most to establish Trilling's formalist reading as the starting point for future debates. And, again, whether Trilling's analysis was *only* a formalist reading is beside the point.[60] What counts for *Huckleberry Finn*'s interpretive history is that later critics, starting with Marx, responded to Trilling's essay as primarily a piece of formalist explication.

With Marx's essay taking the first step, all that remained for the dispute over the ending to become a central problem for the critical history was its incorporation into the discipline's later discourse on *Huckleberry Finn*. This was quickly accomplished by the long string of articles that took up the argument and by the many collections of reprinted essays that included the interpretations of Trilling, Eliot, and Marx.[61] Future arguments did not remain exclusively within the bounds of formalism, but the

[59]Trilling, *Liberal Imagination*, pp. 101, 108, 109.

[60]In fact, Trilling criticized the apolitical formalism of New Criticism in an essay published the same year as his introduction to *Huckleberry Finn*; see Trilling, "The State of American Writing, 1948: A Symposium," *Partisan Review*, 15 (August 1948), 892–93; and William Chace's comments in his *Lionel Trilling: Criticism and Politics* (Stanford, Calif., 1980), pp. 64 and 178. For a much fuller discussion of the larger cultural arena in which Trilling's work participated, see Mark Krupnick, *Lionel Trilling and the Fate of Cultural Criticism* (Evanston, Ill., 1986), esp. chap. 4, and Chace, *Lionel Trilling*, esp. chap. 7. Particularly relevant to my rhetorical perspective is Chace's analysis of Trilling's specific "rhetorical employment" of such terms as "liberalism" (p. 147).

[61]See Thomas Tenney, *Mark Twain: A Reference Guide* (Boston, 1977).

formalist concentration on the text in and of itself continues to focus debate to the present day.[62] This, then, is the rhetorical context as *Huckleberry Finn* passes its centenary. My own ideological interpretation finds the critical history posing the problem of the ending and simultaneously laying out the possible solutions. This history claims that either the "Evasion" episode contradicts what has gone before in the novel or it somehow fits in with it: if the former, it is an artistic failure; if the latter, it's really not a problem at all. One sure way for a new interpretation to join the debate is to choose a side. But a more effective critical strategy would be to show that the traditional solutions to the problem are not—as the critical history would have it—mutually exclusive. This strategy gives us the final step in my rhetorical interpretation: the "Evasion" sequence *is* a problem, but it *does* fit in with the rest of the novel. Indeed, if the concluding chapters are to work, readers must experience the episode as a problem while they are reading so that they can once again participate in the ideological performance.

Past interpretations repeatedly testify to this disconcerting experience as they record the many questions critics have posed about the ending: Is the characterization of Huck and Jim consistent with that in the river episodes? Does the farcical escape betray the earlier social criticism? Does the outlandish humor undermine the previous ideological seriousness? These and other questions particularize the problem in the reading experience as it is stated and restated in past criticism. What we have done here is to make the critical debate itself signify by presenting its questions as evidence of how troublesome many readers have found the "Evasion" episode. From this perspective, the critical solutions to the problem, the specific positions taken in

[62]For the continued preoccupation with the problem of the ending, see, e.g., the very first sentence of Carrington, *Dramatic Unity of Huckleberry Finn:* "The hundreds of books and articles on *Huckleberry Finn* have failed to answer a basic question about the novel: Does the ending belong to the book?" (p. vii); and more recent critical works such as Joel Jay Belson, "The Argument of the Final Chapters of *Huckleberry Finn,*" *Mark Twain Journal,* 21 (Spring 1983), 11–12; Everett Emerson, *The Authentic Mark Twain* (Philadelphia, 1984), pp. 140–41; Forrest G. Robinson, *In Bad Faith: The Dynamics of Deception in Mark Twain's America* (Cambridge, Mass., 1986), esp. pp. 215–17; Harold Beaver, *Huckleberry Finn* (London, 1987), pp. 43–55; and John C. Gerber, *Mark Twain* (Boston, 1988), pp. 104–5.

the debates, are less important than the fact that a problem was experienced in the first place.[63]

In my rhetorical interpretation, the final clash between entertaining humor and ideological seriousness remains, with all its problematic obtrusiveness. But now the two attitudes are no longer simply positions argued for in the critical history; they are concerns developed in the reader's experience of the conclusion. Furthermore, if previously the text enacted its ideological critique *through* the humor, now it does so *despite* the farce. In the novel's earlier staged arguments, the reader released the humor by identifying the grounds on which the rhetorical performances were based. But at the end, readers must separate the comedy from the ideological point they have mastered. Either during or after reading the farce, they must realize that something is wrong, that there *is* a problem with the ending, one that the text will not help solve. Reading the text has created the problem insofar as readers have been persuaded to take the earlier humorous critiques of racism seriously. As a result, they must decide whether the ending shows Twain's ideological retreat or his political realism, whether it contradicts his earlier attack on racism or deliberately represents the impossibility of the ex-slave's freedom. In a sense, it simply does not matter whether the interpretive and evaluative problem is resolved in Twain's favor or not. The fact that the problem appears at all testifies that the novel works, not as a formal unity but as a rhetorical performance in which the reader must participate in order to read at all.

In 1869 Clemens' *Buffalo Express* published a sketch, "A Rural Lesson in Rhetoric," in which a character advises a tem-

---

[63]See chap. 2, sec. IV, above, for a discussion of the critical strategy employed here. The rhetorical perspective developed throughout this chapter is indebted to the version of reader-response criticism discussed in chap. 2, but it attempts to move beyond this rather ahistorical and apolitical approach, especially as it is exemplified in my *Interpretive Conventions: The Reader in the Study of American Fiction* (Ithaca, N.Y., 1982), chap. 3. It also attempts to address Robert Stepto's justifiable criticism that my earlier reading model did not confront "the role that race has played in America in creating [interpretive] communities (black *and* white)": Robert B. Stepto, "Distrust of the Reader in Afro-American Narratives," in *Reconstructing American Literary History*, ed. Sacvan Bercovitch (Cambridge, Mass., 1986), p. 314. One might restate the argument of this chapter: "race" as an ideological target of cultural debate plays a constitutive role in the formation of the reading community posited by my interpretation of *Huckleberry Finn*.

perance lecturer to adapt his words to the understanding of his audience. The speaker is grateful for this, "the best lesson in rhetoric he ever received."[64] In *Huckleberry Finn* the author shapes not only individual words but whole speeches and dialogues to the abilities of his readers. He depends throughout on his audience's help in establishing his novel's engaging humor and its ideological impact. But besides shaping his discourse, Twain rhetorically shapes his readers as well. I am not claiming, however, that the reader changes radically in the course of reading *Huckleberry Finn*. Rather, in depending on the reader's ability to critique false authority, Twain accomplishes a "training of the reader to see with his own eyes," as James Cox says of *Innocents Abroad*.[65] This training helps readers to become more rhetorically aware of the ideological issues they help raise throughout the novel. The very fact that there arises a problem with the ending is due to this training and to the reader's early encounters with the novel's ideological rhetoric, which then directs attention to the concluding interpretive problem. It is this effective rhetorical power, both humorous and serious, racist and antiracist, that makes *Huckleberry Finn* not only a captivating and troubling novel but also a continually important voice in the evolving conversation of American culture.

[64]*Buffalo Express*, 8 November 1869, p. 2.
[65]Cox, *Mark Twain*, p. 54.

4

Cultural Reception and
Social Practices

Some bad boys in Rocky Springs, Claiborne county, captured a
buzzard and tied a lighted turpentine ball to it and turned it
loose. It frightened the life out of all who saw it, the people
regarding it as the sign of destruction of the world.
>   —"Meteoric Gleanings," *Crystal Springs* [Missis-
>   sippi] *Meteor*, 19 May 1883

I wouldn't like the image of Jack Armstrong. I'm too human.
But I don't like being Peck's Bad Boy, either.
>   —John Riggins, Washington Redskins running back,
>   on his off-field responsibilities as a professional foot-
>   ball player in 1985

A common interpretive thread runs through all the
twentieth-century criticism discussed in Chapter 3. Whether
focusing on Twain's wound, his novel's unity, or its reading
experience, critical commentary dramatizes the tension between social critique and entertaining humor, between *Huckleberry Finn's* antiracist performance and its farcical conclusion.
Almost every major academic interpretation has attempted to
come to terms with this perplexing relation of comedic form to
racial commentary.

Early histories of black characters in American literature
praised Twain as a humorist who transcended the racist stereotypes of his period. Sterling Brown, for instance, claimed in
1937 that Jim "is the best example in nineteenth century fiction
of the average Negro slave (not the tragic mulatto or the noble
savage), illiterate, superstitious, yet clinging to his hope for
freedom, to his love for his own."[1] Brown and other literary

[1] Sterling Brown, *The Negro in American Fiction* (Washington, D.C., 1937),
p. 68.

historians singled out the sensitive portrayal of Jim in the first two-thirds of *Huckleberry Finn*, the section I emphasized in my rhetorical analysis of the novel's ideological performance. But, as I also noted, later African-American critics have charged Twain with a more subtle racism in some of these same representations. Ralph Ellison argued in 1958 that "Twain fitted Jim into the outlines of the minstrel tradition," whose "black-faced figure of white fun is for Negroes a symbol of everything they rejected in the white man's thinking about race, in themselves and in their own group." Twain, writing close to Reconstruction and the oral tradition, was not "free of the white dictum that Negro males must be treated either as boys or 'uncles'—never as men."[2]

Even critics who have not accepted such indictments of *Huckleberry Finn* have still complained about Twain's failure to maintain a consistently admirable portrait of Jim throughout the novel. An instance of the more general controversy over the concluding chapters, this critique of *Huckleberry Finn*'s problematic ending centers, as we saw in Leo Marx's 1953 interpretation, on the characterizations of Huck and Jim in the "Evasion" sequence in comparison with those in the earlier river episodes. Both characters, Marx argued, have gone through a surprising transformation that betrays "the failure of the ending." Jim "has been made over in the image of a flat stereotype: the submissive stage-Negro. These antics divest Jim, as well as Huck, of much of his dignity and individuality."[3] Marx's and Ellison's criticisms point not only to the centrality of racism for the novel's academic history but also to the importance of that same issue within its broader twentieth-century cultural reception. Praised as the quintessential expression of democratic equality and true American freedom, *Huckleberry Finn* has also been censored as an example of racist stereotyping and declared inappropriate for school reading lists.[4]

Nothing, then, could be more obvious to a twentieth-century reader than the fact that *Huckleberry Finn* and its critical history

[2]Ralph Ellison, "Change the Joke and Slip the Yoke," *Partisan Review*, 25 (Spring 1958), reprinted in his *Shadow and Act* (New York, 1964), pp. 50–51.
[3]Leo Marx, "Mr. Eliot, Mr. Trilling, and *Huckleberry Finn*," *American Scholar*, 22 (Autumn 1953), p. 430.
[4]See, e.g., Leonard Buder, " 'Huck Finn' Barred as Textbook by City," *New York Times*, 12 September 1957, pp. 1, 29; and the editorial "On *Huck*, Criticism and Censorship," *Interracial Books for Children Bulletin*, 15, nos. 1, 2 (1984), 3.

are preoccupied with the issue of race. It is a fact that has the force of self-evidence, that goes—or should go—without saying. Thus, in looking into the novel's nineteenth-century reception, one is most struck by what's *not* there: no commentary linking *Huckleberry Finn* to the "Negro Problem" of the 1880s. Twain's contemporaries simply did not make the connection, despite the writer's public association with George W. Cable, a southerner deeply enmeshed in the early 1885 debate on the race problem. As we saw in Chapter 3, the public argument Cable initiated still raged when the American edition of *Huckleberry Finn* appeared in February 1885, near the end of the Twain-Cable reading tour.

Apparently no one asked Clemens about the race issue while he toured with Cable.[5] Even more surprising: there is not a single mention of the debate in any of the contemporary reviews of *Huckleberry Finn*.[6] Perhaps this perplexing silence on the novel's attitude toward racism could be explained by the claim that in the 1880s, unlike the 1850s, the novel as a genre was not considered a discourse associated with social commentary on race. But this clearly was not the case, as can be seen in the reactions to Albion Tourgée's novels on Reconstruction, especially *A Fool's Errand* (1879) and *Bricks without Straw* (1880). Though the race problem received far less attention in post-Reconstruction literature than it did before the Civil War, the reception of Tourgée's novels indicates that fictional narratives

[5]At least there is no such question in the known interviews of the period. The relevant interviews are listed in Louis J. Budd, ed., "Interviews with Samuel Clemens," *American Literary Realism*, 10 (Winter 1977), 3–5. See also the detailed account of the Twain-Cable reading tour in Guy A. Cardwell, *Twins of Genius* (East Lansing, Mich., 1953).

[6]A passing comment on one of the *Century* excerpts, however, does make the connection: "In *The Century* [for January 1885] Mr. Cable writes of the negro problem, without doubt the most important question before the American people, and reminds us that the negro, though he has been twice a freedman, is not yet free. . . . Mark Twain dips into the negro problem, too, with a 'Jim' who often wishes, on remembering that before the War he had been worth eight hundred dollars, that he had the eight hundred dollars and somebody else had the 'nigger' " (*Critic*, n.s. 2 [27 December 1884], 307). For a listing of known reviews of the novel, see Victor Fischer, "Huck Finn Reviewed: The Reception of *Huckleberry Finn* in the United States, 1885–1897," *American Literary Realism*, 16 (Spring 1983), 49–57. After an extensive search of mostly southern newspapers, I have located only three additional reviews. The most significant one, by Franklin B. Sanborn, is discussed below and cited in n. 55.

could certainly be read from within contemporary debates over white supremacy.[7]

Perhaps the muted political discussion did make it difficult to relate narratives about antebellum slaves to contemporary arguments over racism toward postwar freedmen. That is, Tourgée's Reconstruction novels represented a time contiguous with and thus more relevant to 1880s problems, but a novel like *Huckleberry Finn* treated a period—pre–Civil War America—and an issue—runaway slaves—that were irrelevant to 1880s race relations. But this explanation does not work, either. Long before Cable spoke out against segregation practices, before he was associated with the "Negro Problem" at all, he published a novel on a period even more remote from the 1880s, and still reviewers readily made the connection between its subject and contemporary problems. Although Cable set *The Grandissimes* (1880) among the Creoles of Louisiana in 1804, reviewers easily interpreted the novel as a parable of 1880s race problems. "The questions," wrote the *Atlantic* reviewer, "which agitated so much of the new nation as regarded Louisiana are, with only slight variations, such as have perplexed the entire body of thoughtful men in the nation ever since the downfall of the Confederacy. Mr. Cable is too sincere an artist to push this parallel, but the reader will make it for himself out of the excellent materials offered."[8]

So why didn't contemporary reviewers find the same parallels in *Huckleberry Finn*? Why didn't they make the connection between the novel's antiracism and current controversies over the race question? The answer developed in this chapter can be put quite simply: The contemporary readers of *Huckleberry Finn* were much more preoccupied by literature's effect on the

[7]On the contemporary reception of Tourgée's novels, see Roy F. Dribble, *Albion W. Tourgée* (1921; rpt. Port Washington, N.Y., 1968), chap. 3; and Otto H. Olsen, *Carpetbagger's Crusade: The Life of Albion Winegar Tourgée* (Baltimore, 1965), chap. 18. On the "comparative inattention" given to race in post–Civil War fiction, see Daniel Aaron, *The Unwritten War: American Writers and the Civil War* (New York, 1973), pp. 332–33.

[8]*Atlantic Monthly*, 46 (December 1880), reprinted in *Critical Essays on George W. Cable*, ed. Arlin Turner (Boston, 1980), p. 14. Also see [Lafcadio Hearn], "The Grandissimes," *New Orleans Item*, 27 September 1880, and [W. C. Brownell], "Cable's *The Grandissimes*," *Nation*, 31 (9 December 1880); reprinted in Turner, *Critical Essays*, pp. 10 and 19, respectively.

"Bad-Boy Boom" than they were on its relation to the "Negro Problem."

Here I am less interested in interpreting the novel than I am in reading the cultural practices that constituted the novel for many readers of the 1880s. To read such cultural practices, one must, as a first step, interpret the rhetoric of a text as participating in the cultural debates of a specific historical period and place, here late-nineteenth-century America. Such analysis does not describe these debates in isolation; instead, it locates the intersecting dialogues of the cultural conversation within the social practices, institutionalized disciplines, and material circumstances that made up American society at the moment the text was produced and at the time it found an audience. In this view, the rhetoric of a text does not simply "reflect" these social practices and circumstances; rather, discursive rhetorical practices are modified extensions and varied repetitions of non-discursive practices. And vice versa, for the institutional and nondiscursive also function rhetorically as repetitions and extensions of the discursive. All of these social practices, running the gamut from persuasion to coercion, are actively involved in the cultural work of social organization, disruption, and reorganization in late-nineteenth-century America.

I. Reading Cultural Practices

On 16 March 1885, the Concord Free Public Library banned *Huckleberry Finn* from its shelves. Defending this act of cultural censorship, the library committee called the novel "trash of the veriest sort": "not elevating" in its plot, "coarse" in its humor, and "irreverent" in its style.[9] To understand this important event in the reception of *Huckleberry Finn,* we will need to place it within the anxiety-ridden discussion of the bad-boy boom in the 1880s. I begin with a somewhat schematic genealogy of nineteenth-century social practices surrounding American youths and lead up to a much more detailed analysis of

[9] "'Huckleberry Finn,'" *St. Louis Globe-Democrat,* 17 March 1885, p. 1. Most of the following citations of nineteenth-century newspaper commentaries will be given in the text in order to provide an immediate sense of the specific time frame in which the rhetorical exchanges took place.

the cultural practices that complicated evaluations of Twain's novel in 1885.[10]

By the early nineteenth century, the Enlightenment view of childhood had penetrated deep into American culture. Even within regions of the country still influenced by vestiges of Puritan ideology, parents no longer simply read youthful character and suppressed its innate weaknesses; rather, they wrote that character and nurtured its potential. Under the pressure of Lockean pedagogy, children had become plastic objects to be shaped, blank texts to be inscribed by adults. Abundant were the nineteenth-century references to the "waxen state of children's minds" and to writing "the law" on "the infantile heart." The child emerged as a "pure, unsullied sheet . . . ready to receive any impression that may be made upon it."[11] And to guide parents in this crucial inscribing there arose after 1825 a revitalized genre, the child-rearing book.

How-to books for parents became especially important to a middle class concerned about a perceived breakdown in family discipline. Lockean pedagogy emphasized a balance between parental affection and filial duty, an emphasis that shifted child rearing toward less authoritarian and more child-centered practices.[12] In the early nineteenth century, some observers thought

[10]I use "genealogy" here in order to emphasize that my purpose is to situate the differences between sets of cultural practices in addition to locating their continuities and homologies. See Michel Foucault, "Nietzsche, Genealogy, History," in *Language, Counter-Memory, Practice: Selected Essays and Interviews*, ed. Donald F. Bouchard, trans. Donald F. Bouchard and Sherry Simon (Ithaca, N.Y., 1977), pp. 139–64.

[11]Lydia H. Sigourney, "Duty of Mothers," *Southern Literary Messenger*, 4 (December 1838), 786; Anon., "Infant Schools," *American Annals of Education*, 3 (July 1833), 296–304; and Rensselaer Bentley, *Pictorial Primer* (New York, 1842), p. 5 (all quoted in Bernard Wishy, *The Child and the Republic: The Dawn of Modern American Child Nurture* (Philadelphia, 1968), pp. 22, 72, 74. Also see Mary Beth Norton, *Liberty's Daughters: The Revolutionary Experience of American Women, 1750–1800* (Boston, 1980), pp. 101, 248.

[12]See the discussion of Lockean pedagogy in Nancy F. Cott, *The Bonds of Womanhood: "Woman's Sphere" in New England, 1780–1835* (New Haven, Conn., 1977), pp. 84–87; Cott, "Notes toward an Interpretation of Antebellum Childrearing," *Psychohistory Review*, 6 (Spring 1978), 4–20; and Jay Fliegelman, *Prodigals and Pilgrims: The American Revolution against Patriarchal Authority, 1750–1800* (Cambridge, 1982). Also, on a related cultural context, see Samuel F. Pickering, Jr., *John Locke and Children's Books in Eighteenth-*

that the changes in these practices had gone too far, that American children were becoming spoiled and unmanageable.[13] Advocating renewed parental authority over unruly children, the advice books chastized fathers for neglecting their duties while encouraging mothers to become more competent in theirs. Indeed, as Bernard Wishy writes, "the principal emphasis of the nurture writers was for *mothers* to reform themselves" so they could form their children.[14] Volumes such as Lydia M. Child's *The Mother's Book* (1831) and Lydia H. Sigourney's *Letters to Mothers* (1838) went through several editions, and simultaneously there developed a new kind of magazine, periodicals such as *Parent's Magazine* and *Mother's Assistant*, directed specifically at parents concerned about child rearing.[15]

The assumptions underlying these most serious publications can be seen at work in more humorous genres as well. In a whimsical piece called "About Babies" in *Putnam's Monthly* in 1855, an old bachelor refers to the new infant as a "little nebulous, pulpy, unshapen thing" and goes on to rhapsodize about "the baby Shakespeare, a little nebulous mass, with here and there a spot of light," who "had once hovered about Warwickshire, and . . . had assimilated everything good, and great, and pleasant, and subtile." The writer concludes that "a baby is a complex and wonderful work of art. Whoever succeeds in perfecting the work deserves all praise—whoever produces a pale and diseased child should at once be put to death."[16]

And of course there were children who became failed works of art, pale and diseased. The Lockean view of successful childhood eventually brought with it a reconception of its negative

---

Century England (Knoxville, Tenn., 1981), esp. pp. 7–12, 204–10. For an argument linking the Lockean doctrine of political tolerance to the emergence of a disciplinary society, see Thomas L. Dumm, *Democracy and Punishment: Disciplinary Origins of the United States* (Madison, Wis., 1987), pp. 66–87.

[13]See Wishy, *Child and the Republic*, pp. 13–16; and John Demos and Virginia Demos, "Adolescence in Historical Perspective," *Journal of Marriage and the Family*, 31 (November 1969), 633–34.

[14]Wishy, *Child and the Republic*, p. 28.

[15]See ibid., pp. 3–78; Cott, "Antebellum Childrearing," pp. 4–20; and Robert Sunley, "Early Nineteenth-Century American Literature on Child Rearing," in *Childhood in Contemporary Cultures*, ed. Margaret Mead and Martha Wolfenstein (Chicago, 1955), pp. 150–67.

[16]"About Babies," *Putnam's Monthly Magazine*, 6 (August 1855), 139, 141, 143; cited in Wishy, *Child and the Republic*, p. 23.

other, juvenile delinquency. Beginning in the mid-1820s, young lawbreakers were housed separately and treated differently from adult criminals. In 1825 the newly formed Society for the Reformation of Juvenile Delinquents founded the New York House of Refuge, the first institution of its kind in the country. The following year local philanthropists established the Boston House of Reformation.[17] These houses for delinquents responded not only to the unprecedented interest in childhood and youth but to the growing anxiety over the lower classes congregating in large eastern cities. The (New York) Society for the Prevention of Pauperism (SPP) complained in 1821: "Thousands of children are growing up in this city, destitute of that superintendence over their minds and morals, so indispensable to render them a valuable acquisition to society." The capitalist metaphor is no accident here. Bourgeois philanthropists ideologically constituted working-class children as both potential labor sources for the production of goods *and* as potential threats to the entire capitalist system. To handle the threat, the SPP called for separate institutions for urban juvenile delinquents: "The youth confined there should be placed under a course of discipline, severe and unchanging, but alike calculated to subdue and conciliate. A system should be adopted that would prove a mental and moral regimen."[18] Houses of refuge attempted to realize these goals, inculcating middle-class values of industry, honesty, and frugality into their deviant charges, so pale and diseased through parental neglect or abuse.

New social practices also targeted middle-class children

[17]For the institutional history of juvenile delinquency, see Joseph M. Hawes, *Children in Urban Society: Juvenile Delinquency in Nineteenth-Century America* (New York, 1971); Robert M. Mennel, *Thorns and Thistles: Juvenile Delinquents in the United States, 1825–1940* (Hanover, N.H., 1973); and Steven L. Schlossman, *Love and the American Delinquent: The Theory and Practice of "Progressive" Juvenile Justice, 1825–1920* (Chicago, 1977). Also see Robert M. Mennel, "Attitudes and Policies toward Juvenile Delinquency in the United States: A Historiographical Review," in *Crime and Justice: An Annual Review of Research*, vol. 4, ed. Michael Tonry and Norval Morris (Chicago, 1983), pp. 191–224.

[18]Society for the Prevention of Pauperism (SPP), *Annual Report* (1821), p. 11, and SPP, *Report on the Penitentiary System in the United States* (New York, 1822), p. 60, both quoted in Mennel, *Thorns and Thistles*, p. 11. The disciplinary management of working-class children within nineteenth-century French society is suggestively analyzed in Jacques Donzelot, *The Policing of Families*, trans. Robert Hurley (New York, 1979), pp. 48–95.

and youths who remained with their families, creating mechanisms for public control and supervision outside the home. "Nineteenth-century Americans did not discover childhood vulnerability. Nor did they invent the notion that children required protection and supervision," observes Barbara Finkelstein. "What they originated was a disposition to define, build and organize learning communities for the young—specialized educational settings in which their moral and cognitive capacities would be especially attended."[19] Thus the early nineteenth century saw the beginning of infant schools, the spread of Sunday schools, and the rapid expansion of first voluntary, then mandatory attendance at common schools. With these institutions of juvenile training complementing such new total institutions as refuges and orphanages, American society constructed its first effective agencies for appropriating traditional family functions, affirming in the process the growing worry about discipline in the home. This expansion of educational institutions produced a marked increase in discussions of educational theory. Inherited from the previous century, theories of moral and mental discipline dominated popular and specialized discussions of educational goals and practices. Not only what was taught but how it was taught received scrupulous attention. Nineteenth-century educators argued that if the student's "mind is to be disciplined, enlarged, those studies must be pursued which compel earnest, continued mental effort."[20] Earnest mental effort would increase intellectual abilities and simultaneously foster industry and dedication among students. Within schools of all kinds, mental and moral training combined to develop and regulate youthful character throughout the century.

These institutional practices were complemented by more

[19]Barbara Finkelstein, "Casting Networks of Good Influence: The Reconstruction of Childhood in the United States, 1770–1870," in *American Childhood*, ed. Joseph M. Hawes and N. Ray Hines (Westport, Conn., 1985), p. 111.

[20] *Report of the Massachusetts Board of Education* (1867), quoted in Herbert Galen Lull, "Inherited Tendencies of Secondary Instruction in the United States," *University of California Publications in Education*, 3 (15 April 1915), 203. Also see Michael B. Katz, "The 'New Departure' in Quincy, 1873–1881: The Nature of Nineteenth-Century Educational Reform," *New England Quarterly*, 40 (March 1967), 15–17; and Katz, *The Irony of Early School Reform: Educational Innovation in Mid-Nineteenth-Century Massachusetts* (Cambridge, Mass., 1968), pp. 117–53.

general cultural practices, including genres of discourse directed not at parents but at children and youths. In the 1820s a number of juvenile periodicals began their long runs, including *The Youth's Companion* and *Peter Parley's Magazine*, the latter a fixture in the Clemens household during Sam's early years.[21] Advice books such as Joel Hawes's *Lectures to Young Men* (1832) targeted adolescents making the transition from childhood to adulthood. Such books assumed that youth was "preeminently . . . the forming, fixing period. . . . It is during this season, more than any other, that the character assumes its permanent shape and color."[22] Another genre was just as concerned with rhetorically shaping its young readers. A sharp increase in the production of didactic juvenile fiction began at the same time as the emergence of new child-rearing guides, parent magazines, houses of refuge, infant schools, Sunday schools, educational theories, juvenile periodicals, and advice-to-youth books. All of these discursive and nondiscursive practices developed traditions and supporting institutions of their own as they interacted among themselves to discipline the young throughout the country.

Didactic fiction for children and its reception cannot be separated from this whole complex of social practices developing in nineteenth-century America. For instance, a major contribution to the wide dissemination and rhetorical aim of juvenile fiction grew out of the Sunday school movement, owing primarily to the publishing activities of the American Sunday School Union (ASSU). Founded in 1824, the ASSU united the Sunday school activities of the major evangelical Protestant sects. In its large publishing enterprise, the organization attempted to avoid sectarian controversy among its members by producing tracts, periodicals, and books that were more generally moral than narrowly religious. Indeed, as Anne Scott MacLeod has pointed out, "there is little useful distinction to be made between most Sunday stories and those produced for children by secular publishing companies."[23] The ASSU's fiction for children became quite influential nationally because it was distributed free to

[21]Albert Bigelow Paine, *Mark Twain: A Biography* (1912; rpt. New York, 1980), 1:14.

[22]Quoted in Demos and Demos, "Adolescence," p. 634.

[23]Anne Scott MacLeod, *A Moral Tale: Children's Fiction and American Culture, 1820–1860* (Hamden, Conn., 1975), p. 23.

Sunday school libraries, which were often the only source of juvenile reading matter in a community. Recognition of such facts requires the cultural historian to interpret a genre tradition, in this case didactic children's fiction, as vitally related to other social practices, historical institutions, and material circumstances. To make the same point in a slightly different way: Jacob Abbott's popular Rollo series of prewar children's novels must be read against the background of all the post-1820 practices I have been describing. In such a cultural context, Abbott's claim "to present models of good conduct for imitation and bad examples to be shunned" makes sense not only as a declaration of his genre's didactic aims but also as a definition of the rhetorical purposes of all the social practices involved in the regulation and reformation of American youth.[24]

II. Narratives of Juvenile Delinquency

The cultural attention to juvenile delinquency persisted throughout the nineteenth century as preventive agencies and reform schools began after 1850 to replace houses of refuge in one of those periodic crusades to reform the reformatories. After the Civil War, concern over young lawbreakers intensified as cities grew, the number of immigrants increased, and industrialism expanded.[25] Abbott's *Gentle Measures in the Management and Training of the Young* (1871), the most famous advice book in the postwar decade, incorporated the new physiological knowledge of the period and heralded the era of the scientific expert in child training, an expert with knowledge soon to be professionalized and institutionalized within the American university.[26] Abbott specifically argued for "right develop-

---

[24]Jacob Abbott, Preface to *Harper's Monthly Story Book* (New York, 1854), p. 58, quoted in Wishy, *Child and the Republic*, p. 58. For a suggestive discussion of middle-class disciplinary theory and adult literature of the period, see Richard H. Brodhead, "Sparing the Rod: Discipline and Fiction in Antebellum America," *Representations*, 21 (Winter 1988), 67–96.

[25]Despite being somewhat time-worn and overused, these demographic and economic explanations remain persuasive parts of most standard histories of postwar changes. See, e.g., Robert H. Wiebe, *The Search for Order: 1877–1920* (New York, 1967), chaps. 2–3; and Jay Martin, *Harvests of Change: American Literature 1865–1914* (Englewood Cliffs, N.J., 1967), chap. 1.

[26]On the academic institutionalization of the child-study movement, see Dorothy Ross, *G. Stanley Hall: The Psychologist as Prophet* (Chicago, 1972).

ment . . . by methods in harmony with the structure and the characteristics of the juvenile mind" and continued to maintain that desirable behavior depended more on the imitation of role models than on direct commands or formal precepts.[27]

Didactic children's literature of the postwar period continued to provide acceptable models for juvenile readers.[28] Stories burlesquing the Sunday school genre testify to its continued prominence. In 1865, for instance, Mark Twain published a sketch with the subtitle "The Story of the Bad Little Boy That Bore a Charmed Life," and five years later appeared its companion piece, "The Story of the Good Little Boy Who Did Not Prosper."[29] Both texts make fun of the conventions of the didactic Sunday school story and its unrealistic portrayal of boys and their lives. A sample parodic incident: Jim, "the bad little boy," once "climbed up in Farmer Acorn's apple tree to steal apples, and the limb didn't break and he didn't fall and break his arm, and get torn by the farmer's great dog, and then languish on a sick bed for weeks and repent and become good. Oh, no—he stole as many apples as he wanted, and came down all right, and he was all ready for the dog, too, and knocked him endways with a rock when he came to tear him." The narrator then sarcastically comments: "It was very strange. . . . Nothing like it in any of the Sunday–school books."[30]

In 1870 William Dean Howells, then editor of the *Atlantic Monthly*, enthusiastically praised another story about bad boys, not a burlesque but a straightforward narrative that still rejected the idealization of children's role models in didactic fiction. In his review of *The Story of a Bad Boy* (1869), Howells wrote: "No

[27]Jacob Abbott, *Gentle Measures in the Management and Training of the Young* (New York, 1871), pp. v, 124.

[28]See, e.g., Gary Scharnhorst with Jack Bales, *The Lost Life of Horatio Alger, Jr.* (Bloomington, Ind., 1985), pp. 86–90, on the popularity of Alger's juvenile fiction, especially *Ragged Dick; or, Street Life in New York* (1868), which established the author's oft-repeated formula of an admirable young hero rising from "rags to respectability" (p. 83).

[29]Mark Twain, "The Christmas Fireside for Good Little Boys and Girls. By Grandfather Twain. The Story of the Bad Little Boy That Bore a Charmed Life," *Californian*, 4 (23 December 1865), 4, reprinted in *Early Tales and Sketches*, vol. 2, ed. Edgar Marquess Branch and Robert H. Hirst (Berkeley, 1981), pp. 407–10; and "The Story of the Good Little Boy Who Did Not Prosper," *Galaxy*, 9 (May 1870).

[30]Mark Twain, "The Christmas Fireside," p. 408.

one else seems to have thought of telling the story of a boy's life, with so great desire to show what a boy's life is, and so little purpose of teaching what it should be; certainly no one else has thought of doing this for the life of an American boy."[31] In this semiautobiographical fiction, Thomas Bailey Aldrich did attempt a more realistic representation of boyhood. He introduces his story by explicitly distinguishing his "bad boy" from "those faultless young gentlemen who generally figure in narratives of this kind. . . . I was a real human boy, such as you may meet anywhere in New England, and no more like the impossible boy in a story-book than a sound orange is like one that has been sucked dry."[32] In the story that follows, Aldrich chronicles the various escapades of a typical boy growing up in small-town America.

In a sense, Aldrich anticipated by more than a decade G. Stanley Hall's scientific claim that "bad boys" weren't doomed to be adult criminals. By separating the view of the adult narrator from his earlier bad-boy self, the author makes it clear to his young and old readers that this sample of "delinquency" is only a temporary stage soon to be outgrown. No special intervention seems necessary. Sometime between the story told and its telling, the bad boy develops naturally into the respectable adult narrator. In this implication and the narrator's indulgent attitude toward the bad boy's pranks, we see a literary preview of Hall's later influential theory of adolescence, a scientific theory advocating a more tolerant attitude toward temporary youthful deviance. Hall suggested that "normal children often pass through stages of passionate cruelty, laziness, lying, and thievery," and that perhaps "a period of semicriminality is normal for all healthy boys." He argued that "magnanimity and a large indulgent parental and pedagogical attitude is the proper one toward all, and especially toward juvenile offenders."[33] Hall's

---

[31]*Atlantic Monthly*, 25 (January 1870), 124. Howells favorably compared Tom Sawyer to Aldrich's hero, Tom Bailey, in his review of *The Adventures of Tom Sawyer* in ibid., 37 (May 1876), 622. I am grateful to John Crowley for bringing the 1870 review to my attention; see his "*Little Women* and the Boy-Book," *New England Quarterly*, 58 (September 1985), 384–99. On 1870s controversies over boy books, see Richard L. Darling, *The Rise of Children's Reviewing in America, 1865–1881* (New York, 1968).

[32]Thomas Bailey Aldrich, *The Story of a Bad Boy* (Boston, 1870), pp. 8–9.

[33]Hall argued for these views in the eighties and nineties. The quotations here are from his highly influential *summa*, *Adolescence: Its Psychology and Its*

arguments did not become influential until the 1890s, and the earlier bad-boy genre that Aldrich helped establish apparently exerted little pressure to change attitudes toward juvenile delinquency. Indeed, the bad-boy book was to have the opposite effect in the 1880s. Aldrich's practices of realistic representation soon evolved into forms that raised anew fears that bad boys in literature produced bad boys in life.

The 1880s stand as a transitional stage in the discussion and management of juvenile delinquency. Reform schools came under increasing attack, while various alternative "child-saving" programs continued to be proposed and implemented. By 1882 nine states had established boards of charity to supervise and regulate their reform schools. Franklin B. Sanborn, the first secretary of the Massachusetts board, had proposed widely copied methods of inspection and reporting; and in 1884, as inspector of charities, he helped establish the Massachusetts Reformatory for Men, which housed first-time offenders sixteen to thirty years old.[34] Sanborn's activities typify the evolving American practices of dealing with juvenile delinquents: more differentiated control, more detailed supervision, more comprehensive discipline.

But the emergence of a disciplinary society is always a somewhat uneven development, a haphazard evolution of routine, supervision, training, and control.[35] In late-nineteenth-century America, proposed changes in prison and reformatory practices often ran into material obstacles to the ideals of efficiency and comprehensiveness, obstacles such as insufficient funding,

---

Relations to Physiology, Anthropology, Sociology, Sex, Crime, Religion and Education (New York, 1904), 1:335, 404, 339. In the first quotation Hall is speaking approvingly of a suggestion by Cesare Lombroso, and in the second he is repeating a claim of his own student Edgar J. Swift.

[34]Mennel, *Thorns and Thistles,* pp. 65–71. Also see Sanborn's own account of his charity work in a 1916 series of articles for the Concord *Minute Man,* reprinted in *Sixty Years of Concord,* ed. Kenneth Walter Cameron (Hartford, Conn., 1976), pp. 42–57.

[35]See Michael Ignatieff, "State, Civil Society, and Total Institutions: A Critique of Recent Social Histories of Punishment," in *Crime and Justice: An Annual Review of Research,* vol. 3, ed. Michael Tonry and Norval Morris (Chicago, 1981), pp. 153–92, for a useful criticism of monolithic concepts of power and totalizing views of change in disciplinary practices. I am grateful to John Bender for bringing this valuable article to my attention and for his helpful suggestions concerning this chapter.

management incompetence, and prisoner opposition. Moreover, the rhetoric of impersonal discipline was occasionally undercut by the periodic reappearance of a personalized, familial vocabulary. Some philanthropists argued that families were the "natural reform schools," and the cottage plan and "placing out" programs enacted this rhetoric of the family in institutional reforms.[36] The organization of urban reformatories into family units or "cottages" and the practice of "placing out" delinquents with farming families in the rural Midwest loosened the grip of certain disciplinary practices. Still, these rhetorical and institutional counterforces to closer supervision and regimented control were only partly effective in opposing the dominant though never entirely successful movement toward intensified and comprehensive discipline in the management of juvenile delinquency.

Underlying these disciplinary practices was the continuing belief in the possibility of reform and the malleability of the young. It was not until the 1890s that radically different views came into wide circulation, evolutionary theories that either optimistically conceived of delinquency as a developmental stage naturally outgrown or pessimistically viewed it as a hereditary trait of irremedial degeneracy.[37] Neither perspective significantly affected the arguments made in the 1880s.

[36]See Mennel, *Thorns and Thistles*, pp. 35–42, 52–56, and Miriam Langsam, *Children West: A History of the Placing-Out System of the New York Children's Aid Society, 1853–1890* (Madison, Wis., 1964). The quoted phrase is from Samuel Gridley Howe, *A Letter to the Commissioners of Massachusetts for the State Reform School for Girls* (Boston, 1854), cited in Mennel, *Thorns and Thistles*, p. 42.

[37]Edgar J. Swift, after interviewing several eminent men of the period, represented the optimistic view in "Some Criminal Tendencies of Boyhood: A Study in Adolescence," *Pedagogical Seminary*, 8 (March 1901), 65–91. In "A Study in Youthful Degeneracy," ibid., 4 (December 1896), another Hall student, George E. Dawson, illustrated the pessimistic turn evolutionary theory could take when applied to the lower classes. Though he explicitly offers some hope, Dawson's study of inherited criminal degeneracy suggests more "despair, because it reveals the true significance of the criminal and defective classes in society. . . . Throughout these groups, physical and mental degeneration has spread like an infectious disease." Heredity and environment have established "plague-centers from which moral and mental disease spreads in every direction" (pp. 225–26). On the changed attitudes and practices of the 1890s and early twentieth century, also see Mennel, *Thorns and Thistles*, chap. 3; Joseph F. Kett, *Rites of Passage: Adolescence in America, 1790 to the Present* (New York, 1977), chap. 8; and Anthony M. Platt, *The Child Savers: The Invention of Delinquency*, 2d ed. (Chicago, 1977).

Perhaps I should pause here and review the episodes in my developing narrative of American childhood. Taking my cue from Foucault, I am describing childhood not simply as a set of behaviors or ideas, not as the way children actually behaved or simply the way they were conceptualized.[38] Rather, my story of childhood in nineteenth-century America involves an analysis of how social practices (including literary and nonliterary discursive practices) targeted, controlled, shaped, and thus constituted childhood throughout the century. In this narrative I have identified three phases or overlapping episodes: first, a post-Revolutionary form of childhood, in which children's identities were formed almost entirely within the traditional nuclear family structure; second, a period from the 1820s through the 1880s, in which children were also institutionally disciplined, inscribed by the whole set of interrelated, extra-familial cultural practices I have been analyzing; and third, the 1890s, during which evolutionary and other scientific ideologies, though still defining childhood and adolescence as special stages of growth, argued for new attitudes toward delinquency, either tolerance or despair. The mid-1880s come at the end of the second phase, when arguments continued to assume that youth was the most impressionable stage of development, that this stage determined future moral and mental growth, and that if the young were protected from corrupting social influences, juvenile delinquency could be prevented.

If anything, the anxiety over late childhood and early adolescence increased in the cultural conversation of the eighties. Both scholarly journals and the popular press described this stage as a crisis, a period of extreme contradiction as well as dangerous vulnerability. In his early 1882 essays on adolescence, G. Stanley Hall calmly described this period of rapid change, when youths received "a new capital of energy and altruistic feeling" but could also suffer from "lack of emotional steadiness, violent and dangerous impulses, unreasonable conduct, lack of enthusiasm and sympathy." This is a time when a child's character must be rewritten, when "the previous selfhood is broken up like the regulation copy handwriting of early school years, and a new individual is in process of crystallization. All is solvent, plastic, peculiarly susceptible to external

[38]See Michel Foucault, *The Use of Pleasure*, trans. Robert Hurley (New York, 1985), pp. 3–13.

influences."[39] More hysterically, Anthony Comstock declared in his *Traps for the Young* (1883): "We speak of youth as the plastic state—the period of all others when the human soul is most easily moulded and character formed. . . . *If parents do not train and instruct their children, the devil will. . . . The devil stations a sentry to observe and take advantage of every point open to an evil influence.*"[40] Nothing in the cultural conversation of the eighties better illustrates this intense anxiety over youth than the repeated expressions of fear concerning the bad-boy boom. Central to this fear, indeed one of its primary causes, was the same assumption that drove the production of didactic literature for children: the assumption that fiction has real, tangible effects on juvenile behavior. As Comstock put it: "Good reading refines, elevates, ennobles, and stimulates the ambition to lofty purposes. It points upward. Evil reading debases, degrades, perverts, and turns away from lofty aims to follow examples of corruption and criminality."[41]

[39]G. Stanley Hall, "The Moral and Religious Training of Children," *Princeton Review*, 10 (January 1882), 43, 45.

[40]Anthony Comstock, *Traps for the Young* (1883; rpt. Cambridge, Mass., 1967), p. 239.

[41]Ibid., p. 5. Assumptions about the bad effects of reading continued to be highly gendered in the eighties: boys' behavior turned criminal after they read dime novels and crime stories, while girls' minds became trivialized and distracted when they read sentimental romances. An 1884 newspaper reprints a letter from a Texas woman, just turned twenty-one, who requests help: "I fear I have seriously impaired my mind by novel reading. Do you think I can restore it to a sound and vigorous condition by eschewing novels and reading only solid works?" The editor responds first by commenting that the writer "proves herself a less hopeless case than most of her sisters in the east, who are not only saturated with the dilute sentimentality of fiction, but who also are completely satisfied with their condition." He then goes on to advise these "young ladies who feed their brains with novels and their palates with confectionery" to avoid "silly or pernicious trash" and shun "the monstrous amount of wishy-washy, sensational or at best neutral fiction which the reading public demands": "Young Women and Novels," *Philadelphia Bulletin*, rpt. *Austin Daily Statesman*, 28 December 1884, p. 2. Also see Edward G. Salmon, "What Girls Read," *Nineteenth Century*, 20 (1886), 515–29, discussed in Elizabeth Segel, "Domesticity and the Wide, Wide World," *Children's Literature*, 8 (1980), 168–75. On the gendered assumptions about reading fiction in an earlier era, see Linda K. Kerber, *Women of the Republic: Intellect and Ideology in Revolutionary America* (Chapel Hill, N.C., 1980), pp. 239–49; and Cathy N. Davidson, *Revolution and the Word: The Rise of the Novel in America* (New York, 1986). For a valuable ethnography of twentieth-century reading habits, see Janice A. Radway, *Reading the Romance: Women, Patriarchy, and Popular Literature* (Chapel Hill, N.C., 1984).

As we have seen and will see again, an extreme causal mimeticism informed the theories and practices of child rearing, educational reform, delinquency supervision, and cultural censorship throughout the nineteenth century.[42] Most character managers believed that specific examples, not abstract precepts, were the most powerful sources of positive and negative changes in juvenile behavior. Thus parents, educators, social workers, and censors all generally accepted the claim that exposure to unmediated role models reproduced those exemplars in the characters of children and adolescents. Such role models were considered unmediated if they were directly experienced by youths, either in face-to-face relations with parents, teachers, and peers or in reader–text relations with fictional and nonfictional discourses. In the 1880s these assumptions determined the rhetorical context for discussion of both the facts of juvenile crime and its supposed causes, the varied texts that provided bad-boy models.

III. The Bad-Boy Boom

Though past Twain scholars have located the *Adventures of Huckleberry Finn* inside the tradition of bad-boy books, the literary tradition itself has never been read within the larger scene of cultural debates and social practices concerned with juvenile delinquency.[43] In other words, though *Huckleberry*

---

[42]Causal mimeticism—the assumption that what is represented or performed is imitated by the reader or spectator—has played a significant role in attacks on literature and drama since Plato. My claim is not that literary evaluations informed by such an assumption are unique to the American 1880s, but rather that such assumptions informed a whole range of discursive and nondiscursive practices surrounding American youths in the eighties and that the particular social arrangement and interlocking relation of these practices give a distinctive historical specificity to certain literary evaluations as acts of cultural censorship. For a suggestive history of one genre's relationship to Platonic mimesis and censorship, see Jonas Barish, *The Antitheatrical Prejudice* (Berkeley, 1981). On late-nineteenth-century literary censorship in general, see John Tebbel, *A History of Book Publishing in the United States* (New York, 1975), 2:609–34.

[43]Still extremely valuable, however, are the discussions of the literary context in Walter Blair, "On the Structure of *Tom Sawyer*," *Modern Philology*, 37 (August 1939), 75–88; Albert E. Stone, Jr., *The Innocent Eye: Childhood in Mark Twain's Imagination* (1961; rpt. Hamden, Conn., 1970), pp. 58–90; and Alan Gribben, "'I Did Wish Tom Sawyer Was There': Boy-Book Elements in *Tom Sawyer* and *Huckleberry Finn*," in *One Hundred Years of Huckleberry Finn:*

Finn has been interpreted within its horizon of literary expectations, the novel's reception has not been adequately located within its extraliterary horizon.[44] In fact, I argue that in the reception of Twain's book, the distinction between literary and extraliterary completely breaks down.

Huckleberry Finn prefigures an aspect of its own reception when it satirically thematizes the potent effect of novels on impressionable young readers. Tom Sawyer's mind is indelibly marked by the romantic adventure stories he admires and then self-consciously imitates throughout the story. During the first meeting of his "highwaymen," Tom guides his gang in their plans for "robbery and murder" and reads an oath binding each member to secrecy under pain of having "his throat cut, and . . . his carcass burnt up and the ashes scattered all around." Responding to Tom's reading, "everybody said it was a real beautiful oath, and asked Tom if he got it out of his own head. He said, some of it, but the rest was out of pirate books, and robber books, and every gang that was high-toned had it."[45] Though sometimes challenging his friend's expertise, Huck is often intimidated by Tom's superior knowledge of book-lore and usually falls in line behind his friend's outlandish schemes. Imitating the imitator, Huck is affected by books at secondhand, as he comes to admire and repeat Tom's book-learned "style" in his own bad-boy escapades. At the end of the novel, Huck repro-

---

The Boy, His Book, and American Culture, ed. Robert Sattelmeyer and J. Donald Crowley (Columbia, Mo., 1985), pp. 149–70. Less valuable are the historical analyses that assume a reductive reflection model of literature and simply use the story in *Huckleberry Finn* as evidence for social attitudes toward delinquency; see, e.g., Hawes, *Children in Urban Society*, pp. 120–23.

[44]See Hans Robert Jauss, "Literary History as a Challenge to Literary Theory," in his *Toward an Aesthetic of Reception*, trans. Timothy Bahti (Minneapolis, 1982), pp. 24, 39–45; and my *Interpretive Conventions: The Reader in the Study of American Fiction* (Ithaca, N.Y., 1982), pp. 167–70. My concern here with discipline and literary reception (rather than production) can be usefully supplemented by Mark Seltzer's analysis of the realist novel's complicity in the social technologies of disciplinary power; see his *Henry James and the Art of Power* (Ithaca, N.Y., 1984).

[45]*Adventures of Huckleberry Finn*, ed. Walter Blair and Victor Fischer (Berkeley, 1985), pp. 9–10. Of course, there is a long tradition of fiction about the effects of reading fiction. On the reception of one such work, see Dominick LaCapra, "*Madame Bovary*" on Trial (Ithaca, N.Y., 1982), esp. pp. 23–52, analyzing the interpretive arguments about the novel during the 1857 court trial and its verdict, which censured (but did not convict) the author.

duces the fantasy of many an 1840s dime-novel reader when he determines to light out for the western territories.

By the 1880s the dime novel had evolved to include urban as well as western settings, detective heroes as well as cowboys.[46] In the westerns still being written, "blood and thunder" increased dramatically, while the detective fictions presented descriptions of crime quite disturbing to parents of boy readers. The turn to increasing violence and crime in dime novels was a response to the sharp decline in the prices of competing books. When cheap reprints of popular classics began to flood the market in the late 1870s, the dime novel needed more than its low price to attract readers.[47] Competition also came from the newspapers, as the *Police Gazette* and other crime weeklies published explicit stories of criminals' practices and their victims' sufferings. In periodical and novel form, then, boys found new, intriguing, and sometimes attractive criminal models to imitate. Or so it seemed to the horrified parents and arbiters of culture in the early 1880s.

An 1884 editorial in the *New York Tribune* began, "The work of the dime novel is being performed with even more than the usual success. The other day three boys robbed their parents and started off for the boundless West." After describing another example of juvenile crime, the writer went on to analyze its causes in detail:

> The class of literature which is mainly responsible for all this folly is distributed all over the country in immense quantities, and it is distinctly evil in its teachings and tendencies. The heroes of the dime novel are almost always thieves, robbers and immoral characters, and the heroines are no better. The stories abound with descriptions of brutality, cruelty and dishonesty. . . . Through reading this pestilent stuff a great many boys are undoubtedly put fairly in the road to ruin. They insensibly acquire a crooked moral vision. . . . They pine for opportunities to emulate the heroes they are reading about.   [10 March 1884, p. 4]

[46]See Albert Johannsen, *The House of Beadle and Adams and Its Dime Novels: The Story of a Vanished Literature* (Norman, Okla., 1950), 1:3; and Edmund Pearson, *Dime Novels; or Following an Old Trail in Popular Literature* (1929; rpt. Port Washington, N.Y., 1968), pp. 138–90. For a suggestive analysis of the dime novel and cultural politics, see Michael Denning, *Mechanic Accents: Dime Novels and Working-Class Culture in America* (London, 1987).

[47]See Raymond Howard Shove, *Cheap Book Production in the United States, 1870 to 1891* (Urbana, Ill., 1937), pp. 1–25.

Five days before this editorial appeared, Anthony Comstock
had spoken in Union Hall, New York City, on the subject "The
Curses of Our City." "What I desire most to impress upon you,"
he said to his listeners, "is the growth of vile literature. . . .
Every publisher of the vile sensational papers for boys is shaping the career of the youth of our country. They glorify crime;
the hero of each story is a boy who has escaped the restraints of
home and entered on a life of crime." Comstock then went on to
support his claims with data gathered in his position as secretary of the New York Society for the Suppression of Vice:

> During the first six months of 1882, 18 persons of minor age were
> arrested for murder in this city and 50 for attempts at murder.
> During the same period in 1883, 26 were arrested on the first
> charge and 86 on the second, nearly all of them having been
> readers of the villainous stuff with which the country is flooded
> and the ideas contained in which led in a majority of cases to the
> commission of the crime.

Later, newspaper editorials used similar rhetorical devices to
support their pleas for cultural censorship, but, as we will see,
they tended to narrativize the data, to present stories rather than
statistics. Comstock ended his lecture by calling for "public
sentiment" to "root out" vile literature and other evils corrupting the young (*New York World*, 5 March 1884, p. 5).

But it was not only fictional and nonfictional descriptions of
crime that inspired attempts at cultural censorship. There also
appeared in the 1880s a comic culmination of the new tradition
of the bad-boy story, *Peck's Bad Boy and His Pa*, published in
1883. George W. Peck, later governor of Wisconsin, created a
character who was more outlandish and perhaps more culturally significant than the bad boy of Aldrich's 1869 novel. This
1880s bad boy was much more antiauthority in his attitude and
sadistic in his pranks. Readers were meant to laugh not at the
boy's innocence but at his success in causing pain for his father
and other adults. Peck's Bad Boy came to symbolize the worst
fears of middle-class parents, and newspapers encouraged these
fears with comments like these from the *Baltimore Day*:

> When we speak of the pernicious influence of the dime novel or
> the Jesse James style of border drama we should not forget that
> there are other and more insidious ways of corrupting youth, and

no better illustration of this could be given than the fact that when a number of boys in Milwaukee, of respectable parentage, were recently arrested for barn burning and other wanton outrages, the boast of one of them to the magistrate was: "I am Peck's bad boy, and don't you forget it." [11 March 1884; reprinted as "Peck's Bad Play," *New York World*, 13 March 1884, p. 4]

At stake here is the shaping of youthful identity, and this boy "of respectable parentage" boasts about the fashioning already accomplished. The disciplinary techniques of family and reform school are no match, it seems, for the rhetorical self-fashioning that produced this bad-boy imitator.[48] At least in this newspaper report, Peck's Bad Boy became a trope used by young lawbreakers for self-definition. How widespread such molding of inner lives came to be remains problematic. But if 1880s juvenile voices are hard to hear, adult voices are not. Whatever juvenile subjects made out of Peck's Bad Boy, many adults were convinced that real bad boys were made out of juveniles subjected to bad-boy fiction. Indeed, Peck's Bad Boy became a rhetorical figure marking a growing concern within the cultural conversation of the mid-eighties, a concern with the special dangers of adolescence and the perceived rise in juvenile delinquency. Unlike earlier worry over the link between pauperism and delinquency, the 1880s anxiety included fear for middle-class youths as well as for orphaned street urchins. Of course, concern over lower-class delinquents continued and was simply compounded by fears that the sons of respectable, bourgeois families were also threatened by corrupting models of bad-boy behavior in and out of texts.[49] One straightforward news account in the *New York World* bore the startling title "Sad Juvenile Depravity / The Astounding Record of One Week's Crimes and Plots / The Bad Boy as a Highwayman." The account strung together reprints of news items from several eastern cities, factual reports that included bits of information such as the following: In Quincy, Massachusetts, "seven young boys" composing the "Jesse James

---

[48]Cf. Stephen Greenblatt, *Renaissance Self-Fashioning: From More to Shakespeare* (Chicago, 1980), pp. 86–88, 119–20.

[49]See Geo. C. Needham, *Street Arabs and Gutter Snipes: The Pathetic and Humorous Side of Young Vagabond Life in the Great Cities, with Records of Work for Their Reclamation* (Boston, 1884), chap. 3, on "pernicious literature" as a source of "youthful debasement."

Gang" were charged with burglary and later confessed that "they were led into crime by reading dime novels." A Philadelphia eighteen-year-old had "been a constant reader of dime novels lately" and had just "tried his hand at forgery." When arrested in Millersburg, Pennsylvania, three teenaged highwaymen possessed "four gold-mounted revolvers, a number of actresses' photographs, and several dime novels" (26 March 1884, p. 2).

In a piece headed "The Bad-Boy Boom," the editors of the *World* analyzed these reports of juvenile crime:

> No one who reads and thinks need be told that the foolish desire on the part of these boys to organize themselves into predatory gangs is not the usual and natural result of mere depravity. Some new influence is at work to produce this comparatively recent symptom. One does not have to look far to find it. The organization of crime has been made fascinating to the undeveloped mind by the novelist and playwright.

The editorial continued: "Thousands of undisciplined youths have imbibed their notions of heroism and their excuse for the violation of law from the tawdry scenes and the precocious Dick Turpins thus represented." The column ended with the question: "What is society doing to stop these poisonous fountains that are sending out their subtle and fetid waters throughout the country?" (26 March 1884, p. 4).

Earlier the *World* had been even more emphatic. An editorial, "Crime among Small Boys," began, "While other nations are giving their attention to the decline of imperialism and the decay of commerce and loyalty, America is called upon to protect itself against the fell swoop of its children." In this bewildering interpretation of national priorities, bad boys distract the country from its dual goals of expansionist politics and economic development. The writer continued: "The whole of this sudden irruption of juvenile depravity is traceable to looseness of discipline and that license of thought and conduct which are permitted nowhere else in the world." The editorial concluded with this clarion call for action against the national menace: "If parents and guardians cannot instruct children so that they will avoid becoming outlaws before their bones are hard, something ought to be done by society to prevent the venders of poisonous literature from misinstructing them" (24 March 1884, p. 4).

As if in direct response to this challenge, Senator John Gilbert soon introduced into the New York State Legislature a bill prohibiting "the sale or exhibition of indecent publications devoted to criminal and police news and criminal deeds, tending to corrupt the morals of youth (*New York Evening Post*, 27 March 1884, p. 1). At the same session, the New York Society for the Prevention of Cruelty to Children presented a petition that not only supported the bill but advocated a ban on the sale of dime novels as well.[50] The following year the Massachusetts legislature passed a similar bill sponsored by the New England Society for the Suppression of Vice.[51] Obviously, intense concern over the textual production of real bad boys was not restricted to the popular press in the eighties.

But that press, which soon would review Twain's bad-boy book, did provide the broadest forum for constructing the social linkage between literary effects and juvenile delinquency. Throughout the nation, not only in New York and Boston, newspapers called for cultural censorship of texts that threatened to corrupt minors. In " 'The Bad Boy' of the Period," the *Detroit Free Press* editorialized: "Most excellent is the intent of the law proposed in the New York Assembly for prohibiting the vicious literature which is turning American boys into savages and rendering it problematical whether the next generation will be either Jesse Jameses or Jay Goulds." Citing the *New York World's* reports of "sad juvenile depravity" (quoted above), the editorial began its analysis:

In the large majority of these cases the boys were readers of the newspapers and books whose heroes are of the type of Jesse James,

---

[50]"New York Legislature," *New York Evening Post*, 27 March 1884, p. 1. The society, incorporated in 1875, aimed to prevent such abuses as "the endangering of the health or morals" of children as well as "kidnapping, abduction, abandonment, improper guardianship, begging, the use of unnatural violence," according to William Pryor Letchworth, "The History of Child-Saving Work in the State of New York," in *History of Child Saving in the United States* (Boston, 1893), p. 199.

[51]Chap. 305, *Acts and Resolves of Massachusetts* (1885), p. 758; *Annual Report of the N. E. Society for the Suppression of Vice, for the Year 1885–1886* (Boston, 1886), p. 11.

"Peck's Bad Boy," or some other infernal scamp who figures in the
vile trash that waylays boys on nearly every street corner. . . . They
are insidiously assailed by this literature, which is either vulgar or
vicious. They become "bad boys," insolent little vandals, without
regard for the rights of person or property. They indulge in what
they call the "tricks" of the "bad boy"—which are really odious
and lawless assaults upon common rights and common decency.
[30 March 1884, p. 4]

Within a year, another bad boy began to tell the public about
his delinquent tricks. Huck Finn's reception is best understood
in the interpretive and evaluative context typified by these
newspaper editorials. Not surprisingly, the *New York World*,
which had been so vocal a few months earlier, headed its review
"Mark Twain's Bad Boy." It began by attacking Twain at his
strongest yet also his most vulnerable point, his status as a
"humorist." Though not yet the cultural institution he was to
become, Mark Twain in the early 1880s was an extremely popular comic satirist. But being called a humorist was not an un-
problematic compliment. Humorous writing had considerably
less cultural prestige than more serious literary modes in late-
nineteenth-century America, a fact that Samuel Clemens recognized and sometimes worried about. Also, as the *World* reviewer argued, there are humorists and then there are "humorists": "Were Mark Twain's reputation as a humorist less well
founded and established, we might say that this cheap and
pernicious stuff is conclusive evidence that its author has no
claim to be ranked with Artemus Ward, Sydney Smith, Dean
Swift . . . or any other recognized humorist above the grade of
the author of that outrageous fiction, 'Peck's Bad Boy.' " *Huckleberry Finn*, the reviewer went on, "is the story (told by himself)
of a wretchedly low, vulgar, sneaking and lying Southern country boy of forty years ago." The review condemned the book's
"irreverence which makes parents, guardians and people who
are at all good and proper [look] ridiculous" (2 March 1885,
p. 6). This judgment by no means represents the opinions of
most reviewers of *Huckleberry Finn*, which received high praise
for its realism and humor in many quarters. But the *New York
World* review does typify a significant phase of the novel's
contemporary reception, a set of interpretive and evaluative acts
best understood in the cultural context I have been developing.
About two weeks after the *World* review, the most famous of

these acts took place: the Concord Free Public Library removed *Huckleberry Finn* from its shelves. This act of cultural censorship received national publicity and inspired debate throughout the country. The *St. Louis Globe-Democrat* quoted one member of the Concord Library committee: Twain's novel "deals with a series of adventures of a very low grade of morality. . . . It is also very irreverent. . . . The whole book is of a class that is more profitable for the slums than it is for respectable people, and it is trash of the veriest sort" (17 March 1885, p. 1). An editorial in the *Springfield* (Massachusetts) *Republican* heartily approved of the library's action in "banishing" the book "on the ground that it is trashy and vicious," and called parts of the book "offensive," comparing their tone to that of a dime novel. Again echoing the rhetoric of earlier attacks on bad-boy literature and periodicals, the editorial concluded by claiming that sample sections of the novel have a low "moral level" and "their perusal cannot be anything less than harmful" (17 March 1885, p. 4).

Not surprisingly, the *New York World* gave its support to the Concord ban. Citing the library committee's judgment of the novel as "trashy and vicious," the newspaper replayed its earlier review in a more understated register: "It is very possible that the book may be as bad as the Concordians pronounce it" (18 March 1885, p. 4). The *World* followed up this editorial with several lighthearted "news items" that kept reminding its readers about the ban. For example, two days after its show of support for the library's action, this notice appeared: "Mark Twain is believed to be in concord with the Concordians in their gratuitous advertisement of 'Huckleberry Finn' as a 'bad' book, but Mr. Comstock has not yet been heard from."[52]

Comstock's voice might not have been heard on this occasion, but Mark Twain's certainly was. In a facetious public letter thanking the Concord Free Trade Club for its invitation to become an honorary member, Clemens also thanked the library committee for its "generous action" in having "condemned and excommunicated" his book, thus doubling its sales (*Boston*

[52]*New York World*, 20 March 1885, p. 4. Mark Twain items also appeared in the *World* on 19 March, p. 4; 2 April, p. 1; 4 April, p. 4; 5 April, p. 4; 6 April, p. 4; and 9 April, p. 4. In some of these items, the *World* took philosophical and political swipes at the Concordians, underlining the fact that the newspaper's agreement with the Concord Library committee was primarily aesthetic-ethical in nature.

Daily Advertiser, 2 April 1885, p. 2). The author continued in the same ironic vein in his other responses to the Concord censorship. Two days after the public letter, he wrote Charles Webster, his nephew and publisher, instructing him to include a "Prefatory Remark" in all future editions of the banned novel. "Huckleberry Finn is not an imaginary person," the preface would read, for he, rather *they*, still live. Huck is really a truthful representation of the boyhood of two well-known gentlemen, "the present editors of the Boston *Advertiser* and the Spring-field *Republican*." These two newspapers had published some of the most negative reviews and editorials on *Huckleberry Finn*, expressing strong support for the Concord ban, a ban Clemens playfully ridiculed in his proposed preface. He concluded by adding that Huck's portrait was "true to the originals, in even the minutest particulars, with but one exception, and that a trifling one: this boy's language has been toned down and softened, here and there, in deference to the taste of a more modern and fastidious age."[53]

The preface was never published as such in any edition of the novel, for this response to the censors was itself censored by Clemens' wife. Still another reaction, more interesting in its implications, appeared a few days later in Clemens' notebook. Here the author read his novel's negative reception, as I have done, through the pages of the *New York World*. Over eight note-book sheets, Clemens copied several sensational news items from the April 9 issue of that newspaper: poisoning, shooting, seduction, suicide, lynching, racism, abortion, murder, ending with " 'Hacked himself to death'—1/2 col.—with the gory & slaughterous details." The sarcastic moral Clemens appended to this gruesome litany cut, as it were, to the heart of the censors' motives: "If you want to rear a family just right for sweet & pure society here & Paradise hereafter, banish Huck Finn from the home circle & introduce the N.Y. World in his place."[54]

Clemens' responses to the negative criticism indicate that he read it as a manifestation of the literary-ethical linkage most cultural arbiters assumed as given. And, more specifically, his

[53]*Mark Twain's Letters to His Publishers, 1867–1894*, ed. Hamlin Hill (Berkeley, 1967), p. 188. For more on Mark Twain's interaction with New York and Massachusetts newspapers, see Louis J. Budd, *Our Mark Twain: The Making of His Public Personality* (Philadelphia, 1983), chap. 6.

[54]*Mark Twain's Notebooks and Journals*, vol. 3, ed. Robert Pack Browning, Michael B. Frank, and Lin Salamo (Berkeley, 1979), pp. 128–30.

notebook reaction to the *World* suggests that he fully recognized how seriously his critics took literary reading as child rearing. Even some of *Huckleberry Finn*'s defenders accepted the premises of the cultural censors. Although he was professionally concerned about juvenile delinquents, Franklin Sanborn still praised the novel in one of its most favorable reviews: "I cannot subscribe to the extreme censure passed upon this volume, which is no coarser than Mark Twain's books usually are, while it has a vein of deep morality beneath its exterior of falsehood and vice, that will redeem it in the eyes of mature persons. It is not adapted to Sunday-school libraries, and should perhaps be left unread by growing boys; but the mature in mind may read it, without distinction of age or sex, and without material harm."[55] While he vigorously rejected the judgment of the Concord Library committee, Sanborn nonetheless accepted the assumptions about juvenile reading that supported its act of censorship.

In perhaps the most rhetorically incisive analysis of the controversy, the *San Francisco Chronicle* did the best job of exposing the interpretation supporting the negative evaluations of *Huckleberry Finn:*

> The action of the Concord Public Library in excluding Mark Twain's new book . . . is absurd. The managers of this library evidently look on this book as written for boys, whereas we venture to say that upon nine boys out of ten much of the humor, as well as the pathos, would be lost. . . . When the boy under 16 reads a book he wants adventure and plenty of it. He doesn't want any moral thrown in or even implied; the elaborate jokes worked out with so much art, which are Mark Twain's specialty, are wasted upon him. [29 March 1885, p. 4]

Clearly, this reviewer thought that the Concord Library committee had misread Twain's novel—not only missed its moral but also misidentified its intended audience. Still other reviewers could see no moral appropriate for young readers, whatever the intended audience. The *Cleveland Leader and Herald*, in its approval of the Concord ban, added its opinion that the novel "cannot be said to have a very high moral tone, but records the adventures of a lot of fishy people who try to outdo each other in mischievousness; very amusing, no doubt, but hardly suitable

[55]Franklin B. Sanborn, "Our Boston Literary Letter," *Springfield* (Mass.) *Daily Republican,* 27 April 1885, p. 2.

for a Sunday school, as Horace Greeley remarked about Byron's poems" (26 April 1885, p. 4).

In light of these contemporary comments, we can see that a significant part of *Huckleberry Finn*'s reception participated in the ongoing cultural discussion of literary effects and juvenile delinquency. Thus I must disagree with Victor Fischer when, in his essay "Huck Finn Reviewed," he claims that "the Concord ban caused a distortion in the reviews that followed it, for few newspapers considered the book simply on its merits."[56] Though the ban did influence later reviews, it is misleading to call this influence a "distortion," for the "merits" of the book are not some transhistorical qualities intrinsic to the novel, which are either recognized or overlooked. Rather, what counts as a "merit" is what the cultural conversation allows to be taken as such. And certainly, as I have tried to show, a novel's relationship to worries over literary effects and juvenile delinquency functioned as a dominant criterion for judging any 1885 book about boys. Anxiety over the bad-boy boom and assumptions about vulnerable readers formed an inextricable part of the rhetorical context in which such books as *Huckleberry Finn* were written, read, and evaluated in mid-1880s America.

In 1884 the New York State Reformatory at Elmira established a class in English literature as "an experiment in a more intensive use of literature for reformative effect."[57] The reformative effect intended went beyond the simple use of good literature to teach good morals. For the reformatory superintendent, Zebulon Brockway, the English literature class also extended a disciplinary strategy of surveillance: the required reading made it possible, he claimed, "to tell with considerable certainty at any moment what occupies the mind of any man."[58] In its second year the course in literary study became mandatory, with examinations being given to determine prisoners' grade standing and progress toward release. Brockway later observed that this edu-

[56]Fischer, "Huck Finn Reviewed," p. 31.

[57]Zebulon Reed Brockway, *Fifty Years of Prison Service: An Autobiography* (New York, 1912), p. 273.

[58]Brockway, "Report of the General Superintendent," *Annual Report of the Board of Managers of the New York State Reformatory at Elmira, for the Year Ending September 30, 1885* (Elmira, N.Y., 1885), pp. 12–13. According to the *Report*, 60.1 percent of the reformatory inmates were between 16 and 20 years old when admitted, and the average period of detention for the current inmates was 16.9 months (pp. 23–24).

cational training in literary taste was particularly enhanced by discussions in the practical morality classes. Visiting lecturers added to these classroom attempts to turn cultural enrichment into ethical improvement.[59] Ironically, one of these uplifting lecturers was Mark Twain, who read from *Huckleberry Finn* during a visit in July 1886.[60]

Another visitor was Franklin Sanborn, longtime friend of Brockway and inspector for the Massachusetts State Board of Charities, the agency that supervised state reform schools for juvenile delinquents. A radical abolitionist before the war, Sanborn was also the secretary of the American Social Science Association (ASSA) and had arranged for Cable to deliver his "Freedman's Case in Equity" lecture before that organization in September 1884.[61] With his dual interests in race relations and juvenile delinquency, Sanborn's final response to a novel about both can stand as a proper coda to this chapter.

While teaching the nation's first course in applied social science, Sanborn took his Cornell students on a field trip to the Elmira reformatory in April 1885, and during the visit he noted the librarian's negative opinion of a certain controversial novel. Subsequently, Sanborn wrote to Brockway: "I have read 'Huckleberry Finn,' and I do not see any reason why it should not go into your Reference Library, at least, and form the subject of a debate in your Practical Morality Class."[62] That debate had in fact already taken place in a much larger cultural arena, a historical context of social practices that made possible the university course, the reformatory classroom, and the reception of *Huckleberry Finn*.

---

[59]Brockway, *Fifty Years*, pp. 273–76.

[60]*Twain's Notebooks and Journals*, 3:244.

[61]See Sanborn to Cable, Concord, Mass., 7 July 1884, George W. Cable Papers, Howard-Tilton Memorial Library, Tulane University. Volumes edited by Kenneth Walter Cameron reproduce relevant essays published by Sanborn in the 1880s; see *Transcendental Youth and Age: Chapters and Autobiography* (Hartford, 1981) and *Ungathered Poems and Transcendental Papers* (Hartford, 1981). On Sanborn and the ASSA, see Thomas L. Haskell, *The Emergence of Professional Social Science: The American Social Science Association and the Nineteenth-Century Crisis of Authority* (Urbana, Ill., 1977).

[62]*The Summary*, a weekly newspaper published by the Elmira Reformatory, quoted in *Critic*, n.s. 3 (30 May 1885), 264. Brockway commented on (what amounts to) the disciplinary aim of *The Summary*, which was "edited and printed by the prisoners under proper censorship" (*Fifty Years*, p. 273). Also see the remarks of "Our Special Correspondent," most probably Sanborn, in "From New York State," *Springfield* (Mass.) *Daily Republican*, 19 May 1885, p. 2.

PART THREE

Neo-Pragmatism and the
Politics of Interpretation

5

Rhetoric, Theory, and Politics

> The trouble about arguments is, they ain't nothing but *theories*, after all, and theories don't prove nothing, they only give you a place to rest on, a spell, when you are tuckered out butting around and around trying to find out something there ain't no way *to* find out.
>
> —Mark Twain, *Tom Sawyer Abroad*

Part Two can be read simply as a practical demonstration of the rhetorical politics at work in various discourses. To place the ideological rhetoric of *Huckleberry Finn* within the 1880s debate over white supremacy, to situate the novel's reception in the context of late-nineteenth-century discursive and nondiscursive practices surrounding juvenile delinquency, and to locate the interpretive arguments about Mark Twain within the interlocking discourses of cultural politics, academic literary studies, and his texts' critical histories—each of these interpretive efforts presented rhetorical analyses as historical narratives. Each extended the perspective proposed in Part One by showing how this rhetorical approach can be applied to critical theory, academic interpretations, literary texts, and cultural reception.

But there is another way to read Part Two: not as a practical application but as a theoretical illustration of rhetorical hermeneutics, especially its claim that interpretive accounts should move from theory to history as quickly as possible. This neopragmatist argument proposes a change of subject for hermeneutics, a move from explaining interpretation in terms of isolated readers and isolated texts to discussing rhetorical exchanges among interpreters embedded in discursive and other social practices at specific historical moments. Rhetorical hermeneutics joins the antifoundationalist debate by supporting the claim that a general Theory of interpretation is impossible. Part Two demonstrates how difficult it is to explain rigorously even a single act of literary interpretation, such as the Concord Library's ban of *Huckleberry Finn* or any twentieth-century academic reading of the novel.

Rhetorical hermeneutics argues that any explanatory attempt must embed the act of interpretation first in its most relevant critical debates (and there may be several); then the act and its participation in ongoing arguments must be situated in the rhetorical traditions within relevant institutional discourses; and then the interpretive act, its arguments, and its framing institutions must be placed within the cultural conversations, relevant social practices, and constraining material circumstances of its historical moment. And of course this moment has its specific temporal history and geographical location within a culture's evolving social, political, and economic formations. The question is: Where does a literary theorist or a cultural historian draw the line? At what degree of microscopic detail, at what level of macroscopic contextualization does one stop in explaining even a single act of interpretation? I argue in Chapter 1 that to explain exhaustively a specific interpretive act, the Theorist must either simply name "context" or "situation" and then fall silent or begin to describe the historical context in an unending act of specification. For a general hermeneutic Theory, this means never beginning or never ending. It is in this sense that a certain kind of theory—foundationalist theory—is impossible. But of course there are other kinds of theorizing. The one I am advocating here is a hermeneutics that leads necessarily to rhetorical history, the type I have been presenting throughout this book, one that does not claim absolute coverage for its narratives but does attempt to make a persuasive case for each of them.

If *Rhetorical Power* can be read either as theory serving practice (a rhetorical perspective applied to various kinds of texts) or as practice serving theory (continual hermeneutic theorizing through illustrations), it is only in the latter view that I claim never to leave off theorizing. That is, to theorize about interpretation, to do hermeneutics, leads me into rhetorical accounts of establishing the meaning of texts, and such accounts become by necessity thick historical descriptions and genealogies of specific interpretive episodes in the cultural conversation at specific times and places. Thus in rhetorical hermeneutics it is

argued *both* that therapeutic theory leads to rhetorical history—
that is, a theoretical critique of realist and idealist foundationalism leads to rhetorical accounts of historical disputes over
meaning—*and* that the theory-versus-history distinction breaks
down; that is, a rhetorical theory of interpretation must be content with providing detailed historical narratives of specific
controversies over textual interpretations and give up the goal of
ahistorical generalizations, statements of the form "interpretation in general always does or should work this way." Such
rhetorical histories resist making foundationalist claims, which
try to ground criteria for correct interpretation outside of historical contingencies, local relations of power, and specific episodes of cultural conversations. From this rhetorical perspective, doing histories of interpretive acts is the only kind of
positive theorizing about interpretation that counts.

Within this framework of viewing *Rhetorical Power,* Part One
(the more "theoretical" chapters 1 and 2) does not justify, explain, or enable Part Two (the more "historical" chapters 3 and
4); rather, the latter simply continues the theoretical/historical
project that the former initiates. From this perspective, Chapter
3 thematizes rhetoric in a literary text and relates it to the
rhetorical context in which that text's ideology was performed.
This rhetorical interpretation is then used as an example of an
interpretive act that can itself be situated in its own rhetorical
context within the interpretive history of the novel it is analyzing. This second step, the situating of its own arguments, is a
continuation of the specific kind of rhetorical theorizing advocated in Chapter 1. Chapter 4 then repeats this theorizing as
detailed historical description by placing another interpretive
act—the banning of *Huckleberry Finn* by the Concord Library—
within the sociopolitical context of debates and practices surrounding the bad-boy boom of the mid-1880s. Instead of making
any foundationalist claims about the relation of an independent
reader and an objective literary text, rhetorical hermeneutics
takes up the interpretive debates over textual meaning at specific historical moments. Rhetorical hermeneutics does not replace all theory with history; rather, rhetorical theorizing about
interpretation leads to and includes rhetorical histories of interpretive disputes, and, conversely, rhetorical histories about
such disputes are, from this perspective, the only type of positive theorizing that rhetorical hermeneutics advocates.

In Part Three, I clarify further the claims of rhetorical hermeneutics, beginning in the present chapter by refining its arguments and adjusting its figures. My route to these ends will be by way of three contemporary American books concerned with reading: Ken Kesey's *One Flew Over the Cuckoo's Nest*, about reading the deviant within; Edward Said's *Orientalism*, about reading the alien without; and Richard Rorty's *Philosophy and the Mirror of Nature*, about reading as such.[1] My purpose here is not to provide anything like a comprehensive interpretation of these extraordinary books, but rather to use an interested reading of them to develop further my case for a rhetorical hermeneutics.

I. Representing Power

Weaving together this trio of disparate texts is the theme of power, both physical and rhetorical. Read from this perspective, *Cuckoo's Nest* emerges as a problematic parable of politics. In the first of its two conflicting views of power, Kesey's novel represents a patient who declaims: "This world . . . belongs to the strong, my friend! The ritual of our existence is based on the strong getting stronger by devouring the weak. . . . The rabbits accept their role in the ritual and recognize the wolf as the strong. In defense, the rabbit becomes sly and frightened and elusive and he digs holes and hides when the wolf is about. And he endures, he goes on. He knows his place. He most certainly doesn't challenge the wolf to combat. Now, would that be wise? Would it?" (p. 62). In this scenario of power, the domination of the weak by the strong determines the social relations and political interaction of the world's players. Domination is a cause, the origin of a repressive and negative form of power. As Kesey would have us see, the patient's description of the world at large applies even more accurately to the microcosm of the psychiatric ward in which the novel's action takes place.

The ward patients are, in their own words, the rabbits of the rabbit world (p. 65), and their wolf is Nurse Ratched, the dominating presence who possesses the power the patients lack. Big

[1]Ken Kesey, *One Flew Over the Cuckoo's Nest* (New York, 1962); Edward W. Said, *Orientalism* (New York, 1978); and Richard Rorty, *Philosophy and the Mirror of Nature* (Princeton, 1979). All further references to these works will be cited in the text.

Nurse aims to have her ward "running like a smooth, accurate, precision-made machine. The slightest thing messy or out of kilter or in the way ties her into a little white knot of tight-smiled fury" (p. 26). Chief Bromden, the schizophrenic narrator, literalizes the machine metaphor and sees Big Nurse wielding "a sure power that extends in all directions on hairlike wires. . . . What she dreams of there in the center of those wires is a world of precision efficiency and tidiness like a pocket watch with a glass back" (pp. 26–27). There at the center Big Nurse wields sovereign power over her world, with everyone "obedient under her beam" (p. 27). She manifests her repressive rule in most spectacular fashion when she uses the ward's rituals of punishment—the Shock Shop and lobotomy—to mark the bodies of intransigent patients with the signs of her sovereignty.

But the reign of Big Nurse is neither absolute nor all-pervasive. In this first depiction of power, there is an outside. A nurse from another ward says, "It's not all like [Nurse Ratched's] ward" (p. 266). And from beyond Big Nurse's regimented kingdom comes a savior, Randle Patrick McMurphy, whom Bromden describes as "a giant come out of the sky to save us" (p. 255). Indeed, the heroic rebellion of McMurphy and the Chief's escape at the novel's conclusion suggest that Big Nurse's repressive power is far from invulnerable or infallible. The final chapter holds out the hope of successful revolt or at least a limited personal triumph.

In *Cuckoo's Nest* this first depiction of power—as sovereign, repressive, spectacular, yet not omnipotent—is juxtaposed to another and very different representation. This second form of power becomes most explicit in the narrator's figurative rhetoric, especially his metaphor of the Combine, "a huge organization that aims to adjust the Outside as well as [Big Nurse] has the Inside" (p. 26). In fact, the Combine successfully abolishes an outside, making everything part of its network of power. But this force is not just repressive; it is also productive. It not only obstructs; it directs, regulates, normalizes. "The ward is a factory for the Combine. It's for fixing up mistakes made in the neighborhoods and in the schools and in the churches" (p. 38). All these institutions of power serve to administer and supervise the lives of men and women, not by repression but through a disciplinary method that produces regimented but individualized behavior. The narrator's mechanistic metaphors express

perfectly this microphysics of power, especially in his description of society's most basic institution, the family. About a
father who returns home after being "repaired" at the hospital,
Bromden says, "And the light is on in his basement window
way past midnight every night as the Delayed Reaction Elements the technicians installed lend nimble skills to his fingers
as he bends over the doped figure of his wife, his two little girls
just four and six, the neighbor he goes bowling with Mondays;
he adjusts them like he was adjusted. This is the way they
spread it" (p. 38). Here the Combine's power pervades the whole
of society through a disciplinary bio-politics regulating both the
individual body and the general population. The ward simply
supports a more general political technology of the body, a form
of power that individualizes and normalizes through a series of
relays connecting the whole populace.

This power is not a property possessed by some and not by
others (as the first depiction of politics would have it). Rather,
power exists as an evolving network of force relations. Any
hierarchy of domination—wolves over rabbits, Big Nurse over
patients—is less a cause of this web of forces than an effect of it.
Thus Bromden nearly gets it right when he says, "It's the whole
Combine, the nation-wide Combine that's the really big force,
and the nurse is just a high-ranking official for them" (p. 181).
Big Nurse simply functions as a part of the Combine, a cog in the
machine—a fact brought out nicely when Bromden uses mechanical metaphors to describe not only the patients but Big
Nurse as well (e.g., pp. 4–5). At such times, Bromden takes Big
Nurse out of the center of power, away from pulling strings or
more precisely away from using wires to control the patients.
The power system of the ward becomes decentered, and Big
Nurse becomes just another force within the system. In this
scenario of disciplinary power, the Combine is less a huge organization holding power than the name for the power network
itself, a network of mechanistic forces that is all-pervasive and
inescapable.

But from the perspective of this second representation of
power, what sense can we make of McMurphy? What part does
he play in this disciplinary society? Though Bromden continually presents McMurphy's rebellion as revolutionary individualism heroically struggling to overthrow the Combine, this
same rebellion gets reinscribed within the power relations as

simply an inevitable point of resistance. McMurphy becomes not a savior "out of the sky" external to the relations of power, but a functioning part of these relations first to last. Bromden himself prepares for this reinscription by citing his father's analysis of social control: "Papa says if you don't watch it people will force you one way or the other, into doing what they think you should do, or into just being mule-stubborn and doing the opposite out of spite" (p. 198). In other words, whether a disciplinary society makes you a passive victim of force or an active participant in the force relation as a point of resistance, there is no way to escape the all-encompassing power system. Bromden's reading of McMurphy's final act of rebellion adds another twist to this analysis of the complicitous nature of resistance: "We couldn't stop him [from attacking Big Nurse] because we were the ones making him do it. It wasn't the nurse that was forcing him, it was our need" that made him perform this last desperate act like "a sane, willful, dogged man performing a hard duty that finally just had to be done, like it or not" (pp. 304–5). McMurphy's heroism thus becomes victimage *not* because he refuses to be a cog in the Combine's machine but because he inevitably accepts his role in the Combine's theater of power. And his resistance is never offstage, never out of control: McMurphy was "resting a second before he came out for the next round—in a long line of next rounds. The thing he was fighting, you couldn't whip it for good. All you could do was keep on whipping it, till you couldn't come out any more and somebody else had to take your place" (p. 303). McMurphy plays the role of rebel, a role that others will take on after he has left the Combine's stage. Thus dominating force and resistance to force, the wolves, rabbits, and rebels, are all part of the same unrelenting, inescapable network of power.

But is there really no escape? Right before McMurphy's final rebellion, the patients hold a secret going-away party for him, and in the middle of the illegal celebration, Bromden exclaims, "Maybe the Combine wasn't all-powerful" (p. 292). But the Chief misses the point. This is a controlled illegality. The disciplinary system in a sense *allows* it to happen as a cordoned-off display of resistance that offers no real threat to the Combine. In fact, the Combine ends up using the display to discipline the patients further: the party's discovery sets off a series of events that includes Billy Bibbit's suicide and McMurphy's death, the only true escapes from the Combine's domination. But what about Bromden's escape from the ward at the end? The novel questions even this hopeful conclusion, for readers must finally ask themselves: From where is the story being told? If we look back at the first chapter, it appears that Bromden is telling this tale from the confines of the hospital. Did the Combine's ward reach out and recapture him? Did he ever really escape?

Thus Cuckoo's Nest presents two very different readings of power, two conflicting political representations. The first depicts a negative force from above, a repressive power possessed by a dominating oppressor, Big Nurse. Here a sovereign exploits torture (the Shock Shop) to sign her patient's body with the debilitating signature of her rule. But in this first representation, domination can be overcome by a resistance outside the power circuit: a rebel, McMurphy, can defeat the rulers, the Combine. The novel ends with Bromden escaping from domination and heading for a pastoral utopia where power is absent. In contrast to this first depiction of power, there is a second that represents a political technology of the body in which power permeates the whole of society as disciplinary method. This form of power is not primarily negative and repressive but positive and productive. It not only prevents collective rebellion: more important, it also controls people through a bio-politics that individuates, normalizes, and programs. This power is not a possession; it is a detailed network of force relations, supremely adaptable and ultimately inescapable. The Combine and McMurphy, the dominating force and resistance to it, are part of the same system. Thus the hegemony of Big Nurse is not the origin of the power relations in the novel; rather, her domination derives from a certain alignment of forces, a certain disciplinary deployment. Domination is an effect of power rather than a cause.

This reading of Cuckoo's Nest as a problematic parable of power thus distinguishes two conflicting political representations.[2] But how do I know this reading is correct? The novel

[2]Not surprisingly, such a reading addresses certain interpretive problems posed by the novel's critical history. Indeed, from the earliest reviews, readers of Cuckoo's Nest have argued over its representation of power and the implications of its conclusion. For a sampling of critical opinion, see the arguments in George Adelman's review in Library Journal, 87 (1 February 1962), 574; David Lodge, "The Mad Authorities," Spectator, no. 7028 (8 March 1963), 299–300; Ruth H. Brady, "Kesey's One Flew Over the Cuckoo's Nest," Explicator, 31 (February

itself poses this same question of accurate interpretation, of true knowledge of meaning. In the first chapter, for example, Bromden introduces his narrative by almost putting it under erasure: "It's still hard for me to have a clear mind thinking on it. But it's the truth even if it didn't happen" (p. 8). Such questioning of its own historical truth includes the ironic ending: Where is Bromden when he tells the story we have just read? What is true about the novel's story? What is its meaning? These interpretive questions open up into the theoretical questions of a general hermeneutics: Is it possible to formulate a general theory of reading that could resolve the interpretive problems of this novel? What is the relation of these problems to a specific theory for reading particular genres of literature, say, postmodernist American fiction? As we've seen, a rhetorical hermeneutics answers no to the first question. But the second hasn't been explicitly addressed. Cuckoo's Nest itself points toward the rhetorical topics involved in answers to both questions: issues of power, meaning, and knowledge. However, though the novel does represent different forms of power and does pose questions about meaning, it does so without emphasizing the close connection between its political representations and its interpretive questions. At one point Bromden does describe the ward's logbook as a text where political manipulation and medical information merge, but Cuckoo's Nest does not generally focus on the relation of power to knowledge, a relation I must develop in order to clarify further my claims for rhetorical hermeneutics.

II. Epistemic Politics and Hermeneutic Imperialism

A second American text provides a more thoroughgoing inquiry into this crucial concept of power-knowledge. Said's *Orientalism* begins by bracketing the question whether Orientalist

---

1973), item 41; Robert Rosenwein, "Of Beats and Beasts: Power and the Individual in the Cuckoo's Nest," *Lex et Scientia*, 13 (January–March 1977), 51–55; and Stephen L. Tanner, *Ken Kesey* (Boston, 1983), pp. 18–51. Because I use *Cuckoo's Nest* in this chapter primarily to clarify the notion of power assumed by rhetorical hermeneutics, this interested reading necessarily excludes many important issues raised in the novel's critical history. In a different rhetorical context, the issue I would most want to address is how the ideological politics of gender shaped the novel's rhetoric and its relation to the 1960s context of cultural production and reception.

discourse corresponds to a true Orient and then goes on to argue that Orientalism produced an interpretation of the Orient which served the interests of European imperialism. Said writes that "knowledge of subject races or Orientals is what makes their management easy and profitable; knowledge gives power, more power requires more knowledge, and so on in an increasingly profitable dialectic of information and control" (p. 36). Orientalist discourse is therefore an "exercise of cultural strength," in which "knowledge of the Orient, because generated out of strength, in a sense *creates* the Orient, the Oriental, and his world" (p. 40). Under these circumstances, it is impossible to separate power and knowledge without radically distorting the human work involved in both.

Said supports his argument through a series of readings of Orientalist texts, which are themselves interested readings of the Orient. These readings of readings are placed in a narrative about modern Orientalism, which Said begins with Napoleon's invasion of Egypt in 1798. Said argues that the subsequent French occupation of the country (1798–1801) "gave birth to the entire modern experience of the Orient as interpreted from within the universe of discourse founded by Napoleon in Egypt, whose agencies of domination and dissemination included the Institut [d'Égypte] and the *Description* [*de l'Égypte*]" (p. 87). The French published the *Description* in twenty-three volumes from 1809 through 1828. Said refers to this lengthy discourse as "that great collective appropriation of one country by another" (p. 84) and reads it as an "Orientalist projection" of Egypt which was "enabled and reinforced by Napoleon's wholly Orientalist engulfment of Egypt by the instruments of Western knowledge and power" (p. 86). Among the many aims of this Orientalist appropriation, Said lists attempts "to instruct (for its own benefit) the Orient in the ways of the modern West; to subordinate or underplay military power in order to aggrandize the project of glorious knowledge acquired in the process of political domination of the Orient; to formulate the Orient, to give it shape, identity, definition with full recognition of its place in memory, its importance to imperial strategy, and its 'natural' role as an appendage to Europe" (p. 86). Of course, the result of this historical organization of power-knowledge was the specific hierarchy of European "superiority" over Oriental "inferiority." With such texts as the *Description* helping to establish European domination, Orientalism became "an accepted grid for filtering through the Orient into Western consciousness" (p. 6), and thus relevant acts of interpretation always took place within a specific complex of power-knowledge associated with this grid of Orientalism. Power-knowledge, an issue neglected in *Cuckoo's Nest*, is central to the story *Orientalism* has to tell.

To apply this theme directly to my claims for rhetorical hermeneutics, we must turn to a text standing behind Said's and my own, Michel Foucault's *Discipline and Punish*. "We should admit," Foucault writes, that power produces

> knowledge (and not simply by encouraging it because it serves power or by applying it because it is useful); that power and knowledge directly imply one another, that there is no power relation without the correlative constitution of a field of knowledge, nor any knowledge that does not presuppose and constitute at the same time power relations. These 'power-knowledge relations' are to be analysed, therefore, not on the basis of a subject of knowledge who is or is not free in relation to the power system, but, on the contrary, the subject who knows, the objects to be known and the modalities of knowledge must be regarded as so many effects of these fundamental implications of power-knowledge and their historical transformations.[3]

Said's *Orientalism* shows precisely the way "power and knowledge imply one another," but we need a third American text, Rorty's *Philosophy and the Mirror of Nature*, to help connect these historical claims about power-knowledge with theoretical claims about reading. In the passage quoted from *Discipline and Punish*, Foucault argues that the knowing subject and the subject known are simply functions of power-knowledge and their historical transformations. What exactly does this mean? Read alongside Rorty's new pragmatism, Foucault seems to claim that theories about isolated knowers investigating independent objects—or theories of readers reading texts—ignore the historical context of power-knowledge in which knowing

[3]Michel Foucault, *Discipline and Punish: The Birth of the Prison*, trans. Alan Sheridan (New York, 1977), pp. 27–28. For Said's disagreements with Foucault's analytics of power, see Said, *The World, the Text, and the Critic* (Cambridge, Mass., 1983), pp. 178–247, and Said, "Foucault and the Imagination of Power," in *Foucault: A Critical Reader*, ed. David Couzens Hoy (Oxford, 1986), pp. 149–55.

and reading take place. Theoretical questions such as "Does the interpreter create the text or does the text control the interpreter?" assume a misleading distinction between text and interpreter, a distinction between elements mistakenly removed and isolated from the historical configuration of power-knowledge in which they are embedded and of which they are a function. To make this point clearer, we must look more closely at *Philosophy and the Mirror of Nature*.

III. Pragmatist Readings

The story Rorty tells about epistemology begins with the Cartesian invention of the mind, an internal space that seeks a way of accurately representing external space. Rorty's philosophical narrative translates easily into a tale of recent theories of reading: on one side of the conflict we find Lockean realism arguing for direct or indirect access to an independent and preexisting meaning in the text, a text with objective facts that are reflected in correct interpretations; on the other side we have Kantian idealism arguing that the minds of readers constitute the meaningful text, a text whose facts are constructed by readers who share interpretive conventions that determine correct interpretations. Rorty demonstrates how Lockean realism and Kantian idealism are caught up in similar logical confusions and lead to similar dead ends. I will not rehearse his arguments here (I provide some of my own in Chapter 1), but will instead move on to his conclusions. Calling for an end to epistemology, Rorty proposes a theoretical discourse that focuses not on the *confrontation* between knower and object—the controlling visual metaphor of traditional epistemology—but on the *conversation* among knowers. Such an anti-epistemology becomes, in literary theory, an anti-Theory of reading, which I have been calling rhetorical hermeneutics.

Rhetorical hermeneutics begins by rejecting the project of Theory, defined as the attempt to construct a foundationalist account of reading in general, because such a project inevitably leads to the dead ends of textual realism and readerly idealism. Following Rorty's pragmatist suggestion, rhetorical hermeneutics proposes to set aside the problem of explaining interpretation in terms of the characteristics of readers and the elements of texts and to focus instead on the rhetorical dynamics among

interpreters within specific cultural settings. In such a hermeneutics, theory soon turns into rhetorical history. More precisely, it becomes a collection of more or less related histories of
conversations about texts. These conversations consist of rhetorical exchanges taking place within traditions of arguments
and figures, and these traditions of specific rhetorical practices
are themselves part of the micropractices that make up a culture
at any historical moment.[4] Thus rhetorical hermeneutics describes the ebb and flow of the cultural conversation and rejects
foundationalist attempts to ground knowledge, interpretation,
and reading outside the rhetorical context of history.

This pragmatic change of subject allows rhetorical hermeneutics to dispense with many pseudo problems troubling contemporary theories of reading—for example, the endless questions
about whether texts or readers determine meaning. We are left
instead with problems that we can address without falling into
the bottomless bogs of essentialism and foundationalism. There
are still legitimate questions about the certainty of our readings
that need to be asked. But rhetorical answers will, as Rorty puts
it, make our certainty "a matter of conversation between persons, rather than a matter of interaction with nonhuman reality." In other words, rather than waste time idealistically seeking to discover how a reader's mind determines a text's shape or
realistically seeking to discover how a text causes a reader's
certainty, a rhetorical hermeneutics gives up the notion of theoretical foundations altogether, gives up the notion that truths
"are certain because of their causes rather than because of the
arguments given for them." In attempting to justify our interpretations of texts, we come to see that we are "looking for an
airtight case rather than an unshakable foundation" (p. 157)
either in readers' minds or in independent texts.

Putting aside realist and idealist foundationalism, however,
does not mean that just anything goes. Arguments are always
embedded in historical circumstances, rhetorical traditions,

---

[4]For more on this background of cultural micropractices, see Hubert L. Dreyfus, "Holism and Hermeneutics," *Review of Metaphysics*, 34 (September 1980),
9–11; Dreyfus and Paul Rabinow, *Michel Foucault: Beyond Structuralism and
Hermeneutics*, 2d ed. (Chicago, 1983); and Dreyfus, "Beyond Hermeneutics:
Interpretation in Late Heidegger and Recent Foucault," in *Hermeneutics: Questions and Prospects*, ed. Gary Shapiro and Alan Sica (Amherst, Mass., 1984),
pp. 66–83.

episodes of cultural conversations—all of which make certain arguments appropriate and others inappropriate at particular moments. Furthermore, rejecting realist and idealist epistemology does not mean that references to textual details or interpretive frameworks are ruled out of bounds. Quite the contrary. Justifying a reading by pointing to the particulars of texts or assumptions is a very effective critical strategy. But such rhetorical maneuvers have nothing to do with epistemological theories, which take these maneuvers out of their historical contexts of argument and place them into the ahistorical space in which general accounts of reading attempt to dwell. Referring to textual details during an argument is just not the same as trying to construct a general realist theory of reading that applies to the relation of reader and text, a relation outside any particular rhetorical context.

As we set aside the questions of realism and idealism and turn our attention toward rhetorical exchanges, we must look more closely at the way Rorty characterizes the cultural conversation, in which literary interpretation functions. Sometimes he seems to imply that the conversation is a rather pleasant affair involving polite conversants who should be more interested in keeping the talk flowing than in resolving disputes or winning arguments. Into this rather pacifistic tableau we need to reintroduce Foucault's more combative model of power-knowledge. When asked who were the subjects opposing each other in his view of power, Foucault once responded, "This is just a hypothesis, but I would say it's all against all. . . . Who fights against whom? We all fight each other. And there is always within each of us something that fights something else."[5] If we take Foucault

[5]"The Confession of the Flesh," trans. Colin Gordon, in Foucault, Power/ Knowledge: Selected Interviews and Other Writings, 1972–1977, ed. Gordon (New York, 1980), p. 208. In the same volume, see "Truth and Power," pp. 114–15 and 123, for Foucault's comments on the war metaphor. Also, cf. the use of the same figure in Jean-François Lyotard, The Postmodern Condition: A Report on Knowledge, trans. Geoff Bennington and Brian Massumi (Minneapolis, 1984), p. 10 ("to speak is to fight") and pp. 16–17 (on this "agonistic aspect of society" in which "interlocutors use any available ammunition, changing games from one utterance to the next: questions, requests, assertions, and narratives are launched pell-mell into battle"). Also see Fredric Jameson, The Political Unconscious: Narrative as a Socially Symbolic Act (Ithaca, N.Y., 1981), p. 13. A useful cautionary note is struck by Kenneth Burke in his comments on war as a "constitutive anecdote" for rhetorical analyses: A Grammar of Motives (1945;

seriously here, we must view the cultural conversation as a complex rhetorical struggle of everyone with everyone, a conversation traversed by uneven power relations, a rhetorical conflict implicated in social formations of race, class, gender, age, and nation. In various episodes of the conversation, there are rhetorical allies and enemies, strategic moves to dominate the field, battles to win arguments decisively, and sometimes grudging or graceful retreats. Rhetorical practices are simply the discursive form of the micropractices that make up the social arrangement of power-knowledge at any historical moment. Put a little differently, in this depiction of the cultural conversation, rhetorical power describes the argumentative forces at work within the particular historical contexts in which interpretive knowledge emerges.

A brief return to Said's *Orientalism* will help me sum up the various points of this chapter. I noted in passing that Said brackets the question whether Orientalist discourse corresponds to a real Orient. In one place he writes, "It is not the thesis of this book to suggest that there is such a thing as a real or true Orient (Islam, Arab, or whatever). . . . On the contrary, I have been arguing that 'the Orient' is itself a constituted entity" (p. 322). Or again: Orientalism was and is "a system of opportunities for making statements about the Orient. My whole point about this system is not that it is a misrepresentation of some Oriental essence—in which I do not for a moment believe—but that it operates as representations usually do, for a purpose, according to a tendency, in a specific historical, intellectual, and even economic setting" (p. 273). These purposes and tendencies are specifically rhetorical: Orientalist discourse attempts to persuade others to see the Orient and the Oriental according to the tropes and arguments of Orientalist representations.

By denying the existence of an "objective" Orient, Said does not make an idealist claim, nor in condemning Orientalist distortions does he make a realist claim. He takes no stand on epistemological issues at all. Any anti-essentialism or antireal-

---

rpt. Berkeley, 1969), pp. 328–33; also see Burke, *A Rhetoric of Motives* (1950; rpt. Berkeley, 1969), pp. 20–23, on division and identification. For Burke, rhetoric involves the use of language for competition *and* cooperation; see "Rhetoric and Poetics" in his *Language as Symbolic Action* (Berkeley, 1966), p. 296.

ism in Said's book remains pragmatic rather than idealist, as he rejects any notion of an Orient independent of representations produced in rhetorical contexts of power-knowledge. And his criticism of Orientalism as biased distortion is not a fall into epistemological realism but rather a recognition of the interested nature of all representations, his own included. *Orientalism* is self-consciously an act of persuasion at the service of rhetorical interests *opposed to* those of Western Orientalism. Idealist and realist epistemologies remain completely irrelevant here. What remains relevant is the historical context of rhetorical power that Said describes and the cultural conversation in which *Orientalism* participates.

It is to such complex rhetorical histories of power-knowledge that a rhetorical hermeneutics must draw our attention. In sum, this rhetorical perspective attempts to describe the historical circumstances of various rhetorical exchanges rather than address questions about whether texts or readers determine interpretations. Rhetorical histories thus replace foundationalist Theory.

Rhetorical hermeneutics provides no answers to such foundationalist questions as: How can we get a general Theory of reading for adjudicating critical interpretations? How can we identify *the* relation between reader and text so that we can achieve correct interpretations? These are simply the wrong questions to ask. They lead back to all the problems of textual realism and readerly idealism and ignore the specific rhetorical context of power-knowledge. This claim does not mean that we should give up putting forward interpretations or defending them. On the contrary, arguing for or against interpretations is precisely what we can never give up entirely. It is only foundationalist justifications that a rhetorical hermeneutics calls into question for interpretive arguments.

From this neo-pragmatist perspective, there are at least two responses to the question: Can my earlier reading of *One Flew Over the Cuckoo's Nest* be theoretically justified? The answer is no if such justification means appealing to a general Theory of reading that guarantees correct interpretations outside the context of interpretive arguments. The answer is yes if such justification means appealing to a specific "theory" or reading of contemporary American texts which itself must be developed and defended within a particular rhetorical context and tradition of arguments about postmodernist fiction.

I want to emphasize that I am not saying that interpreting *Cuckoo's Nest* is impossible. I provided an interpretation in the first section of this chapter, and I have said nothing since to take it back. There I argued that the novel's representations were ironically poised between a depiction of repressive power possessed by an oppressor whose control might be escaped *and* a view of productive power whose relations of force include points of resistance co-opting rebellion as a necessary function of the power network. Thus my interpretation suggests that the novel's meaning is undecidable. But, again, I am not saying that *Cuckoo's Nest* is radically indeterminate in some absolute sense (whatever that would mean). Like any other reading, claims about a text's "undecidability" and "indeterminacy" are simply interpretations to argue for or against in particular historical (primarily academic) contexts. Indeed, the indeterminacy of one novel or of postmodernist American fiction in general is clearly an interpretation that can be defended quite effectively among some groups of academic critics. The point here is not that interpretations cannot be accepted or rejected; rather, it is that any literary explication participates in the rhetorical politics of interpretation, a politics embedded in institutional structures and specific cultural practices.

6

Truth or Consequences

There's another trouble about theories: there's always a hole in
them somewhere, sure, if you look close enough.
—Mark Twain, *Tom Sawyer Abroad*

At least one hole in rhetorical hermeneutics can be easily identified: the absence of a history of its own rhetoricity.
Though I have foregrounded its theoretical figures, such as "cultural conversation," I have not yet provided an explicit history
of its arguments. This chapter tries to fill the gap by tracing and
demonstrating the agonistic relationship of rhetorical hermeneutics to other recent antifoundationalist theories. While Rorty
and others have been reinterpreting American pragmatism for
contemporary philosophy, a small group of literary theorists
have introduced similar arguments into debates over literary
interpretation and poststructuralism.[1] The effects of these arguments constitute the plot of the story I present in the next two
sections.

I. Against Theory Again

The consequence of my reading "Against Theory" by Steven
Knapp and Walter Benn Michaels stands as an excellent il-

---

[1]Besides Rorty's work, see also Richard J. Bernstein, *Praxis and Action: Con-
temporary Philosophies of Human Activity* (Philadelphia, 1971) and *Beyond
Objectivism and Relativism: Science, Hermeneutics, and Praxis* (Philadelphia,
1983). And more generally see John Rajchman and Cornel West, eds., *Post-
Analytic Philosophy* (New York, 1985); Kenneth Baynes, James Bohman, and
Thomas McCarthy, eds., *After Philosophy: End or Transformation?* (Cambridge,
Mass., 1987); and Evan Simpson, ed., *Anti-Foundationalism and Practical Reasoning: Conversations between Hermeneutics and Analysis* (Edmonton, Al-
berta, 1987). For related issues being debated in legal hermeneutics, see Sanford

lustration of how persuasion works in theoretical discourse.[2] Before reading the essay, I thought I fully understood Stanley Fish's theory of interpretive communities. Fish's theory seemed a consistent elaboration of the claim that facts are created, not found. What we take to be independent facts are actually constructions of our interpretive assumptions and strategies. From this perspective, texts do not determine interpretations; interpretations constitute texts. Furthermore, interpretive practices are never idiosyncratic; that is, acts of making sense are always a function of shared beliefs or interpretive conventions. Every individual interpreter is a member of an interpretive community: "Since the thoughts an individual can think and the mental operations he can perform have their source in some or other interpretive community, he is as much a product of that community (acting as an extension of it) as the meanings it enables him to produce."[3]

Such a grounding of interpretation in communities defends Fish's hermeneutic theory against the charge of relativism, the bugbear of the Anglo-American critical tradition since the heyday of New Criticism. New Critics claimed to avoid interpretive relativism by grounding meaning objectively in the autonomous text. Later, E. D. Hirsch tried to show that New Critical theory and practice resulted in the very relativism the New Critics abhorred; Hirsch argued that one must give priority to authorial intention in order to determine valid or correct interpretations.[4] Fish's theory of interpretive communities holds that interpretation produces both textual meaning and authorial intention, but he avoids relativism by showing that there are always correct interpretations, determined by communities rather than individuals. Individual interpreters are not free to see or describe any textual meaning they want (the fear of the New Critics), nor is meaning made radically indeterminate (the complaint of

Levinson and Steven Mailloux, eds., *Interpreting Law and Literature: A Hermeneutic Reader* (Evanston, Ill., 1988).

[2]"Against Theory," *Critical Inquiry*, 8 (Summer 1982), reprinted in *Against Theory: Literary Studies and the New Pragmatism*, ed. W. J. T. Mitchell (Chicago, 1985), pp. 11–30 (hereafter cited in text as AT).

[3]Stanley Fish, *Is There a Text in This Class?: The Authority of Interpretive Communities* (Cambridge, Mass., 1980), p. 14.

[4]E. D. Hirsch, Jr., *Validity in Interpretation* (New Haven, Conn., 1967), and *The Aims of Interpretation* (Chicago, 1976).

Hirsch against the anti-intentionalists). Rather, correct interpretations always exist and can be (are already) determined. It's just that because interpretive communities can change, so too can what counts as a correct interpretation.

So went my understanding of Fish's position before I read "Against Theory." After reading it, however, I became convinced that my previous understanding was incomplete. To approach "Against Theory" and eventually reveal *its* incompleteness, we can begin with a literary example of the two hermeneutic accounts that Knapp and Michaels reject on their way to rejecting theory in general.

In George Orwell's *1984* the Party maintains its absolute power over the people of Oceania by completely controlling all individual acts of interpretation. Through material and ideological coercion, the Party imposes its way of making sense on its people and achieves "the persistence of a certain world-view and a certain way of life" which forms the basis of its totalitarian rule.[5] This hermeneutic imperialism guarantees that the people will continue to be "without any impulse to rebel" because they are "without the power of grasping that the world could be other than it is" (p. 173). O'Brien, the spokesman for the Party, points out the philosophical assumption underlying its successful politics of interpretation: "Reality is inside the skull. . . . Nothing exists except through human consciousness" (p. 218). Since the Party controls interpretation, it controls human consciousness and thus manipulates reality itself. One would-be rebel, Winston Smith, tries to resist the Party by attacking its hermeneutics. He champions common sense, autonomous facts, external reality, and the empirical method. Though elsewhere Orwell supports Smith's philosophical stance, in *1984* he allows O'Brien to win the argument (both rhetorically and politically) during the final confrontation between Smith and the Party spokesman.[6] O'Brien argues that "reality exists in the human mind, and no where else. Not in the individual mind, . . . only in the mind of the Party, which is collective and immortal. Whatever the Party holds to be truth *is* truth. It is impossible to

<hr>

[5]George Orwell, *1984* (1949; rpt. New York, 1961), p. 173; all further references to this work will be cited in the text.

[6]See Gerald Graff, "Politics, Language, Deconstruction, Lies, and the Reflexive Fallacy: A Rejoinder to W. J. T. Mitchell," *Salmagundi*, 47–48 (Winter–Spring 1980), 88–89.

see reality except by looking through the eyes of the Party"
(p. 205). Smith is not able to counter O'Brien's arguments, and
ultimately the Party is successful in achieving its goal: "We
shall squeeze you empty, and then we shall fill you with ourselves" (p. 211). Smith submits by internalizing the Party's
worldview and adopting its hermeneutic theory.

It is inevitable that Smith must lose, not only because he
confronts the overwhelming power of the state but also because
he presents such a weak case for his hermeneutic position. As
O'Brien points out, Smith holds that "the nature of reality is
self-evident" (p. 205). He fails to understand that his common-
sense "facts" are as much a product of interpretation as are the
Party's; and he clings to a naive realist ontology and a simplistic
common-sense epistemology that O'Brien demolishes from his
dominant political position, through a more sophisticated hermeneutic argument, a form of idealism he calls "collective solipsism" (p. 219).

Knapp and Michaels would find neither Smith's realism nor
O'Brien's idealism to be satisfactory as a hermeneutic theory.
They write that "a realist thinks that theory allows us to stand
outside our beliefs in a neutral encounter with the objects of
interpretation; an idealist thinks that theory allows us to stand
outside our beliefs in a neutral encounter with our beliefs themselves" (AT, p. 27). A realist like Smith is mistaken when he
assumes that "the object exists independent of beliefs" and that
"knowledge requires that we shed our beliefs in a disinterested
quest for the object" (AT, p. 28). An idealist like O'Brien avoids
this mistake when he implies that "we can never shed our
beliefs," but he commits his own kind of error when he equates
knowledge with "recognizing the role beliefs play in constituting their objects" (AT, p. 28). This constitutive hermeneutics is
a necessary corollary of both O'Brien's collective solipsism and,
at times, Fish's theory of interpretive communities.[7] In the same
way that O'Brien claims that the Party's collective mind creates
reality, Fish sometimes argues that interpretive communities
create what they claim merely to be discovering or describing.
Of course, O'Brien and Fish perceive themselves as living
within radically different arrangements of hermeneutic power.
O'Brien sees himself as the extension of an interpretive commu-

[7]See Fish, "Interpreting the *Variorum*, " in *Is There a Text?*, p. 171.

nity (the Party) that completely dominates the world of 1984. Fish, on the other hand, claims that his world contains many competing communities, each vying for interpretive hegemony for its set of beliefs, values, and ideologies.

Despite such differences in their sociological accounts, O'Brien and Fish end up in the same theoretical contradiction. During his debate with Smith, O'Brien's epistemological idealism leads him to imply that a true believer within the Party could somehow get outside the Party's beliefs. Knapp and Michaels argue that Fish makes a similar move when he claims to have a *theory* of interpretation through which he distances himself from his own interpretive assumptions. This theory allows him to argue that previous literary critics' "assumptions were not inferior but merely different" from his own.[8] As Knapp and Michaels point out, Fish is claiming here that "no beliefs are, in the long run, truer than others" (AT, p. 29). But this claim assumes a "position from which we can see our beliefs without really believing them. To be in this position would be to see the truth about beliefs without actually having any" (AT, p. 27). Since Fish himself admits there is no such standpoint outside belief, he has clearly contradicted himself. Theories like Fish's and O'Brien's which admit the absolute primacy of belief in practice cannot turn around and claim to escape belief in theory.

Knapp and Michaels ultimately argue that *all* theories cannot avoid similar contradictions or incoherencies whenever theory attempts to prescribe critical practice. They demonstrate how some typical theorists base their methodological prescriptions on the prior separation of entities that are in fact logically inseparable (intention and meaning, language and speech acts, knowledge and true belief). Theorists make these false separations so that they can prescribe moving from one entity to the other to arrive at meaning or truth. Thus, if theory is understood as an attempt to describe so that it can have prescriptive consequences, then it is incoherent and should be abandoned. Theory, properly understood, has no consequences.

Knapp and Michaels' arguments are convincing as far as they go. Their attack on some foundationalist theories did show me a contradiction in Fish's theory which I had previously failed to notice, and it finally persuaded me to abandon an idealist her-

[8]Fish, *Is There a Text?*, p. 368.

meneutics I had developed in the last chapter of my book *Interpretive Conventions*. However, the conclusion that Knapp and Michaels draw from their arguments—that theory is inconsequential and should therefore stop—does not necessarily follow. True, foundationalist theory does not have consequences in the exact way it claims to have consequences. Nevertheless, such theories do have results of a very precise kind, as I noted in Chapter 1 and will now argue more fully.

The work of Edward Said illustrates how one kind of theory can have disruptive consequences both inside and outside the discipline of literary studies. In *Orientalism* and other writings Said assumes a sort of ideological hermeneutics as he examines Orientalism as "the enormously systematic discipline by which European culture was able to manage—and even *produce*—the Orient politically, sociologically, militarily, ideologically, scientifically, and imaginatively during the post-Enlightenment period."[9] Through the project of Orientalism, Europe imposed a self-serving meaning in an apparently disinterested way. In effect, it constructed an Orient that was ripe for domination. The imperialist West did exactly what the Party in *1984* tries to do: determine reality by controlling interpretation. The Party is simply more self-conscious about its "hermeneutics of power."[10]

Said's project has been to reveal the ideological interests behind the hermeneutic power of Western discourse about the Islamic Orient. But Said further claims that *all* descriptions of the Orient (not only those by European and American Orientalists) are perspectival constructions rather than objective representations:

> I do not mean to suggest that a "real" Islam exists somewhere out there that the media, acting out of base motives, have perverted. Not at all. For Muslims as for non-Muslims, Islam is an objective and also a subjective fact, because people create that fact in their faith, in their societies, histories, and traditions, or, in the case of non-Muslim outsiders, because they must in a sense fix, personify, stamp the identity of that which they feel confronts them collectively or individually. This is to say that the media's Islam, the

[9]Edward W. Said, *Orientalism* (New York, 1978), p. 3; emphasis added.
[10]The term is Gerald Graff's in "Textual Leftism," *Partisan Review*, 49 (1982), 566.

Western scholar's Islam, the Western reporter's Islam, and the Muslim's Islam are all acts of will and interpretation that take place in history, and can only be dealt with in history as acts of will and interpretation.[11]

Said grounds these acts of hermeneutic will in "communities of interpretation," and thus his theory resembles that of O'Brien and Fish, though not in their more epistemologically idealist moments.[12] Said escapes the "beliefless neutrality" objection discussed above. However, like O'Brien and Fish, he would agree with the assertion in "Against Theory" that there is no "condition of knowledge prior to and independent of belief" (p. 26). If Knapp and Michaels are correct that "no general account of belief [similar to their own] can have practical consequences," then the epistemologies of O'Brien, Fish, and Said, which also posit the primacy of belief, should also be inconsequential (p. 28). But such accounts can and do have consequences. In the world of 1984, the theory of collective solipsism provides a philosophical base for totalitarian domination. In the realm of American scholarship and politics, Said's theoretical assumptions guide his practical analyses of Orientalism, and these analyses have had very definite consequences, as the debates within the New Republic, New York Review of Books, History and Theory, and other journals testify. Indeed, one Humanities Report article noted that "the position Said represents [in Orientalism] has produced a set of semi-academic study groups and has implications for government and foreign policy."[13]

But how exactly can a hermeneutic theory that, according to Knapp and Michaels, should have no consequences result in these rhetorical and political effects? In Said's case, the reason is that when he reveals Orientalist representations as based on interested belief rather than impersonal truth, objectivists read his demystifying project as (successfully or unsuccessfully) undermining the validity of Orientalist interpretations, and Orien-

---

[11]Said, Covering Islam: How the Media and the Experts Determine How We See the Rest of the World (New York, 1981), p. 41. See also Orientalism, pp. 273 and 322.

[12]Said, Covering Islam, p. 41.

[13]Colin R. MacKinnon, "Talking Back: Orientalism and the Orientals," Humanities Report, 4 (February 1982), 5.

talism's victims read this same project as providing support for the objectivity of their own self-interpretations. These appropriations of Said's discourse can occur because a demonstration that others' asserted truth is actually interested belief always *counts as* a critique of their assertions in the present arena of critical and political discussion. In such an arena, to expose asserted truth as "mere" belief is to have the effect of undermining that truth even though the debunker elsewhere insists that *all* truth is perspectival belief. Even in an essay in which Said foregrounds the perspective from which he makes his analysis (for example, in "Zionism from the Standpoint of Its Victims"), his discourse still has the rhetorical effect of proof or propaganda (depending on whether the reader is convinced or not by his arguments).[14]

But such political consequences are only the most far-reaching results of theory. More limited but just as real are the effects of theoretical prescriptions within the discipline of literary studies. Even if it is granted that all foundationalist theories are based on logical mistakes (such as separating intention and meaning), such theories still have consequences for critical practice. All we need do is remember the effects of New Critical proscriptions against the intentional and affective fallacies. The critics persuaded by these theoretical prohibitions avoided extrinsic approaches and directed their analyses to intrinsic elements in the literary text itself—image patterns, symbolic structures, and so forth. More recently, theories of undecidability have changed the interpretive practices of many within the discipline: instead of looking for unities, they look for disunities, contradictions, incoherencies. Theory does change practice.

Knapp and Michaels come close to addressing this methodological objection when they discuss whether intentionalist theories have consequences. They argue that "nothing in the claim that authorial intention is the necessary object of interpretation tells us anything at all about what should count as evidence for determining the content of any particular intention."[15] True

[14]See Said, "Zionism from the Standpoint of Its Victims," *Social Text*, 1 (Winter 1979), 7–58; revised in Said, *The Question of Palestine* (New York, 1979), pp. 56–114.

[15]Knapp and Michaels, "A Reply to Our Critics," *Critical Inquiry*, 9 (June 1983); reprinted in Mitchell, *Against Theory*, p. 101.

enough, for a foundationalist theory that simply makes claims about the relation of intention and meaning—but what intentionalist theory stops there? For example, assuming that texts with intentions can be corrupted, textual-biographical critics claim that a valid interpretation must reconstruct the author's composing process; thus they are consistent with their theory in advocating the close examination of manuscript stages and biographical evidence in the act of interpretation. Here methodological consequences follow logically from an intentionalist Theory.[16]

But such methodological consequences may not be exactly what Knapp and Michaels mean by consequences. Fish's related argument for Theory's inconsequentiality suggests that my objection is entirely beside Knapp and Michaels' point:

> Interpretation is a function of the way human beings know, of what it is possible and not possible for the mind to do, of epistemology; and epistemology—the conditions of human knowing— is logically independent of any account one might give of it. I could be wrong about the way interpretation works, or I could be right; but the fact of my being either right or wrong would have no bearing whatsoever on the interpretive act I (or anyone persuaded by me) might perform.[17]

In this sense, Fish would argue, accurate or inaccurate Theory has no consequences.

I agree that having a correct or incorrect account of interpretation has no effect on whether critics can actually do interpretations. They interpret in any case. But, again, having this rather than that hermeneutic account does affect the kind of interpretation done. One account, for example, might restrict critics to the published text; another might encourage them to examine manuscript material and biographical evidence. Fish, Knapp, and Michaels would not, I suppose, call these effects theoretical because, over and above such methodological prescriptions, the Theorist claims that the correctness of his or her account determines the effects it has. The anti-Theorists argue that since this Theoretical claim can't be true, the hermeneutic account has no

---

[16]See Hershel Parker, *Flawed Texts and Verbal Icons: Literary Authority in American Fiction* (Evanston, Ill., 1984).

[17]Fish, "Fear of Fish: A Reply to Walter Davis," *Critical Inquiry*, 10 (June 1984), 705.

methodological consequences. But delimiting "methodological consequences" in this way is certainly misleading. True, Theories do not have the kind of consequences a Theorist thinks they have in the way he or she thinks they have them. Still, the *attempt* to do the impossible (to have a correct Theory that guarantees valid interpretations because it is correct) does have consequences for practice which directly follow from the theoretical attempt, consequences such as critics talking about the author's mind or becoming preoccupied with textual indeterminacies or focusing on historical context.

Here we finally reach the limits of Knapp and Michaels' account of theory. Their description turns out to be as incomplete as my previous understanding of Fish's work was incomplete. Theory sometimes does claim to be what Knapp and Michaels define it as, but theory always *functions* differently. In fact, theory is a kind of practice, sometimes a peculiar kind when it claims to escape practice. But the impossibility of achieving this goal does not prevent theory (of various kinds) from continuing, nor does it negate the effects it has *as persuasion*. It is telling that Knapp and Michaels do not call for the end of critical practice even though they reject criticism's claim to find meaning objectively in autonomous texts, intentions, or reading experiences. Michaels has pointed out, correctly, that such practice misconceives its function: the meanings it claims to find are actually determined completely by the beliefs it assumes.[18] Similarly, foundationalist theory claims to be in a neutral position beyond belief and turns out not to be, yet as theoretical practice it can still affect other practices as persuasion. Theory can simply continue doing what all discursive practices do: attempt to persuade its readers to adopt its point of view, its way of seeing texts and the world. Whether or not successful persuasion takes place as a result of misunderstanding, theory can be consequential as rhetorical inducement and thus will probably not be abandoned soon.

In their conclusion to "Against Theory," the authors write:

The theoretical impulse, as we have described it, always involves the attempt to separate things that should not be separated: on the ontological side, meaning from intention, language from speech

[18]See Walter Benn Michaels, "Saving the Text: Reference and Belief," *MLN*, 93 (December 1978), 771–93.

acts; on the epistemological side, knowledge from true belief. Our point has been that the separated terms are in fact inseparable. It is tempting to end by saying that theory and practice too are inseparable. But this would be a mistake. Not because theory and practice (unlike the other terms) really are separate but because theory is nothing else but the attempt to escape practice. Meaning is just another name for expressed intention, knowledge just another name for true belief, but theory is not just another name for practice. [Pp. 29–30]

Though they deny it here, Knapp and Michaels do seem to separate theory and practice. They could have said that theory is just another name for metapractice (practice about practice). Instead they chose to imply a distinction between two kinds of discourse that are similar in function: theory is an instantiation of practice even when it claims to escape from practice. Why do Knapp and Michaels ignore this fact? Strangely, this implied separation of theory and practice can be seen as strengthening rather than weakening their argument. Indeed, it confirms at least part of it. Not unlike Theoretical discourse, "Against Theory" separates the inseparable—theory from practice—in order to prescribe practice—the abandonment of theory. Of course, whether Knapp and Michaels' theory has consequences depends entirely on whether it persuades readers to take its ingenious arguments seriously.

II. Antiprofessionalism

One person who has taken "Against Theory" seriously indeed is Stanley Fish, who made a similar argument about the inconsequentiality of foundationalist theory in Is There a Text in This Class? and who clarified his position further in a response to the Knapp-Michaels essay.[19] In "Consequences," Fish approves the neo-pragmatist argument of "Against Theory" and implies that he accepts the authors' critique: "I am in agreement with Steven Knapp and Walter Benn Michaels, who are almost alone in agreeing with me and who fault me not for making the 'no consequences' argument but for occasionally falling away from it." Fish goes on to describe the rhetorical strategy of any anti-

[19]Fish, Is There a Text?, p. 370; Fish, "Consequences," in Mitchell, Against Theory.

foundationalist argument: "It is always historicist; that is, its strategy is always . . . to demonstrate that the norms and standards and rules that foundationalist theory would oppose to history, convention, and local practice are in every instance a function or extension of history, convention, and local practice." He then quotes from Rorty's pragmatist antifoundationalism: "There are no essences anywhere in the area. There is no wholesale, epistemological way to direct, or criticize or underwrite the course of inquiry. . . . It is the vocabulary of practice rather than of theory . . . in which one can say something useful about truth."[20] It is this historicist pragmatism that also animates my own rhetorical hermeneutics and its localized rhetorical histories of particular cultural practices.

However, what especially concerns me here is the turn Fish's most recent work has taken, his use of what might be called a neo-pragmatist concept of professionalism to attack antiprofessionalism. In his critique Fish ends up covering over what is really at stake in the professionalism debate by ultimately collapsing the distinction he initially posits between right and left antiprofessionals, that is, between the discipline's reactionaries and its reformists. He first describes the profession of literary studies in terms of "all its attendant machinery, periods, journals, newsletters, articles, monographs, panels, symposia, conventions, textbooks, bibliographies, departments, committees, recruiting, placement, promotion, prizes, and the like."[21] For Fish, this professionalism defines the only institutional structures in which the disciplinary work of academic literary studies has any meaning and value. Thus, even antiprofessional arguments within the discipline can be heard only within the assumptions and practices of professionalism, and whatever institutional success a specific antiprofessional argument has can be defined only in professional terms. Fish claims, then, that the institution's choice is never *whether* to be professional but

---

[20]Fish, "Consequences," pp. 106, 112, quoting Richard Rorty, *Consequences of Pragmatism (Essays 1972–1980)* (Minneapolis, 1982), p. 162.

[21]Stanley Fish, "Profession Despise Thyself: Fear and Self-Loathing in Literary Studies," *Critical Inquiry*, 10 (December 1983), 351. Also see Fish, "Professional Anti-Professionalism," *Times Literary Supplement*, 10 December 1982, p. 1363, and his "Anti-Professionalism" and "Resistance and Independence: A Reply to Gerald Graff," both in *New Literary History*, 17 (Autumn 1985), 89–108 and 119–27.

rather *how* to be. Antiprofessional arguments always turn out to be polemics against a particular form or aspect of professionalism, polemics that are crucially enabled by the very professional practices they purport to attack. This holds true whether the antiprofessional attacks come from the reactionary right or the radical left within the discipline.

I find much of this argument persuasive, but it does have its problems. Fish's attempt logically to exclude antiprofessional challenges depends crucially on his prior assertion that professionalism exhaustively accounts for all activities within contemporary literary studies. We might join both Edward Said and Gerald Graff and ask whether professionalism indeed covers the field.[22] Are there not positions within a wider cultural politics which academic critics can occupy and from which they can speak, positions that are outside the ground covered by professionalism? Cannot a theologian or a politician or my mailman talk to a group of professional literary critics and be heard simultaneously as talking to that group *and* as still being outside it? I agree with Fish that such talk must be heard from within some assumptions and practices. The question is: Would we want to characterize all of these practices as professional? If professional procedures are contained withiǹ a larger set of social practices, then certainly it is possible not only for my mailman but for critics themselves to talk to professional colleagues from outside professional assumptions. This fact does not mean that they will necessarily be successful in getting a professional audience to listen as, say, nonprofessional citizens, nor is there any guarantee that nonprofessional arguments heard as such won't immediately be turned into a professional project. It is just that professionalism doesn't quite cover the field all the time. It's not *always* the only game in town.

During World Wars I and II, for instance, it became possible to talk in an MLA session as a citizen to fellow citizens. Of course, such examples are open to an objection: Don't proposals to change the discipline differ in kind from patriotic appeals to support the war effort?[23] That is, unlike general nationalistic

22Edward W. Said, "Response to Stanley Fish," *Critical Inquiry*, 10 (December 1983), 373; and Gerald Graff, "Interpretation on Tlön: A Response to Stanley Fish," *New Literary History*, 17 (Autumn 1985), 115–16.

23See, e.g., the various kinds of appeals in James Taft Hatfield's opening remarks to a 1917 MLA Central Division session on Germanic Languages, *PMLA*,

petitions, aren't specific proposals to reform the discipline necessarily heard and responded to only from within professional assumptions and procedures? I don't think so. For just as arguments for and against the national government entered into professional conferences in the 1960s, so too did such arguments directly influence debates about changing the profession and about being professional at all. It is possible to take a position within a broader cultural politics even when we criticize the professionalism of our fellow professionals. We must simply acknowledge how difficult it is to place ourselves even temporarily in some extraprofessional position and still get a hearing. Perhaps we must grant that Fish's analysis of antiprofessionalism within academic literary studies is accurate *historically:* for over a century, MLA antiprofessionals have almost always worked entirely within the professional practices they attack. But this is an *empirical* claim, not the logical one Fish insists on.

And even if we do grant that Fish's analysis accurately describes how antiprofessionalism has functioned in the past, we should not stop there. Is it true, as Fish also argues, that because literary antiprofessionalism is often (Fish would say always) self-contradictory in its project—attacking what enables it— that it should stop, especially because its only effect is to add to our continuing embarrassment and defensiveness? For Fish, antiprofessionalism is like foundationalist theory: both projects want to get outside the practices they comment on. And just as theory, in Fish's view, has no consequences because its goal is impossible, so too antiprofessionalism has no antiprofessional consequences because its goal is incoherent.

In order to see how misleading this claim is, we must look more closely at the tight fit between Fish's case against theory and his case against antiprofessionalism. In his attack against foundationalist theory, Fish argues that theory tries to get outside the practices it desires to guide and that since such an escape is impossible, theory has no consequences. But Fish is

---

33 (1918), xlvi; Kuno Francke's 1917 MLA Presidential Address, "The Idea of Progress from Leibniz to Goethe," *PMLA*, 33 (1918), lxix and lxxxvii–lxxxviii; Thomas Edward Oliver's 1917 MLA Central Division Chairman's Address, "The Menace to Our Ideals," *PMLA*, 33 (1918), lxxxix–cxv; and Robert Herndon Fife's 1944 MLA Presidential Address, "Nationalism and Scholarship," *PMLA*, 59 (1944), suppl., 1282–94.

very misleading here. What he actually means is that theory has no *theoretical* consequences, that is, it does not have the consequences it claims as theory (the consequence of getting outside practice). If someone presents an example of "theory" that does have the consequences of its claims, Fish responds in one of two ways: he says either that the so-called theory does have consequences but it's not really a theory or that it is a theory but the consequences it has are not theoretical ones.[24] This is a cagy maneuver on Fish's part, but it ends up making an interesting point at the expense of covering over the important institutional consequentiality of theory. Theory and its consequences become so narrowly defined as to make Fish's argument, if not trivial, at least misleading. As I argue above, theory does have very practical rhetorical consequences, unique to theory, even though these consequences are not what many theorists think they are.

The same holds true for antiprofessionalism. Fish claims that literary antiprofessionalism tries to escape the professional practices it attacks, but since it relies on those same practices and thus can never escape them, antiprofessionalism cannot have the consequences of its claims. Again, as with his argument against theory, Fish is both correct and misleading at the same time. Insofar as antiprofessionalism requires professional structures, Fish is right to say that it can't very well do away with them. But he is misleading when he suggests that this means there are no possible consequences unique to antiprofessional arguments. On the contrary, antiprofessional arguments are important rhetorical strategies adopted by those who want to change the profession, and these arguments can have very specific consequences within the institutionalized discipline: new emphases in critical discourses, new topics in theoretical debates, new values in pedagogical practices, even new criteria in professional standards of training, hiring, and promoting. Antiprofessionalism can foster changes, can have consequences.

The only consequence antiprofessionals cannot achieve is the one they sometimes seem to want: to deprofessionalize the profession. The closest that reactionary antiprofessionals of the Right could come to this goal would be to deinstitutionalize the discipline, to enact and argue for a return to the preprofessional status of literary studies outside the academy, a status the "dis-

[24]See Fish, "Consequences," pp. 130–31n.

cipline" held before its incorporation into the American university in the late nineteenth century. Such an unlikely nostalgic return to origins would not mean, however, that literary studies would cease to be a set of discursive and nondiscursive practices functioning against a background of other social practices; rather, it would simply mean that the practices constituting literary studies would no longer be of the kind we now characterize as "professional."

The reformist antiprofessionals of the Left present a very different alternative, a proposal with which I agree. It is not a preprofessional utopia they want but a postprofessional revolution, or better, not an absence of professionalism but a radically new kind of professionalism. The history of academic professions has been the history of increasing specialization, narrowing areas of expertise, greater and greater fragmentation of knowledge and authority. The result is more professional disciplines and fewer interdisciplinary professionals. Antiprofessionals of the Left seek, as a first step, to reverse this trend and promote for literary studies a form of professionalism that works against isolating the study of literature from the study of cultural practices generally. This proposal is not merely old Interdisciplinary Studies dressed up in a new guise. It is more like a politicized American Studies program taking over the whole discipline. It is a redefinition of literature, requiring literary studies to become cultural studies, with culture being conceptualized as the network of rhetorical practices that are extensions and manipulations of other practices—social, political, and economic.[25] In other words, reformist antiprofessionals see their goal not in a preprofessional past but in a cultural studies future. Still, even this radical polemic, as different as its dream is from today's professionalism, takes place in a thoroughly

[25]See, e.g., the new undergraduate major in English and Textual Studies in the English Department at Syracuse University, described in the collectively written essay "Not a Good Idea: A New Curriculum at Syracuse" (unpublished; available on request). The theory of pedagogy assumed in that text is consistent with the program I am advocating here: The new curriculum at Syracuse "poses *as a question* what it means to read, write, and interpret texts, and foregrounds what is at stake in the different ways these activities are undertaken" at the present moment (p. 3). Instead of "privileging a particular body of culturally sanctioned texts," such a curriculum emphasizes "the modes of critical inquiry one can bring to bear on any textual object and the political implications of such modes" (p. 1).

professionalized rhetorical context, and its consequences will be felt most immediately not in a nonprofessional discipline but in a discipline with a professional shape different from today's. Fish is correct, then, when he argues that antiprofessionalism cannot easily escape the context of the profession. But he is wrong when he implies that antiprofessional arguments could have no significant antiprofessional consequences. Surely they could: deinstitutionalizing the discipline, as the reactionaries would have it, or making the discipline over into a politicized cultural criticism, as the radicals desire, would be significant changes indeed. And these consequences are certainly possible—if not probable—scenarios. Despite all the misunderstandings between the professionals and the antiprofessionals, there really is something at stake: a new vision for literary study and its role in cultural politics.

III. The Rhetoric of Rhetorical Theory

What I have tried to do in this chapter is provide a rhetorical history of my rhetorical hermeneutics. This story is a narrative of arguments, those that worked and those that misfired. It is the story of being persuaded to change and changing in not being persuaded. That is, insofar as Knapp, Michaels, and Fish convinced me that the idealist hermeneutics of my conclusion to *Interpretive Conventions* was misguided, I have changed my mind and moved toward a neo-pragmatist theory that rejects both idealism and realism. But insofar as they have not persuaded me to accept their overemphasis on Theory's inconsequentiality, I have defined my rhetorical hermeneutics at least partly against their views. My point is that the rhetorical history of my theory is a function of an agonistic relationship to other theories, including those of other current neo-pragmatists.[26]

I claim that this same rhetorical situation holds for all theo-

[26]As one of my readers points out, there are broader narratives in which this more limited one could be embedded in order to expand the rhetorical history of rhetorical hermeneutics; for example, the loosely connected development of a "school of suspicion," including Marx, Freud, and Nietzsche and more recently Althusser, Lacan, and Foucault. (The quoted phrase is from Paul Ricoeur, *Freud and Philosophy: An Essay on Interpretation*, trans. Denis Savage [New Haven, Conn., 1970], p. 33.) An even older tradition of Sophistic rhetoric could also be cited. (For relevant interpretations of the Sophists, see Martin Heidegger, *The Question Concerning Technology and Other Essays*, trans. William Lovitt [New York, 1979]; Richard Rorty, *Philosophy and the Mirror of Nature* [Princeton,

ries. All theories can be defined quite precisely by the arguments they make in relation to implicitly or explicitly competing theories. The only difference here, perhaps, is that a rhetorical hermeneutics must be more historically specific and rhetorically explicit about its situation because it claims that historical and rhetorical detail should constitute any hermeneutic analysis, including its account of its own theorizing.

Problems may arise with such rhetorical self-consciousness. One danger is that rhetorical candor will be read as narcissistic self-indulgence, that it will be seen not as a necessary theoretical move required by rhetorical theory but as another case of theory's fashionable rereading of itself—self-critique as self-display. There's no easy way that a consistent rhetorical theorist can avoid this complaint. He or she can only hope that a sympathetic reader understands that a rhetorical theory cannot pretend to be outside of its own rhetorical history by ignoring that history in its account of itself. A rhetorical hermeneutics can be truly rhetorical only if it locates itself within, not above, its own history.

A still greater danger for a rhetorical hermeneutics is that a demonstration of its rhetoricity will undermine its persuasiveness as theory. This is the rhetorician's nightmare: By arguing that there is no appeal outside rhetorical exchanges, have I undercut the rhetorical force of my own theory? Does rhetorical candor detract from rhetorical effectiveness? The answer is yes *only* if the arguments of this rhetorical theory have not been entirely persuasive. That is, if you believe that there must ultimately be an appeal outside rhetoric, then you would find my theory unconvincing both because of its contrary claim *and* because it reaffirms this claim in its own rhetorical history of itself. However, if you are convinced by my rhetorical claims, then an admission of their rhetorical grounds is not only unsurprising but absolutely necessary. For rhetorical candor is the rhetorical theorist's obligation, not his embarrassment.

One other problem must also be faced head on. It is again the

1979], p. 157; Jasper Neel, *Plato, Derrida, and Writing* [Carbondale, Ill., 1988], pp. 204–9; and, in places, Jean-François Lyotard and Jean-Loup Thébaud, *Just Gaming*, trans. Wlad Godzich [Minneapolis, 1985], pp. 73–83.) However, as important as these traditions may ultimately be, they are less important for an agonistic account of my rhetorical hermeneutics than the more local rhetorical context (i.e., the actual historical debates with the neo-pragmatists Knapp, Michaels, and Fish).

question of consequences, the consequences of rhetorical her-meneutics. Certain traditionalists in hermeneutics and conser-vatives in politics will worry about its purported relativism and anarchic nihilism, claiming that in such a theory anything goes and all is permitted. Some radical revisionists may accuse this same theory of liberal pluralism and political quietism, not because "anything goes" but because "everything stays" in such theories; nothing is changed because all is (supposedly) toler-ated. Both of these critiques of rhetorical pragmatism derive ultimately from concerns about the relation of politics to herme-neutics.

Traditionalists want to preserve a foundationalist theory that can separate the political from the ethical, the epistemological, and the aesthetic. Without theoretical foundations, the tradi-tional argument goes, we have interpretive relativism, which leads inevitably to the political pollution of these autonomous areas of inquiry, ending in might making right. Only theories of the good, the true, and the beautiful allow us to avoid such dangerous nihilism. What I am arguing here is that such founda-tionalist theories are both unnecessary and impossible.[27] They are unnecessary because rhetorical exchanges about the good, the true, and the beautiful are always historically specific argu-ments already constrained by historically specific practices, tra-ditions, assumptions, ideologies, and so forth, which are part of the historically specific arrangements of power-knowledge. Fur-thermore, such rhetorical historicity cannot be escaped, and thus foundationalist projects are as impossible as they are un-necessary. Every attempt to appeal to some general, transhistori-cal set of hermeneutic principles is automatically involved in a specific context of rhetorical politics, and such appeals do not end debate but provide new grounds for potential disagreement. It is not that theoretical appeals are inconsequential; it is just that they do not provide an escape from the historically situated debates they are designed to govern. Rhetorical politics is insep-arable from hermeneutics, and by necessary extension from ethics, epistemology, and aesthetics as well.

It is not the danger of confusing politics with other intellec-

---

[27]Rorty, Consequences of Pragmatism, chap. 9; and Fish, Is There a Text?, chaps. 13 and 16, and "Fiss v. Fish," Stanford Law Review, 36 (July 1984), reprinted in Levinson and Mailloux, Interpreting Law and Literature, pp. 251–68.

tual and social spheres that bothers some critics of rhetorical pragmatism. For the radical revisionist, such antifoundationalism simply leads to the *wrong* mix of politics and hermeneutics. More precisely, the charge from the Right is that rhetoric leads to chaos, the inability to choose correctly; for the Left the problem is that rhetoric leads to political quietism, the inability to choose at all. From the latter perspective, rhetoric functions simply to maintain the status quo, because a rhetorical theory derived from antifoundationalism provides no grounds from which to criticize unjust social relations. This negative critique is simply the traditional foundationalist argument of the conservatives but from the other side of the political spectrum. And the answer is the same: No universal, objective idea of Justice and no ahistorical foundationalist theory of how such Justice should be implemented is necessary for specific interpretations, arguments, and resistances to take place. All such practices are historically grounded in specific rhetorical and political situations that provide the contemporary (and only) available arguments and justifications for defending, reforming, or revolutionizing the status quo.[28]

[28]This is not, however, a very satisfying argument against other kinds of objections: (1) that antifoundationalist theories can easily be used as deconstructive strategies for debilitating any political resistance that continues to appeal to absolute notions of transcendental Justice and foundationalist theories of implementation; and (2) that antifoundationalism as rhetorical pragmatism becomes still more debilitating when combined with (even revised versions of) Foucauldian notions of power because such notions offer little hope that resistance will not be co-opted. Regarding objection 1: If indeed it can be shown that at the present moment rhetorical pragmatism does lead to a politically reactionary result, then the rhetorical theorist committed to other results must combat such "misappropriations" (as I have tried to do in this and the following chapter). The theory itself thus becomes the site of the struggle it describes. In response to objection 2: see the attempts to argue for a more positive political reading of Foucault in Mark Poster, *Foucault, Marxism, and History: Mode of Production versus Mode of Information* (Cambridge, 1984), esp. pp. 157–69; David Couzens Hoy, Introduction to *Foucault: A Critical Reader*, ed. Hoy (New York, 1986), pp. 13–20; Mark Maslan, "Foucault and Pragmatism," *Raritan*, 7 (Winter 1988), 94–114; and Michel Foucault, "The Ethic of Care for the Self as a Practice of Freedom: An Interview," trans. J. D. Gauthier, S.J., in *The Final Foucault*, ed. James Bernauer and David Rasmussen (Cambridge, Mass., 1988), pp. 1–20. In any case, more needs to be done to ensure that rhetorical pragmatism realizes the radical potential that Cornel West suggests for neo-pragmatism in general; see his *American Evasion of Philosophy: A Genealogy of Pragmatism* (Madison, Wis., 1989).

Conclusion

The ABM Treaty
Interpretation Dispute

We can take the final step in my argument by returning to Chapter 1 and the statutory interpretation that introduces its proposal of a rhetorical hermeneutics. In June 1978 the Carter administration published a summary of presidential directives concerning future space activities. "The United States is committed," the summary says, "to the principles of the exploration and use of outer space by all nations for peaceful purposes and for the benefit of all mankind."[1] In making this claim, the summary echoed the opening statement of the Space Act of 1958: "The Congress hereby declares that it is the policy of the United States that activities in space should be devoted to peaceful purposes for the benefit of all mankind."[2]

In March 1982 Robert Cooper, director of the Defense Advanced Research Projects Agency for the Reagan administration, reinterpreted "peaceful purposes" before the House Committee on Armed Services: "The basic policies that we are operating under today . . . [include] maintaining the full right to use space for peaceful purposes which we interpret to include military uses of space to promote peace in the world."[3] I suggested at the

[1]"United States Space Activities: Announcement of Administration Review, June 20, 1978," *Weekly Compilation of Presidential Documents*, 14 (26 June 1978), p. 1136.

[2]"National Aeronautics and Space Act of 1958," *United States Statutes at Large* (Washington, D.C., 1959), vol. 72, pt. 1, p. 426.

[3]*Hearings on Military Posture and H.R. 5968 [H.R. 6030], Department of Defense Authorization for Appropriations for Fiscal Year 1983*, before the Committee on Armed Services, House of Representatives, 97th Cong., 2d sess. (Washington, D.C., 1982), pt. 5, p. 561.

beginning of Chapter 1 that this ironic reading stems from the misinterpretation of an antimilitaristic text by a government with a militaristic ideology. How else, I implied, can one explain the semantic collapse of "peaceful purposes" into its diametrical opposite, "military uses"? But this simple explanation does not survive the argument it initiates. First of all, the use of the term "ideology" can very easily fall into the essentialist trap I try to avoid throughout this book. That is, to claim that the Reagan administration ideologically projects a militaristic meaning on an antimilitaristic text could suggest that ideological interpretation ignores the actual meaning in the text and that there is a nonideological reading that avoids this mistake. To suggest the former is to reinvoke all the essentialist problems of the realist/idealist debate over interpretation, and to suggest the latter is to misunderstand ideology as an avoidable blindness to objective truth rather than as a rhetorical activity constituting interpretation as a politically interested act of persuasion.

It is possible, of course, to disagree with the Reagan administration's reading of "peaceful purposes." One does not, however, have to wax Theoretical to do so. Instead, one "simply" argues a counterinterpretation, making such rhetorical moves as pointing to the text, citing the traditional interpretation, and invoking the consensus. Such moves are as ideological as those of the Defense Department in that they are interested attempts to persuade an audience to interpret the text in a nonmilitaristic manner. No easy appeal to hermeneutic foundationalism provides a way out of this rhetorical politics of interpretation.

If foundationalist theory cannot resolve the interpretive dispute, at least rhetorical theory can help explain it. Here again we move from hermeneutic theory to rhetorical history. In this case, I will use a brief history of a related interpretive controversy about the militarization of space to demonstrate exactly how theories of interpretation function less as constraints on reading than as resources for arguing. That is, formalist, intentionalist, and other theories do not provide guarantees of correct interpretation or algorithms for resolving interpretive disputes, but in particular historical contexts they do make available to disputants additional rhetorical tactics for continuing specific arguments over meaning.[4]

[4]This is not to say that every theory (foundationalist, rhetorical, or whatever) is always equally available to every political position. Rather, the strategic

Consistent with the Space Act of 1958, the Senate ratified the 1972 Anti-Ballistic Missile Treaty with the Soviet Union. This treaty contained a crucial provision as Article V (1): "Each Party undertakes not to develop, test, or deploy ABM systems or components which are sea-based, air-based, space-based, or mobile land-based."[5] For thirteen years, through three administrations, this short text was interpreted not only as outlawing the militarization of space but as prohibiting even the *development and testing* of space-based ABM systems.[6]

On 23 March 1983, President Ronald Reagan announced his Strategic Defense Initiative (SDI), a program to develop an ABM system based on new technologies that could "intercept and destroy" incoming offensive missiles. The president promised that this program would be "consistent with our obligations" under the ABM Treaty.[7] It soon became clear, however, that at some future date the development of "Star Wars" would certainly bump up against the treaty's explicit constraints. Nevertheless, the Reagan administration continued to uphold the tra-

utility of a theory depends on, among other things, its affiliations, prestige, and implications at specific times and places. Thus the rhetorical opportunities offered by a particular theory's use are neither completely unlimited at a given moment nor eternally fixed across different rhetorical contexts. For discussion of different political uses made of the "same" theory, see Sanford Levinson, "Introduction," in *Interpreting Law and Literature*, ed. Levinson and Steven Mailloux (Evanston, Ill., 1988), p. 10, on intentionalist theory; and Gerald Graff, "The Pseudo-Politics of Interpretation," *Critical Inquiry*, 9 (March 1983), 602–5, on objectivist theory. Also see Edward W. Said, "Traveling Theory," *Raritan*, 1 (Fall 1982), 41–67, rev. in Said, *The World, the Text, and the Critic* (Cambridge, Mass., 1983), pp. 226–47; and the discussion of Said's argument by Paul Bové, *Intellectuals in Power: A Genealogy of Critical Humanism* (New York, 1986), pp. 209–37.

[5]"Treaty between the United States of America and the Union of Soviet Socialist Republics on the Limitation of Anti-Ballistic Missile Systems," 26 May 1972, *United States Treaties and Other International Agreements* (Washington, D.C., 1973), vol. 23, pt. 4, p. 3441.

[6]For a helpful historical overview, see Paul B. Stares, *The Militarization of Space: U.S. Policy, 1945–1984* (Ithaca, N.Y., 1985); and on the public debates and secret negotiations leading up to the signing of the ABM Treaty, see John Newhouse, *Cold Dawn: The Story of SALT* (New York, 1973), and the accounts by two of the American negotiators, Gerard Smith, *Doubletalk: The Story of the First Strategic Arms Limitation Talks* (Garden City, N.Y., 1980), and Raymond L. Garthoff, *Detente and Confrontation: American-Soviet Relations from Nixon to Reagan* (Washington, D.C., 1985), chaps. 3–5.

[7]"Address to the Nation. March 23, 1983," *Weekly Compilation of Presidential Documents*, 19, no. 12 (28 March 1983), pp. 447–48.

ditional interpretation of Article V (1). For example, its *Fiscal Year 1985 Arms Control Impact Statement* reported: "The ABM Treaty prohibition on development, testing and deployment of space-based ABM systems, or components for such systems, applies to directed energy technology (or any other technology) used for this purpose. Thus, when such directed energy programs enter the field testing phase they become constrained by these ABM Treaty obligations."[8]

This interpretation held throughout 1984 and most of 1985. Then, on 6 October, National Security Adviser Robert McFarlane offered a new reading of Article V (1). In a televised interview on *Meet the Press*, McFarlane claimed that the treaty "approved and authorized" development and testing of space-based ABM systems "involving new physical concepts," presumably directed energy weapons such as lasers or particle beams.[9] This radical reinterpretation provoked immediate controversy. As one newspaper put it: "This startling pronouncement by a high official, almost a 180-degree reversal of the longstanding U.S. position on the treaty, was a shock to the ABM Treaty's negotiators and other arms control advocates, to U.S. allies in Europe and arms control minded members of Congress."[10] Like the Defense Department's earlier reading of "peaceful purposes" to include "military uses," McFarlane's statements ironically reinterpreted a ban as an approval of the militarization of space.

Eight days later, Secretary of State George Schultz took up this new interpretation in a speech to the North Atlantic Assembly, a speech that clearly set out to create an opening for the revised reading: "The treaty can be variously interpreted as to what kinds of development and testing are permitted, particularly with respect to future systems and components based on new physical principles." The traditional interpretation, once so obvious, was thus declared problematic, and room was immediately established for a new, less restrictive interpretation that allowed for what had previously been prohibited: "It is our

---

[8]*Fiscal Year 1985 Arms Control Impact Statements* (Submitted to the Congress by the President Pursuant to Section 36 of the Arms Control and Disarmament Act), 98th Cong., 2d sess. (March 1984), p. 252. Also see *Fiscal Year 1986 Arms Control Impact Statements*, 99th Cong., 1st sess. (April 1985), p. 37.

[9]*Department of State Bulletin*, 85, no. 2105 (December 1985), p. 33.

[10]Don Oberdorfer, "ABM Reinterpretation: A Quick Study," *Washington Post*, 22 October 1985, p. A10.

view, based on a careful analysis of the treaty text and the negotiating record, that a broader interpretation of our authority is fully justified." Out-of-laboratory testing of SDI technology would now fall outside the constraints of the ABM Treaty. Having asserted the validity of this new interpretation, Schultz then attempted to distance its consequences from actual policy: That the "broader interpretation" is "fully justified" is, "however, a moot point" because "our SDI research program has been structured and, as the President has reaffirmed last Friday, will continue to be conducted in accordance with a restrictive interpretation of the treaty's obligations."[11]

This attempt to depoliticize the new interpretation, to separate "simply reading" the text from political policy making, did not satisfy the critics. On 22 October the House Subcommittee on Arms Control, International Security, and Science convened to discuss the "ABM Treaty interpretation dispute."[12] The record of this hearing provides a discursive context for analyzing the arguments supporting the old "restrictive" and the new "broader" interpretations of Article V (1) of the ABM Treaty and thus for "explaining" its reinterpretation. Only when such a rhetorical analysis is done within the historical narrative I have outlined can the hermeneutics of the argument become clear. No appeal to foundationalist theory can resolve such disputes, but a rhetorical history can determine how theoretical appeals function within the institutional exchanges of a specific political controversy.

The most outspoken administration representative at the hearing was Abraham Sofaer, legal adviser to the secretary of

[11]George Schultz, "Arms Control, Strategic Stability, and Global Security" (address before the 31st Annual Session of the North Atlantic Assembly, San Francisco, 14 October 1985), *Department of State Bulletin*, 85, no. 2105 (December 1985), p. 23.

[12] *ABM Treaty Interpretation Dispute: Hearing before the Subcommittee on Arms Control, International Security, and Science of the Committee on Foreign Affairs, House of Representatives*, 99th Cong., 1st sess., 22 October 1985 (Washington, D.C., 1986) (hereafter cited in text by page number). For another analysis of these hearings, see Abram Chayes and Antonia Handler Chayes, "Testing and Development of 'Exotic' Systems under the ABM Treaty: The Great Reinterpretation Caper," *Harvard Law Review*, 99 (June 1986), 1956–71; and for a more recent contribution, *The ABM Treaty and the Constitution: Joint Hearings before the Committee on Foreign Relations and the Committee on the Judiciary, United States Senate*, 100th Cong., 1st sess., 11 and 26 March and 29 April 1987 (Washington, D.C., 1987).

state. Following the rhetorical strategy of his boss, Sofaer began by problematizing the traditional interpretation of the ABM ban: "My study of the treaty led me to conclude that its language is ambiguous and can more reasonably be read to support a broader interpretation" (p. 5). Noting that the "restrictive interpretation rests on the premise that article V (1) is clear on its face" (p. 5), Sofaer suggested that such a view ignores the document's ambiguities and proceeded to argue that a broader interpretation was just as plausible and in fact more reasonable. To establish good reasons for the broader interpretation, Sofaer appealed to several hermeneutic criteria: the language of the document, the intentions of the negotiators, relevant canons of construction, and, surprisingly, the postnegotiation tradition of interpreting the treaty.[13]

The rhetorical effectiveness of these appeals depends on the acceptability of the relevant hermeneutic theories that constitute these criteria as guideposts for correct interpretation. Thus a formalist theory undergirds the appeal to the language in the text; an intentionalist theory supports the study of the negotiator's mental purposes; a historicist theory justifies the use of interpretive history; and a theory of neutral principles provides a rationale for legal canons of construction.[14] Although these theories are often developed as foundationalist accounts of interpreting, here we will see that they are best viewed as rhetorical resources rather than hermeneutic foundations in debates over meaning.

Sofaer began his arguments with a formalist appeal, but it was not only the advocates of the broad reinterpretation who pointed directly to the text. So did the advocates of the restrictive view: John Rhinelander, former legal adviser to the ABM Treaty negotiators, stated emphatically that "*the prohibitions are clear from*

---

[13]On good reasons in argumentation, see Chaim Perelman and Lucie Olbrechts-Tyteca, *The New Rhetoric: A Treatise on Argumentation*, trans. John Wilkinson and Purcell Weaver (Notre Dame, Ind., 1969); Karl Wallace, "The Substance of Rhetoric: Good Reasons," *Quarterly Journal of Speech*, 49 (October 1963), 239–49; and Wayne C. Booth, *Modern Dogma and the Rhetoric of Assent* (Notre Dame, Ind., 1974).

[14]On the last, see Herbert Wechsler, "Toward Neutral Principles of Constitutional Law," *Harvard Law Review*, 73 (November 1959), 1–35, and the objections in Mark V. Tushnet, "Following the Rules Laid Down: A Critique of Interpretivism and Neutral Principles," *Harvard Law Review*, 96 (February 1983), 804–24.

the text of the Treaty, particularly Article V (1)" (p. 58), and similarly Leonard Meeker and Peter Didisheim, both of the Union of Concerned Scientists, claimed in a statement submitted to the committee: "The ordinary meaning of the treaty's terms are self-evident [*sic*]. The Administration's argument that the treaty permits the development and field testing of [space-based] ABM weapons and components based on new physical principles cannot qualify as an interpretation 'in good faith'" (p. 117). Sofaer rejected any clear or self-evident meaning in the language of Article V (1) and in his formalist argument produced ambiguity by reading various parts of the treaty against each other. Thus he claimed that Agreed Statement D (negotiated at the time of the original treaty) suggests that Article II (1)'s definition of "ABM system" refers only to technology current in 1972, and therefore the prohibitions in Article V (1) do not constrain development and testing of systems based on future technology, such as that involved in SDI.[15] Congressman Henry Hyde found this formalist appeal persuasive, declaring that "the plain intent of those English words leaps out at you" and noting, "There isn't much of a conflict as I see it here between the English language and the interpretation [Sofaer] found that fits within the four corners of this document" (pp. 25, 43).

Others were not so easily convinced, and the rhetorical ground soon shifted from formalist claims about the text to intentionalist arguments about the negotiating history. Sofaer announced this shift early in his interpretive argument: "Under international law, as under U.S. domestic law, once an agreement has been found ambiguous, one must seek guidance in the circumstances surrounding the drafting of the agreement. Thus, in the present situation, once we concluded that the treaty is ambiguous, we turned to the negotiating record to see which of

---

[15]Ironically, one of the few jocular exchanges during the hearing provided the most revealing theoretical comment on the treaty disagreement, foregrounding for a brief moment the interpretive work required to produce the disputed ambiguity (or, indeed, any meaning) in the text:

Chairman Fascell: Do you find anything in agreed statement D that is ambiguous?

Mr. Sofaer: No, I think that is a pretty straightforward section. I am sure that if I worked at it, though, Congressman—

Chairman Fascell: I know you are a good lawyer, but that is too good. I think we better take a recess and go vote. [*ABM Treaty Interpretation Dispute*, pp. 20–21]

the possible constructions most accurately reflects the parties' intentions" (p. 7). This move toward the broader interpretation was questioned in two ways by the advocates of the restrictive reading. First, the rule invoked for guidance in interpretation immediately became the new occasion for interpretive controversy: Rhinelander declared that Sofaer's interpretation rested "on a new canon of construction, never before heard of, that the *unambiguous* text of a treaty should be distorted to give an agreed interpretation [Agreed Statement D] an independent and amendatory role" (p. 173). Second, when Sofaer began filling in the intention behind the text, this new source for guidance marked out still another area of interpretive controversy: even if the negotiators' past intentions do have priority over the present words on the page, it still remains to be determined what those intentions actually were.

The argument over the negotiators' original intentions becomes especially interesting when the negotiators themselves turn up on both sides of the dispute. Gerard Smith, former chief of the U.S. delegation to the ABM negotiations, criticized the administration's revisionism and remembered the negotiators' intentions as supporting the restrictive interpretation of Article V (1) (pp. 21–26). In contrast, Paul Nitze, also a member of the original negotiating team and now special adviser to the president for arms control, strongly endorsed the administration's new, broader interpretation. Certainly an appeal to a ground of intention fails to resolve the interpretive dispute when the appeal ends up supporting both sides of the argument.

The thoroughly rhetorical nature of the intentionalist "ground" becomes even more obvious in this exchange between Nitze and Congressman Lee Hamilton at the hearing:

> Mr. Hamilton: Ambassador Nitze, I am curious about your interpretation of this treaty through this 13-year period. If I understood you correctly a moment ago, and I may not have, you suggested that you have been persuaded by recent legal interpretation that the agreement says something that you didn't think it said at the time you participated in the crafting of the treaty; is that correct?
>
> Mr. Nitze: That is approximately correct. I think the facts of the matter are that it is hard to recollect exactly what one thought at the time 13 years ago. I know that some time thereafter I was asked a question about the treaty which differs from what I now understand to be the negotiating record.

> Mr. Hamilton: Well, what then comes through to me is that for 13 years you at least, by your silence on this important point, have given us all the impression that this treaty is to be interpreted restrictively, but now you say that the lawyers have persuaded you that you reached an agreement that you didn't know you reached? [P. 41]

This exchange demonstrates that the establishment of past intention, like the construction of present meaning, can depend crucially on specific acts of persuasion. The example seems so striking because the person persuaded to a different view of the past is the same person whose original intention is at issue.

But if the rhetoric of interpretation cannot be permanently grounded in the text, intention, or interpretive rules, perhaps the history of interpretations will serve. Ralph Earle, former director of the U.S. Arms Control and Disarmament Agency, suggested just this option in defense of the traditional, restrictive interpretation: "It would be a unique episode in international negotiations to have a completely unambiguous record, especially in a bargaining process requiring $2\frac{1}{2}$ years. But be that as it may, the 13-year record for the parties holding the original version [the restrictive interpretation] should carry far greater weight than some statements reportedly inconsistent with the final language of the Treaty" (p. 23). Rhinelander developed this reception argument further by citing still another guiding principle: "The Vienna Convention on the Law of Treaties and the A[merican] L[aw] I[nstitute] Restatement of the Foreign Relations Law of the United States . . . stress the importance of subsequent *practice* in interpreting a treaty," and "subsequent practice, including statements, of *both* the US and the Soviets *reinforce* the historic [restrictive] interpretation of the ABM Treaty" (p. 173). The turn to interpretive history, then, would seem to decide the matter: the restrictive interpretation has been the traditionally accepted (and thus privileged) reading of the treaty. After all, isn't there at least agreement that the administration's interpretation is in fact a new one?

Not so, says Sofaer: "We do not accept the premise that this administration is departing from a consistent record of 13 years of statements of the restrictive view" (p. 40). In fact, he claimed, the broader interpretation was not new, but old, and the administration's view was not so much a reinterpretation as the remembering of a forgotten tradition. Indeed, Sofaer concluded his lengthy narrative of past readings of the treaty with this moral: "The 'broad' view of the Treaty has as strong a basis as the 'restrictive' view for being called 'traditional' or accepted" (p. 212). Rhinelander provided a detailed critique of Sofaer's interpretive history (pp. 186–99), but this response leaves untouched the fact that Sofaer was still able to make that history an effective part of his case.

After all the rhetorical exchanges, the congressional hearing ended somewhere close to where it began: in radical disagreement over the interpretation of the ABM Treaty. The text is clear, one side claims; no it's not, replies the other. If the text is ambiguous, both rhetorical lines of reasoning suggest, then we can turn to the negotiating record. Still no resolution. Since this record of intentions is itself ambiguous, we can turn to the treaty's thirteen-year interpretive history. But even here both sides are able to appeal to that "same" history to support their antagonistic cases. No appeal to theories or principles resolves the dispute, for the theories themselves become the new sources of controversy because of their theoretical claims or their practical applications. Which theories are relevant to the interpretive dispute? How should a relevant theory's principles be interpreted before being applied? Once interpreted, how should the principles be applied to govern this case? If the relevant theory is apparent (say, intentionalism), if its principles are clear (discover the negotiators' original intentions), if the principles can then be applied (ask the negotiators and check the negotiating record), we are still left with the problem of interpreting and arguing over texts, recollections, histories.

Thus, once again we see that theories are not foundational but rhetorical, establishing no permanent grounding or guiding principles guaranteeing correct interpretation but certainly providing much rhetorical substance for interpretive debate. That this debate is political through and through is perhaps too obvious to require mention, but the ABM Treaty interpretation dispute does thematize its politics more obviously then most interpretive arguments. In defending the Reagan administration's reinterpretation of the treaty, Congressman Hyde accused the critics of mixing politics with simply reading the text: "You are seeing a lot of people who have little use for the SDI, and they are going to assert an interpretation of the ABM Treaty which obstructs development of that system" (p. 43). One of these "obstructionists," Gerard Smith, raised similar questions from the other side, asking: "Why did the administration decide to float this new treaty version just 6 weeks before a summit at which the ABM Treaty was expected to be an important part? Was it an exercise in playing hard ball? A gesture of machismo? . . . Or was it a bargaining ploy looking to a summit accommodation somewhere between the Soviet presummit position of no research at all and the Reagan new version of no limits on strategic defense development?" (p. 22). Both the administration and its critics accused the other side of illegitimately mixing politics with interpretation.

In contrast, it has been the argument of this chapter and of the entire book that textual interpretation and rhetorical politics can never be separated. Indeed, the failure of hermeneutic foundationalism is just another instance of the fact that interpretations can have no grounding outside of rhetorical exchanges taking place within institutional and cultural politics. In Nitze's insistence that there is a clear "distinction between a legal interpretation and a [government] policy" (p. 19), we see another example of a theoretical attempt to separate a textual interpretation from its context of rhetorical power.[16] In this case, it is not only bad hermeneutics; it is also dangerous politics.

Again, I want to counter a possible misunderstanding of my argument here. I am certainly not saying that it is impossible to disagree effectively with the Reagan administration's absurd reinterpretation of the ABM Treaty. One does not, however, have to become a foundationalist theorist in order to do so. Instead, as I noted earlier, one simply and rigorously argues for a counterinterpretation, making such rhetorical moves as pointing to the text, citing the authors' intentions, noting the traditional reading, and invoking the consensus—just as the supporters of the restrictive interpretation did at the congressional hearing. The resulting interpretation is, of course, just as contingent as the militaristic reading and could be just as open to further debate. To admit this contingency, to recognize the rhetorical politics of every interpretation, is not to avoid taking a position. Taking a position, making an interpretation, cannot be avoided. Moreover, such historical contingency does not dis-

---

[16]Nitze was explaining that the Reagan administration believed the broader interpretation to be correct but had decided as policy to act according to the more restrictive interpretation, at least temporarily.

able interpretive argument, because it is truly the only ground it can have. We are always arguing at particular moments in specific places to certain audiences. Our beliefs and commitments are no less real because they are historical, and the same holds for our interpretations. If no foundationalist theory will resolve disagreements over poems or treaties, we must always argue our cases. In fact, that is all we can ever do.

Index

Library of Congress Cataloging-in-Publication Data
Mailloux, Steven.
  Rhetorical power/Steven Mailloux.
    p. cm.
  Includes index.
  ISBN 0–8014–2245–0.—ISBN 0–8014–9602–0 (pbk.)
  1. Criticism. 2. Rhetoric. 3. Hermeneutics. I. Title.
PN81.M38 1989   801'.95—dc20   89–42878